DATE DUE			

UNCERTAIN YEARS
Chinese-American Relations, 1947–1950

Studies of the East Asian Institute
Columbia University

UNCERTAIN YEARS
Chinese-American Relations, 1947–1950

Edited By

DOROTHY BORG and
WALDO HEINRICHS

Columbia University Press—New York—1980

Library of Congress Cataloging in Publication Data
Main entry under title:

Uncertain years.

  Includes bibliographical references and index.
  1. United States—Foreign relations—China—
Addresses, essays, lectures.   2. China—Foreign
relations—United States—Addresses, essays, lectures.
3. United States—Foreign relations—1945–1953—
Addresses, essays, lectures.   4. China—Foreign
relations—1912–1949—Addresses, essays, lectures.
I. Borg, Dorothy, 1902–   II. Heinrichs, Waldo H.
E183.8.C5U43   327.73051   79-28297
ISBN 0-231-04738-X

Columbia University Press
New York   Guildford, Surrey

Copyright © 1980 Columbia University Press
        All rights reserved
Printed in the United States of America

Contents

v

Introduction

IN 1976 the East Asian Institute of Columbia University instituted a project on the study of American-Chinese relations, 1947–1950. The entire undertaking involved the writing of a number of papers; their presentation at a conference of about thirty scholars held at the Seven Springs Center, Mount Kisco, New York from June 9–11, 1978; and the publication of this volume which contains both the papers and summaries of the conference. The project was largely funded through the Luce Fund for Asian Studies. The manuscript was for the most part edited by Dale K. A. Finalyson and owes much to her fine craftsmanship. Due to the pressure of time additional editorial assistance was needed. Anita M. O'Brien attended to many essentials, including the provision of that most vital of tools—the index. Further help and valued support were given by Gilda M. Roberts.

The crucial years, beginning with the Chinese Communists' victorious drive to power in 1947 and ending with the outbreak of the Korean War in 1950, were years of uncertainty in Chinese-American relations. The kind of relationship the United States and the emerging Chinese Communist state might establish was still very much in question. In all probability it would not be an easy one, but this did not dictate that it would essentially be hostile. The present volume considers in detail why the United States and the Chinese Communists did not reach an accommodation in the 1947–1950 period and instead embarked upon an historic enmity that was to last for almost a quarter century with far-reaching and often disastrous consequences.

The project that led to the publication of *Uncertain Years: Chinese American Relations, 1947–1950* was originally suggested in 1976 by a small group of scholars. They felt the decisive moment had come to undertake an intensive study of the origins of the prolonged hostility that had existed between the Chinese Communists and the United States. The People's Republic of China (PRC) and the United States appeared to be moving toward the normalization of their relations. Current events were therefore revitalizing the question of whether their estrangement could have been avoided.

In addition, by this time scholars were beginning to gain access to a wealth of primary sources, indispensable for any comprehensive research on the relations of the United States with both the Chinese Communists and the Chinese Nationalists in the 1947–1950 period. The American government was opening its relevant diplomatic and military archives and the volumes of the *Foreign Relations of the United States* series for the period were nearing completion. (In fact they were all published in time for use in this book, including a long-delayed volume for 1949 that contains documents on some of the most critical issues of that year.) Many collections of private papers that had an important bearing on American-Chinese relations from 1947 to 1950 were becoming available for research. There was, of course, no prospect of obtaining access to a comparable body of Chinese primary sources. But Dr. V. K. Wellington Koo, who served as Chinese ambassador in Washington throughout the 1947–1950 period, had just opened for the use of scholars the vast collection of his documents—including official communications, private memoranda, and an oral history of over 11,000 pages—deposited at Columbia University.

It was also felt in 1976 that the climate of opinion in America had changed sufficiently to allow for a degree of objectivity hitherto absent in the study of the causes of enmity between the U.S. and the PRC. Few books had been written on the relations of the United States and the Chinese Communists.

Those published at the height of the Cold War with rare exceptions were bitterly hostile to the PRC. Those published after the outbreak of the conflict in Vietnam tended to extend the prevailing intense opposition to U.S. policy toward Vietnam to include U.S. policy toward the PRC. It was not until the mid-1970s that some of the passions of the earlier years gradually dissipated.

More than a year before the convening of the conference at the Seven Springs Center, the authors of the essays published in this book jointly worked out a basic plan. For the most part the authors were specialists in American-Chinese relations, trained in both American and Chinese studies. The plan was above all based on the principle of undertaking a multinational study that would deal with the policy of each of the three major participants in Chinese-American relations throughout the 1947–50 period—the United States, the Chinese Communists, and the Chinese Nationalists—and their interaction. Because of the abundance of American primary sources there were to be several papers on the policy of the United States dealing with both its political and its military aspects. The original scheme called for one essay on the Chinese Nationalists and one on the Chinese Communists. But as it became evident during the course of the conference discussions that there were two markedly different schools of thought concerning the policy of the Chinese Communists, a second paper was written subsequently.

The conference discussions were an exceptionally valuable addition to the entire project. Members of the conference represented different approaches. Some were historians, some political scientists. Most were specialists in either American or Chinese foreign policy, but a substantial number, like the authors of the papers, were specifically trained in the study of American-Chinese relations. As a group their political convictions covered a wide spectrum.

In keeping with the papers, the conference discussions focused almost exclusively on the origins of the enmity between the United States and the Chinese Communists and were remarkably detailed and suggestive. The conference proceedings were recorded in full, and the summaries published in this volume are based on an extensive use of the tapes. The summaries define the major issues and give the substance of the arguments advanced by conference members, which ranged from agreement with the general tenor of the papers to fundamental opposition.

Neither the discussions nor the summaries attempted to reach definitive conclusions. *Uncertain Years: Chinese-American Relations, 1947–1950* seeks rather to provide a needed, comprehensive account of Sino-American relations during a crucial period in their history. In doing so it brings to light and critically assesses new information, raises new questions, defines areas of disagreement, and, it is hoped, will sharpen the focus of further inquiry.

UNCERTAIN YEARS
Chinese-American Relations, 1947–1950

PART I
United States Policy

Roosevelt and Truman: The Presidential Perspective

Waldo Heinrichs

THE FIRST session of the Conference on Chinese-American Relations devoted itself mainly to United States policy toward China in the 1944–48 period, the years preceding the collapse of Nationalist rule on the mainland and Communist triumph. The main topics included in the discussion were Franklin Roosevelt's postwar plans, the Truman administration's early Cold War policies, assistance to Chiang Kai-shek, and the Marshall mission. The central concern of the conferees was determining when and under what circumstances the goal of blocking Soviet expansion became the overriding objective of American policy toward China.

Some discussants argued that the Cold War originated during World War II and arrived in East Asia, more particularly in China, as early as elsewhere if not earlier. In their eyes, the dominant feature of American China policy from the mid-forties was its anti-Soviet character. Others dissented, maintaining that the Cold War emerged gradually and took hold in East Asia later than in Europe and other parts of the world, as late as 1949 and even 1950, the time of the outbreak of the Korean War. According to the latter view, Chinese and regional circumstances counted for more than global concerns in shaping American policy.

Martin Sherwin, in a provisional paper that provoked great interest, traced containment back to World War II China policy. He contended that, although President Roosevelt's

3

views were based primarily on wartime considerations, the postwar extension of American influence and likely competition with the Soviet Union were never far from his mind. Europe, to be sure, was the main stage, but East Asia had a special significance.

China in particular, Sherwin stated, seemed to Roosevelt a "vortex that could draw Russia and America into dangerous confrontation." The president sought to strengthen the Kuomintang regime into a "stable anti-Soviet government" that would act as a "natural barrier" against Soviet influence and a counterweight to Soviet power. It soon became evident, however, that Chiang's regime was too weak and corrupt to fulfill what Sherwin termed a "containment-by-proxy" function. Roosevelt tried to sustain the regime by averting civil war and broadening the government to include a Communist minority. Sherwin felt that in view of the complexity and ambiguity of Roosevelt's whole approach to foreign policy he might have chosen a different course once the war was over. But as it was, he bequeathed to Harry Truman the concept of a China policy based on the idea of using the Chinese Nationalists to keep the Russians at bay, a concept which became the core of Truman's whole containment policy.

Locked in place at Roosevelt's death, the iron logic of containment governed Truman's policy from 1945 to 1950. Truman's personal qualities, favoring firmness, clarity, and confrontation, reinforced the Rooseveltian inclination toward containment. "Overarching concern with the expansion of Soviet influence," Sherwin asserted, "bound Truman's European and Asian policies together infusing them with a coherence that was otherwise lacking." In Truman's overall view of the world, China was "the Eastern Europe of Asia." Under these circumstances, the object of the Marshall mission was to achieve an internal political settlement that would make it impossible for the Soviets to penetrate China through indigenous Communist forces. The Soviet Union might then resort to open aggression but such overt action would at least serve as a clear warning to the American people of Soviet intentions. As evidence of the importance that the Truman administration attached to China, Sherwin cited the Clark Clifford memorandum of 1946, written months before the Greek crisis, which declared that a deteriorating situation such as existed in China inevitably paved the way for Soviet aggrandizement.

In Sherwin's judgment, Truman sensibly avoided the China quagmire and pursued "containment by proxy" in the more advantageous circumstances of Greece. But it was the prior crisis of containment in China that established Congressional receptivity to Dean Acheson's overly alarmist analysis of Soviet global aims on February 26, 1947, and to the ensuing Truman Doctrine and assistance programs for Greece and Turkey. Thenceforth American commitments deepened and expanded but the essential objective, traceable to Roosevelt and China, of keeping Soviet influence within manageable limits remained the same. American intervention in Korea in June 1950, Sherwin asserted, was simply an epilogue to a well-established policy of world containment; "containment by proxy became containment by confrontation."

Thomas Paterson agreed with Sherwin respecting the centrality and continuity of containment, but differed in emphasis. For Sherwin China was the precipitating agent of containment thinking; for Paterson European-Middle Eastern sources seemed at least equally important. Sherwin stressed the Rooseveltian matrix of containment, Paterson the matured Truman dogma. While Sherwin dwelt on the persistence of Roosevelt's basic notion of using other nations to check the Soviets, Paterson highlighted the tactical differences between the two presidents. "Roosevelt," Paterson said, never "conjured up the ugly Communist specter that haunted Truman and Acheson." In Paterson's view, the success or failure of containment heavily depended on local conditions. Among the limiting factors in China were the vastness and unmanageability of the country; the lack of any popular loyalty to the government and of any genuine determination to fight; and Chiang's resistance to reform. In contrast, in Greece there were such favorable elements as the tractability of the government and the prior existence of institutions for the exercise of containment.

Containment, according to Paterson's interpretation, failed in China but not for want of trying. Failing to recognize the conditions within China that imposed limits on the implementation of a containment policy, Americans fell into the "terrible delusion" that they could shape events there. Containment, as Americans defined it, could not logically be bound by geographical lines or perimeters but had to be invoked anywhere a Soviet threat seemed to exist. America's few policemen had to watch all exits; they guarded a constantly shifting frontier that permitted no distinction between what was vital and what was peripheral.

In the spirited discussion that followed these comments, a number of conferees questioned the continuity and centrality of containment policy as depicted by Sherwin and Paterson. For some, containment was relevant to China policy, but in a more spasmodic, pragmatic way. They believed that concern over Soviet expansion in China varied widely in intensity and depended more on local and regional developments than on global Cold War axioms. Policy modes of the two presidents differed radically and in Truman's case changed almost yearly. For others, these variables and differences lay at the heart of China policy in the 1944–48 period, and containment was largely irrelevant.

To Ernest May, profoundly different world views and historical perceptions animated Roosevelt and Truman. Roosevelt experienced international affairs before World War I, then that war itself, and the interwar years in an intense, personal way: "Sarajevo was an event in his head." Consequently Roosevelt's sense of international relations was far richer than that of Truman, who had probably not begun to think much about world affairs until the mid-thirties, the era of totalitarian aggression. Roger Dingman suggested that Roosevelt's China policy partially reflected the thinking of his cousin Theodore Roosevelt, in the sense that toward an area of marginal importance the relevant policy was one of appeasement, in the earlier, nonpejorative sense of the term. Akira Iriye applied different "lessons" of history. He argued that one of the governing ideas of American policy makers in the 1940s was that the autarkic '30s had been a costly mistake and that therefore policy should return to the international cooperation characterizing the 1920s, when of course China had also been torn by civil war and unable to contribute to international stability. In that era too China had been unimportant to the United States.

A number of conferees doubted that China figured enough in Roosevelt's thinking to affect his ideas about postwar relations with the Soviet Union. Understanding the presidency as a job, a unique one but still a job, might help explain this policy dimness of China, May suggested. He likened the presidency to the Supreme Court, where the incumbent is able only to judge those questions brought before him and rarely, because of intense pressure of time, able to elicit and define the kinds of questions he wishes to decide. China, in May's estimation, was not a question being pushed at Roosevelt the way questions relating to Europe, for example, were intruding on his time. More likely Roosevelt, so far as he thought about China, did so glancingly, conceiving it as a nation that after all had always expelled its invaders or, as Michael Hunt suggested, as one that could not in any case become a great power for another quarter century or so. Roosevelt was probably dubious of the revolutionary content of the Chinese Communists' program, it was noted, and of their ability soon to contest power successfully on a national scale. In this minimalist view, even a patched-up united democratic China might, however, prevent stresses in American bipartisan foreign policy and in Soviet relations.

So far as China did present itself as a problem for decision, discussants argued, it was within the context of the war with Japan, the immediacy and importance of which was all too easy to ignore in retrospect. With China a "shambles" in the wake of the Japanese offensive of 1944, James Reardon-

Anderson pointed out, simply uniting China so as to resist Japan was more than sufficient to preoccupy policy makers.

Hunt saw a more constructive element in Roosevelt's China policy, one unrelated to the Soviet Union. He saw the president engaged in symbolic politics with respect to China. To compensate for inadequate wartime aid, Roosevelt acted on the fiction that China was already a major power and hence should be treated with public consideration. Furthermore, Roosevelt anticipated that when China finally realized its potential as a great power, relations would be smoother if a tradition of respect for Chinese sovereignty and equality had been established. Therefore, in Hunt's view, he deliberately sought to avoid past imperialist practice of playing one faction off against another in China and steadfastly adhered to the existing legitimate government regardless of its failings.

Another motive, Robert Donovan asserted, was that "Chiang and his chic, Westernized, Wellesley-educated wife had captured the affection and trust of millions of Americans." In January 1945, "as sensible a legislator as Representative Mike Mansfield equated Chiang with China itself."

Critics of the continuity thesis found it particularly hard to reconcile the Yalta agreement with containment. Its major concessions to the Soviet Union in China hardly squared with confrontationist policy. Given Chinese weakness, said Dingman, the trick for Roosevelt was to design a system that would facilitate accommodation of interests and avoid confrontation. Yalta served that purpose. According to Iriye, the Yalta system meant that the United States would not be concentrating on the Asian mainland. Instead it would achieve security through control of the Pacific, the Philippines, Okinawa, and Japan. In this system Japan was very important to America and China was unimportant.

Paterson had presented Yalta as a more complex form of containment, in which Roosevelt was seeking to use the Soviets to contain the Chinese Communists by securing Moscow's support of Chiang's regime, while at the same time he

sought to use Nationalist China as a check against the Soviets. However, to several participants the more broadly one
construed containment the more meaningless the term became. Agreeing that Roosevelt saw the Soviet Union as an
adversary, Bruce Cumings felt that he was "just not what we
would call a containment thinker." Containment bespoke
clarity; Roosevelt inclined to ambiguity. Containment represented division and dichotomy, Roosevelt inclusiveness.
"FDR threw a net of good cheer and deserved rewards over
his enemies," said Cumings, "thus hindering their movements but still leaving them something." Yalta was a means
of hamstringing the Soviets by "embracing, enveloping, en-
rolling" them in multilateral agreements. Containment, on
the other hand, represented to Cumings a fall-back position, a
postwar compromise between Rooseveltian internationalists
who would have preferred agreement with the Soviets and
Roosevelt's opponents who favored the rollback of Soviet
power.

Trusteeships for Korea and Indochina, the build-up of
China as a great power, and the unilateral occupation of
Japan impressed Cumings as brilliant strategies devised by
Roosevelt for orderly transition in the wake of the disintegra-
tion of the Japanese empire. He urged the conference not to
lose sight of this larger historical context. The impact of Japanese imperialism on Asia had been overwhelming, in his
view. It had carried all before it, not only making a rump
regime of the Kuomintang but also spawning resistance
movements in the Philippines and Malaya, destroying Dutch
rule in the East Indies, and severely weakening France in Indochina. Japanese industrialization and rule had so rear-
ranged northeast Asia that Manchuria and Korea hardly existed as such, all their linkages running to Tokyo. In 1945
profound forces of change were loose in Asia impinging on
American policy not only immediately but for the rest of the
decade. Whatever discontinuities existed in American policy,
wartime Asia was inextricably linked with the immediate
postwar years and the later '40s.

Whether or not an adversary relationship with the Soviet Union framed American China policy, conference members agreed that the transition from Roosevelt to Truman had little immediate impact on policy. Even if the new president had not committed himself to carry on the policies of his illustrious predecessor, he would have found it extremely difficult to disengage the United States from the Chiang regime. "For Truman in his early months and years in office to have turned his back on Chiang," said Donovan, "would have been regarded not only as a repudiation of Roosevelt and an affront to public opinion, but as a challenge to Republican doctrine in Congress." A more parochial and simplistic outlook prevailed at the White House, but, as May pointed out, it took several months for Truman just to define his job as president and China was not one of his most pressing problems. When Patrick Hurley resigned as ambassador and China briefly did command the president's attention, according to May, "Truman reached out for a way of getting rid of the problem by turning it over to General George Marshall, who would keep it off his desk."

Steven Levine saw a more active interest in China, at the start of the Marshall mission. Marshall was sent, he argued, because Washington believed the Soviet Union was pursuing a forward policy in China, especially Manchuria. However, by the late spring of 1946, Marshall concluded that the Soviets were not behaving as anticipated. Instead of seeking an active role in the mediation between Chinese Communists and Nationalists, they were lying low and indeed withdrawing troops from China. This discovery made it possible for American policy makers to disengage China from their containment thinking and revert to their familiar image of China as a swamp of internal strife. A China returning to the warlord condition of the 1920s could be discounted because it was uncontrollable and therefore of no advantage either to the Soviet Union or the United States. Paradoxically, Levine added, even though the Marshall mission failed in its ostensible purpose of unifying China, it succeeded in its larger purpose of stopping Soviet advance there.

To those who tended to minimize its policy significance, China seemed to count for even less during the next two years, from late 1946 until late 1948. Admittedly the Clifford memorandum attached no less importance to China than Europe and—as Donovan stated—George Elsey, who actually wrote it, was merely reflecting what Truman heard "all the time, day in and day out." Nevertheless, Donovan and May agreed that the memorandum was probably intended less for its effect on policy than on Henry Wallace and his followers who were attacking administration foreign policy in a bleak election year. Michael Baron contended that after 1946 the Truman policy makers, far from seeking any involvement in the Chinese situation, were "desperately trying to avoid applying the containment doctrine to China." They feared great power embroilment as in Spain in the 1930s and hoped that a hands-off policy would encourage a similar Soviet posture.

Evidence presented suggested that from late 1948 onward Truman took a more active role in China policy. While usually deferring to Acheson and by no means sanguine about Nationalist prospects, the president repeatedly chose the route that would favor them or work least injury to them. Baron pointed out that three weeks before the election of November 1948, Truman strongly advised against closing the American naval base at Tsingtao, then surrounded by Communist forces. Finally in December, after the Chinese Nationalists withdrew from the port, he relented. At the same time he rejected the advice of aid administrators that economic assistance continue in Communist-held areas. Warren Cohen, in the following paper, describes a number of critical presidential interventions in 1949: Truman dismissed the recommendation to cut off aid to the disintegrating Nationalist regime, rejected talks with Chinese Communist leaders, and insisted on respecting the undeclared Nationalist blockade of mainland ports.

In some degree these presidential interventions could be explained by American domestic politics. Some of them appeared to be aimed less at providing concrete assistance to ensure the survival of the Nationalists than at avoiding the appearance of hastening their defeat. With the election of 1948 Truman was president in his own right. Having removed any possible threat from the left by his resounding defeat of Henry Wallace, Lawrence Weiss pointed out, Truman was free to broaden his consensus by accommodating the right, where strongest pro-Nationalist sentiment lay. While agreeing with Walter LaFeber that Truman was little constrained by public opinion itself, several discussants saw the president as particularly sensitive to Congress and its leadership, frequently consulting the latter on China policy.

No less plausible was the viewpoint that Truman was responding to unfolding events in China as he perceived them. At some point, "quite late," May suggested, Truman came to perceive the Chinese and the Soviets as the same. Then he ceased to ignore China, for China now was part of his Communist problem and he could think about it. Whether that point occurred with the Chinese Communist victories of the fall of 1948 or spring of 1949, or as late as the Sino-Soviet Alliance of 1950 or even the Korean War, was difficult to establish. But clearly, as LaFeber noted, a more decisive Truman emerged in 1949–50.

Acheson, His Advisers, and China, 1949–1950

Warren I. Cohen

Prologue: Preparing to Live with a Communist China

IN HIS memoir, *Present at the Creation*, Dean Acheson wrote of the misfortune of having Chiang Kai-shek's regime collapse on him shortly after he became secretary of state. His predecessor, George C. Marshall, had tried to prevent Chiang's defeat. Marshall and his advisers were convinced that the Chinese Communists were in league with the Soviet Union. They were convinced that Communist control of China would have adverse effects on American interests there and on the world balance of power. Admiration for Chiang and optimism about his prospects were never part of their intellectual baggage, but they agreed on the advisability of supporting resistance to the forces of Mao Tse-tung.[1]

For the Truman administration, the debate on aid to the Kuomintang focused on questions of how much and what kind. Within the Department of State a consensus on the primacy of European affairs emerged. The cost of reconstructing and defending Europe would be enormous. Like the architects of victory in World War II, the men planning the containment of Soviet influence assigned a very low priority to aid to China. Moreover, Marshall and W. Walton But-

[1] Ernest R. May, *The Truman Administration and China, 1945–1949* (Philadelphia: Lippincott, 1975), pp. 20, 25–26; Steven I. Levine, "A New Look at American Intervention in the Chinese Civil War: The Marshall Mission and Manchuria," draft manuscript in my possession.

13

terworth, who returned from China to become director of the Office of Far Eastern Affairs in August 1947, did not believe that the Kuomintang government needed substantial aid. They assumed that the Chinese had adequate reserves of gold and foreign exchange. Intensely suspicious of Chinese profiteering, they demanded reform of financial as well as political and military practices.[2]

Modest economic aid was agreeable to Marshall and his staff, and they responded readily to demands from Congressional friends of Chiang's regime. Military assistance, advisory groups, and troop support were very different matters, however. Unlike the Joint Chiefs of Staff, Marshall did not believe limited military assistance could affect the outcome of the Chinese civil war. He had a low regard for Chiang as a strategist and firsthand experience with the Chinese leader's resistance to advice. Marshall suspected Chiang's interest in American military advisers was an attempt to draw the United States into war with the Communists.[3]

Marshall and Butterworth were determined to avoid a commitment to provide Chiang with the means to victory because they feared the burden on the United States would be unbearable, "of uncertain magnitude and indefinite duration." It might also provoke countervailing Soviet action. If the Kuomintang reformed, it would not need much American assistance. If it did not, no amount of American assistance would enable an unpopular regime to suppress its internal enemies.[4]

The policy of limited economic assistance, dictated by Marshall's concerns, was further rationalized by the observations of George Kennan, chief of Marshall's Policy Planning

[2] May, Truman and China, pp. 28–31; W. Walton Butterworth, Draft Oral History Interview, July 6, 1971, by Richard D. McKenzie and Theodore S. Wilson, Harry S. Truman Library, Independence, Mo. (hereafter cited as Butterworth Oral History).

[3] May, Truman and China, pp. 30–32; memorandum of Marshall and Butterworth conversation with secretary of the army and staff, June 11, 1948, U.S. Department of State, Foreign Relations of the United States (hereafter FR), 1948, 8:90–99.

[4] May, Truman and China, pp. 39–40.

Staff (PPS). Kennan had a low estimate of China's importance in the Cold War. If the Kuomintang collapsed, it would be "deplorable" but probably not "catastrophic." China lacked the resources to become a great power for a long time. He also argued that if the Chinese Communists succeeded in taking over most of China, their dependence on Moscow would diminish. In a rare bow to Congressional and public demands, Kennan recommended, in November 1947, that the United States give Chiang the "minimum aid necessary to satisfy American public opinion and, if possible, to prevent any sudden and total collapse of the Chinese Government."[5]

In the last months of Marshall's tenure as secretary of state, the demise of the Kuomintang government seemed imminent. American intervention was ruled out on the ground that the weakness of Chiang's regime precluded success. Moreover, the Russians had played an insignificant role in the Communist victory. Their absence from Communist-controlled areas, combined with knowledge of Tito's split with Stalin earlier in 1948, allowed some comfort for American impotence. Mao's victory could not be denied, but perhaps China could be prevented from becoming "an adjunct of Soviet power."[6]

Persuaded he could do no more, Marshall left office resigned to a Communist victory in China, buoyed only by the faint hope that Mao, like Tito, would choose to rival Stalin rather than become another Soviet satellite.

Acheson and His Team[7]

Acheson was a commanding presence as secretary of state. Nothing seems clearer than the fact that the opinion neither

---

[5] Kennan memoranda for Robert Lovett, June 23, 1947, and for Marshall, November 3, 1947, Records of the Policy Planning Staff (hereafter PPS), box 13, "China 1947–1948" file, National Archives.

[6] PPS memorandum, Butterworth concurring with "underlying findings," September 7, 1948, *FR, 1948*, 8:146–65.

[7] The biographic sketches that follow have been based primarily on extensive reading of documents; see also nn. 8–14 below.

of his subordinates, of Congress, nor of the public, could sway him once he had made up his mind. The president, however, open to such influences, could and did on occasion reject, modify, or otherwise impose his wishes on Acheson's recommendations.

Acheson had little interest in Chinese affairs. In 1946, however, he had worked in support of Marshall's effort to avert the civil war and had shared the frustration Marshall suffered in his dealings with Chiang. He had no intention of enduring any such nonsense in 1949. He was aware that the Communists were on the verge of victory, regretted the situation, but was quite content to follow the course upon which Marshall had settled. As new questions arose, he relied for information and analysis on Butterworth, who became his assistant secretary for Far Eastern affairs; Dean Rusk, his deputy undersecretary and later Butterworth's successor; and his close friend and alter ego Philip C. Jessup, appointed ambassador-at-large. Although he looked less to Policy Planning than had Marshall, Acheson often received ideas from Kennan and from John P. Davies, the PPS specialist on China. In 1950 John Foster Dulles was brought into the department, at Rusk's suggestion, to attempt to salvage bipartisan support for policy toward Asia. Despised by Acheson, Dulles nonetheless served him loyally, working primarily with Rusk and, to a lesser extent, with Jessup.[8]

Eager to contain Soviet influence everywhere, Acheson was, however, an Atlanticist for whom Western Europe was the highest priority. His principal concerns in 1949 were European recovery and creation of the North Atlantic Treaty Organization. Stopping communism across the Pacific was also highly desirable, but a task of lesser importance. He had little interest in Asia beyond a determination to link Japan, like Germany, to the West. Jessup, Rusk, Kennan, and Davies

---

[8] Acheson's *Present at the Creation: My Years in the State Department* (New York: Norton, 1969) is the most revealing source of his thought and personality. My interviews with Jessup, October 1, 1976, and with Rusk, April 9, 1977, were also useful.

were troubled by his neglect of East Asia, but they had little effect on his policy recommendations prior to the Korean War. He allowed them only symbolic acts, shows of concern—nothing that required a major commitment of American resources or power.

Jessup was a Columbia professor, highly regarded for his work on international law. A friend of long standing, with previous experience in the department, he saw himself as Acheson's general counsel, the confidential adviser who had to understand all operations. He tackled special assignments and was generally available as a whetstone for the secretary's mind. He had a particularly good relationship with Rusk, with whom he had worked closely on United Nations affairs in 1948, and he drew Rusk into his relationship with Acheson.[9]

Jessup was less attracted to realpolitik than were Acheson and Kennan, more likely to think in terms of right and wrong than in terms of power, more likely to seek peaceful, legalistic solutions to problems than to flaunt American strength. His military experience in World War I had led him close to pacifism, to an abhorrence of the use of force. In the 1930s he had supported the neutrality laws and in 1940 had joined America First. Eager to keep America from war, he had favored the appeasement of Japan. In the context of the late 1940s, he was a universalist rather than an Atlanticist, ready to apply right principles to Asia as well as to Europe. He was more eager to help weak countries, more sympathetic to victims of colonialism than were men like Acheson and Kennan. And he was more optimistic about the potential of the United Nations.

Although Jessup had long served in prominent posts with the Institute of Pacific Relations, Asia had never engaged him intellectually. Nonetheless, when problems with policy toward China plagued Acheson, he passed them on to Jessup. To serve the secretary, either by obtaining infor-

[9] Jessup interview.

mation for him or by protecting him, was Jessup's purpose in Chinese affairs.

Rusk had served briefly in the China-Burma-India Theater during World War II, and of Acheson's principal advisers he was the most concerned about the plight of the Chinese people. Like Jessup, he was a universalist, as concerned with Asia as with Europe, uncomfortable with Kennan's contemptuous disregard for the weak of the less-developed world. As a southern liberal, he was intensely sensitive to the slighting of colored peoples anywhere. Loyal to Marshall and Acheson, aware that the Communist conquest of the Chinese mainland could not be prevented, he was nonetheless troubled about the suffering of non-Communist Chinese and sought opportunities to spare them from Mao's rule. He was also like Jessup in his desire to work through the United Nations, to strengthen that organization.[10]

As deputy undersecretary, Rusk was involved in everything of importance that came before the department. He took on additional responsibilities for East Asian affairs because of Acheson's disinterest. He endeared himself to the secretary by volunteering to handle a variety of politically awkward questions. His most precious quality was his ability to soothe congressmen—the fools Acheson tried in vain to suffer. His relationship with Dulles was also important. Given Acheson's difficulty tolerating any Republican leaders, Rusk and Dulles became the instruments of bipartisanship. It was natural for Rusk to replace Butterworth when, early in 1950, political pressure on policy toward China intensified. Rusk, alone of the Acheson loyalists, had credibility with the Republican leadership in Congress.

Butterworth was a career foreign service officer who had served one tour in China, administering the embassy during the Marshall mission and for some months afterward. He had no particular affection for China and was condescending to-

[10] Warren I. Cohen, "Dean Rusk," in Robert H. Ferrell, ed., *American Secretaries of State and Their Diplomacy,* forthcoming.

ward those of his colleagues who, through birth or service
there, had formed attachments to the country or its people.
He prided himself on his lack of any illusions about China or
about any special relationship between Americans and Chinese that gave the United States particular responsibility for
the protection of that country. Intellectually, he was close to
Kennan, who had wanted him assigned to Moscow in 1945.
Princetonian, conservative, he was staunchly anti-Communist and contemptuous of liberals who scrupled to work
with the likes of Franco. He was incredulous about Marshall's efforts to draw the Communists into a coalition government in China. But his fiscal conservatism forced him to
question the value of aid to Chiang's regime. He did not like
the Chinese Communists, but he was not one to squander
money on their defeated opponents, especially when he did
not approve of T. V. Soong's financial legerdemain. The Chinese embassy in Washington and its friends in Congress saw
Butterworth as the evil genius behind the policies of Marshall and Acheson. They were delighted when he was reas-
signed in 1950, although Ambassador Wellington Koo con-
fessed to finding his replacement, Rusk, inscrutable.[11]

Kennan was the department's leading specialist in Soviet
affairs. He was the most articulate proponent of containing
the Soviet Union and of "realism" in foreign policy. Brush-
ing aside public or Congressional opinion, sterile legalism,
misguided faith in international organization, and charitable
concerns about Africans, Chinese, or Jews, he determined the
national interest and advised the secretary how best to serve
it. In Marshall's day Kennan had been greatly admired. Acheson admired him less and often turned to Rusk or to Jessup
for planning. Worst of all, Kennan was a complainer, another
species for which the secretary had little patience. During

[11] Butterworth Oral History; also V. K. Wellington Koo Diary, entries for January
13, 1949, and February 16, 1949, V. K. Wellington Koo Papers, box 217, Butler
Library, Columbia University; memorandum of conversation with J. Leighton Stuart,
Philip Fugh present, August 13, 1949, Koo Papers, box 130; and Koo Diary, entry for
April 20, 1950, box 217.

Acheson's tenure Policy Planning declined in importance, and Kennan eventually left the department.[12]

On Chinese affairs Kennan's record was generally sound. He had underestimated the ease with which the Communists would gain control of the mainland, but he had no illusions about the Kuomintang. His rationale for acquiescing in a Communist victory went unquestioned in the department in 1949. The idea for a public explanation of American policy toward China that developed into the White Paper appears to have been his. But Kennan had little to offer on the other questions of importance to Acheson, such as what to do about recognition and the island of Formosa, although he offered one incredibly bizarre recommendation for handling the latter.

Davies had been born in China, of missionary parents, and had been posted there as a foreign service officer, much like John S. Service. They were strikingly different, however. No one could accuse Davies of being sentimental about the Chinese, of being a Sinophile. He was extraordinarily detached, much given to analyses of Chinese character reminiscent of the 19th century treaty port mentality. But he found the Chinese Communists different from other Chinese, more likely to generate real power, to become a force against the Russians whom he had come to despise in the 1930s. His goal was to use them, as he had earlier sought to use the Kuomintang regime. Of Chiang's government he once wrote that it had failed "to perform as ordered by Washington." When he encountered the Communists, he wondered how they might be drawn into "dependence upon the United States." He seemed to have little more understanding of or sympathy for the national aspirations of the Chinese than men who had never had contact with China. Davies' influence on Kennan in 1949 and 1950 is difficult to measure. His ideas for managing the Chinese Communists after they came to power were as incredible as those of his chief regarding

12 Kennan's *Memoirs: 1925–1950* (Boston: Little, Brown, 1967) is revealing, as is most everything he writes; Rusk interview.

Formosa. His insistence on scolding (*ma*, in Chinese) them for subservience to the Russians, as a means of provoking them to behave more like nationalists, was reflected in the letter of transmittal of the White Paper and in countless public pronouncements by Acheson and Rusk, including the latter's notorious "Slavic Manchukuo" speech of 1951.[13]

Dulles was a prominent lawyer, Republican Party spokesman on foreign policy, and leader of the bipartisan foreign affairs establishment. Had Thomas Dewey been elected president in November 1948, it was generally assumed that Dulles would have been his secretary of state. Still governor of New York in 1949, Dewey appointed Dulles to a vacancy in the U.S. Senate instead. Defeated in a special election a few months later, Dulles was available to the department in 1950 for the task Rusk had in mind: containing Republican harassment. He did not have much luck reining in the wild jackasses of his party, but he was successful in persuading Koo and some of Chiang's supporters that Rusk was friendlier than Butterworth. He was useful as a go-between for the department with its critics. Evidence in Koo's files leaves no doubt that, unlike Secretary of Defense Louis Johnson, Dulles' first loyalty was to the administration.[14]

Throughout 1949 the department was subject to intense pressure to change course and help Chiang reverse the tide. In 1950 the principal opposition demand was for the defense of Formosa. The pressure came from antiadministration forces in Congress and the mass media and from a Department of Defense whose highest echelons were in collusion with Chiang's agents.[15] Acheson held steady, refusing to be diverted by ignorant congressmen. He resisted Pentagon pressures fiercely and generally with success. Almost always,

[13] John Paton Davies, Jr., *Dragon by the Tail* (New York: Norton, 1972), *passim*.

[14] Koo memoranda of conversations with Dulles are most useful for this period. Koo Papers.

[15] See Koo memoranda of conversations with Assistant Secretary Paul Griffiths, June 3, 1950, and with Secretary Louis Johnson, June 30, 1950, Koo Papers, box 180.

he had the president's support. On several important occasions, however, the president resisted the secretary of
state's advice and delayed significantly actions the department was prepared to take.

Between the time Acheson took office and the onset of
the Korean War, the department's concerns regarding China
fell into three general areas. First, there was a need to determine policy toward the retreating Kuomintang and whatever
factions emerged. Second, a decision had to be made about
Formosa. Third, policy toward the emerging Communist
regime had to be defined. In each area Acheson's intent was
thwarted, in several instances by the perceived need for temporary delays in order to win a national consensus, and in
every instance by the Korean War and the Sino-American
conflict that developed from it.

Policy toward the Kuomintang Regime:
Maneuver of Disengagement

Ten days before Acheson was sworn in, the National Security
Council (NSC) agreed to continue efforts to prevent China
from becoming "an adjunct of Soviet power." Council
members also agreed that efforts toward China would be "of
lower priority" than efforts where the benefits to American
security were "more immediately commensurate" with the
expenditure of resources.[16]

By the end of January all of China north of the Yangtze
was in Communist hands and Mao's legions were massing at
the river. Chiang went home to Fenghua and left the government in the hands of Li Tsung-jen, who began peace overtures to the Communists. To Acheson and others in Washington it seemed clear that the time had come to stop aid. On
February 3 the NSC recommended that the United States suspend shipments to China. Several days later, however, Congressional leaders urged the president not to take any formal

---

[16] NSC 34/1, January 11, 1949, FR, 1949 9:474–75.

action. That their concern was not for the fortunes of the Kuomintang but rather to soothe their colleagues and constituents was manifest in their willingness to have shipments delayed by informal action. Truman accepted the advice. Aid would not be suspended, but ways would be found to slow shipments. American political leaders feared that a public announcement of the cessation of aid would lead to the immediate collapse of the Kuomintang regime, and that they would be held responsible. Acheson had his orders.[17]

By the end of February General Albert C. Wedemeyer, more sympathetic to Chiang than most American leaders, had concluded that it would be worse than useless to send aid to Chiang's forces: it would be seized almost immediately by the Communists. In mid-March Acheson wrote to Senator Tom Connally, chairman of the Senate Foreign Relations Committee, to oppose a bill calling for $1.5 billion in aid for China, insisting that even massive military assistance would not reverse the tide. But he agreed that it would be undesirable to cut off aid to Kuomintang-controlled areas "precipitously." Several days later, addressing the committee in executive session, Acheson was franker. He reported that he was persuaded by his advisers "that at the present time to continue aid to anybody in China is going to have the opposite result from what we want to achieve."[18]

A few weeks later Acheson indicated confidence that he had won the support necessary to end aid to the Kuomintang and to seek an accommodation with the Chinese Communists. He told Ernest Bevin, the British foreign secretary, that Chiang's regime was "washed up," that the Communists now had a free hand in China. The Chinese people were tired and further aid to the Kuomintang would anger them. "We had,"

[17] Memorandum by Marshall S. Carter, February 7, 1949, Acheson memorandum of conversation with Truman, February 7, 1949, and memorandum by Sidney W. Souers for National Security Council, February 8, 1949, ibid., pp. 485–87.

[18] Butterworth memorandum of meeting with Wedemeyer, February 25, 1949, and Acheson to Connally, March 15, 1949, ibid., pp. 490–91, 607–9; U.S. Senate, Executive Session of the Committee on Foreign Relations, March 18, 1949, Historical Series, 81st Congress, p. 41.

he explained to Bevin, "abandoned the idea of supporting the regime and were only extending to June 2 a further 58 million dollars under the China Aid Act." It was difficult to withdraw support publicly, but he thought "the extreme supporters of Chiang Kai-shek in Congress were gaining a better appreciation of realities." Most significantly, Acheson promised Bevin, "The U.S. henceforth will pursue a more realistic policy respecting China."[19]

In mid-April Wellington Koo, near despair over his failure to win adequate American support for his government, met with Dulles. He reported finding Acheson preoccupied with Europe and blamed Marshall's influence for the State Department's indifference to China's plight. Dulles agreed and added that Senator Arthur H. Vandenberg, the key Republican foreign policy spokesman in the Senate, would no longer press for aid. The State Department had persuaded Vandenberg that the Kuomintang could not win, no matter how much aid the United States sent.[20]

By the spring of 1949 Acheson was persuaded that the consensus necessary to withdraw support from the Kuomintang had been obtained. On June 2, when the China Aid Act expired, the United States would cease wasting its resources. Kuomintang China was dead. There remained only the need for last rites, to persuade the American people. Acheson turned to an earlier recommendation by Kennan that the public be informed of the reasons for American policy before it was misled by partisan criticism. Marshall had read the suggestion to the cabinet in November 1948, but Truman had rejected it. The people needed the facts, but to reveal Chiang's ineptness and the corruption of his regime would be tantamount to the United States' delivering the final blow. Nine months later, however, Truman agreed that the time had come. He supported Acheson over the objec-

[19] Memorandum of Acheson-Bevin conversation, April 4, 1949, FR, 1949, 7:1138–41.

[20] Memorandum of conversation with Dulles, April 18, 1949, Koo Papers, box 130.

tions of the secretary of defense and the Joint Chiefs, and "The China White Paper" was published. Awareness of the ties between Chiang's lobbyists and Republican critics may have facilitated the decision.[21]

Acheson's determination to publish the White Paper, despite concern over Mao's "leaning to one side" speech, strong opposition from the Pentagon, reservations within the department and on Capitol Hill, and while the Kuomintang still held Canton, is explicable only as a decision to drive in the last nail. He was determined to end American involvement in the Chinese civil war, to quash in advance any new onslaught by Chiang's American friends, and to prepare for an accommodation with the Communist regime. Acheson failed, but not for want of trying. His *bête noire*, Chiang Kaishek, escaped to Formosa and reopened the issue on a basis less susceptible to Acheson's arguments.

Farewell to Formosa

The question of what to do about Formosa stirred the most controversy within the Department of State and a sharp struggle between State and Defense. It revealed Kennan at his most absurd and Acheson at his most resolute. Had Acheson prevailed, there was every likelihood of early diplomatic relations between the United States and the People's Republic. But war came to Korea first, and Acheson, isolated on the issue, was forced to retreat—but he never surrendered.

In May 1947, before the outcome of the Chinese civil war was apparent, Butterworth had seen in the tension between native Formosans and their Kuomintang "liberators" a situation of great potential interest to the United States.[22] When

[21] Kennan to Marshall and Marshall to Lovett, November 26, 1948, FR, 1948, 8:214–15, 220; Jessup for Acheson, July 20, 1949, Joint Chiefs of Staff for Secretary of Defense, July 21, 1949, Acheson to Truman, July 29, 1949, FR, 1949, 9:1376–81, 1388–90.

[22] Butterworth to Secretary of State, May 1, 1947, 123 Butterworth, Wm. W. Jr. HH, National Archives.

Acheson returned to the department in January 1949, he found agreement on the desirability of keeping the island out of Communist hands: its strategic value was obvious. The question that remained was how to achieve this goal without driving the Chinese Communists closer to the Russians or intervening so blatantly as to offend the international community.

Davies and Butterworth warned against sending military forces to Formosa. To do so would facilitate Communist subversion there. Instead, the United States should foster the Formosan independence movement, which would have a strong motivation for denying the island to any mainlanders. Then, if it were necessary for the United States to intervene, it could act in support of self-determination for the Formosans, a morally justifiable position that would win considerable international support. The United States had to keep its distance, disguise its interest, and separate the island from the Chinese civil war by discouraging the further influx of mainland Chinese. These ideas were incorporated into NSC 37/2, signed by the president on February 4, 1949.[23]

The Joint Chiefs preferred to station naval units on Formosa or to offer some other indication of American willingness to use force, as a means of deterring a Communist attack. Acheson was troubled by leaks from the Pentagon which spotlighted American interest in the island. He argued that it was essential to avoid "an American-created irredentist issue just at the time we shall be seeking to exploit the genuinely Soviet-created irredentist issue in Manchuria and Sinkiang." To prevent the Chinese Communists from becoming an adjunct to Soviet power, it was necessary to focus on Soviet imperialism and to "carefully conceal our wish to separate the island from mainland control."[24]

The vision of an independent Formosan regime, free of

[23] Davies note, January 14, 1949, PPS Records, 1947–1953, box 13, "China 1949" file; NSC 37/2, Harry S. Truman Papers, PSF/box 205, Truman Library.

[24] Joint Chiefs of Staff to Secretary of Defense, February 10, 1949, and Acheson to Truman, March 3, 1949, Truman Papers, PSF/box 205.

Kuomintang taint, proved to be a fantasy. Within a few months it was painfully clear that the independence movement was weak and that Chiang Kai-shek's supporters dominated the island. The Economic Cooperation administrator there reported that Formosa had become "the redoubt of the Gimo's favored elements, the very people whose selfishness, corruption and short-sightedness have destroyed their regime on the mainland." Livingston Merchant, sent by the department to investigate conditions, stayed on the island for several months and came to the same conclusion. An autonomous Formosa was not possible. He recommended that the United States abandon its effort to deny the island to the Communists and urged his government "to guard its moral position not only on Formosa and in China but throughout all Southeast Asia by minimizing its association with a governing group which has already in a larger theater demonstrated its incompetence and unpopularity." [25]

Accepting Merchant's analysis, Butterworth and Kennan offered new approaches for separating the island from mainland control. Butterworth proposed calling for a special session of the United Nations to discuss Formosa. The goal would be a UN-supervised plebiscite in which the people would vote for either mainland control or, more likely, some sort of UN trusteeship pending independence. Kennan advocated a more direct approach to ridding the island of the Kuomintang scourge. He thought Formosa of greater strategic importance than the Joint Chiefs would concede, and he was disgusted by defeatism in the Department of State, where everyone told him "we should reconcile ourselves to the prospect of Formosa's falling into the hands of the Chinese Communists." Further inaction was not permissible. Kennan advocated the use of American forces to throw Chiang's army out of Formosa and the Pescadores and, under American pro-

---

[25] Allen Griffin to Harlan Cleveland, forwarded to Butterworth, April 29, 1949, Merchant to Butterworth, March 6, 1949, Merchant to Secretary of State, May 4, 1949, Merchant memorandum for Butterworth, May 24, 1949, FR, 1949, 9:318–20, 297, 324–26, 337–41.

tection, to create a regime independent of mainland control. He proposed sending the mainland Chinese already on the island "elsewhere," but indicated a willingness to let Chiang stay as a political refugee. Kennan knew the sensibilities of some of his colleagues might be offended but thought his plan would be executed the way "Theodore Roosevelt might have done it," with "resolution, speed, ruthlessness and self-assurance."[26]

Acheson was unmoved by either proposal. He accepted Merchant's conclusion as well as his analysis. Prepared to bury the Kuomintang wherever its flag was raised, he preferred to abandon the effort to hold the island. If Chiang's unregenerate followers controlled Formosa, it was doomed to fall to the Communists. They would merely repeat the errors that had lost the civil war. An American effort on the island would be wasted and have adverse effects on the attempt to wean Mao away from Stalin. In August 1949 he won his case at a meeting of the NSC. The Joint Chiefs conceded that military measures would be unwise, even if economic and diplomatic approaches to the problem failed. A few weeks later Butterworth and Merchant told British officials they expected Formosa to be taken by the Communists, probably by infiltration.[27]

Within the department Jessup and Rusk joined Butterworth, Kennan, and Davies in seeking alternatives to the Communist conquest of Formosa. In September Jessup pressed for involvement of the UN. Rusk brushed aside arguments that Chiang would reject a UN trusteeship, urging that he be asked. He warned that public opinion would demand American action short of military intervention. Acheson conceded nothing more than continuance of an extraordinarily

[26] Butterworth for Rusk, June 9, 1949, and Kennan memorandum PPS 53 (enclosure dated June 23, 1949), July 6, 1949, ibid., pp. 346–50, 356–64.

[27] Memorandum by State for National Security Council, August 4, 1949, Joint Chiefs of Staff to Secretary of Defense, August 17, 1949, memorandum of conversation with British officials, September 9, 1949, ibid., pp. 369–71, 376–78, 388–90.

modest economic assistance program. He advised the president that the CIA estimated that Formosa would be under Communist control by the end of 1950.[28]

Early in November the department's senior officers and leading specialists on Chinese affairs met and concluded that the United States should not seek to detach Formosa from China by force or through a UN trusteeship. One possibility was left open. If another country initiated the action, the United States might support steps leading to Formosan self-determination.[29]

Pressure on the department's position mounted in November and December 1949 as the Kuomintang government, its friends in the United States, General Douglas MacArthur, the Joint Chiefs, and Republican political leaders urged action to deny Formosa to the Communists. Chiang's supporters had been buoyed in October when Truman had signed a Mutual Defense Assistance Act that included an appropriation of $75 million for the "general area of China." They found, to their consternation, that Acheson did not intend to use the money to aid the regime on Formosa. Communism in Asia would indeed be contained, but he insisted there was no Chinese basis of resistance. He would not have the United States appear before all Asia as the supporter of the discredited Kuomintang. Driving the Joint Chiefs relentlessly, Acheson forced them to retreat. NSC 48/2, dated December 30, 1949, repeated the goal of seeking to deny Formosa to the Communists by economic and diplomatic means but stressed Acheson's contention that self-help by the Kuomintang was the key to success. NSC 48/2 also stated clearly that economic and diplomatic means might fail, and that the Joint Chiefs had reaffirmed their unwillingness to use overt military action. The United States would fall back, therefore,

[28] "Discussion of Far Eastern Affairs in Preparation for Conversation with Mr. Bevin," September 13, 1949, 890.00/9–1349, National Archives; State Department Report, October 6, 1949 (NSC 37/8), Truman Papers, PSF/box 205.

[29] Memorandum of meeting, November 2, 1949, FR, 1949, 9:160–62.

on a position based on the Philippines, the Ryukyus, and Japan. Farewell to Formosa.[30]

On January 2, 1950, Rusk informed the British that the United States would not "become engaged in the defense" of Formosa. The Kuomintang still had funds with which it could purchase military supplies, but the United States would not allow Chiang to purchase bombers and heavy tanks which, in Communist hands, might be used against Hong Kong. Three days later Acheson met with two of Chiang's staunchest supporters in the Senate, William Knowland (R-California) and H. Alexander Smith (R-New Jersey). He told them bluntly and in considerable detail why the United States would do nothing and must "be prepared to accept what appears to be the real possibility of its [the Kuomintang regime on Formosa] collapse." At an executive session of the Foreign Relations Committee a week later, Smith pursued Acheson. If the United States would regret the fall of Formosa, why not aid the regime? Acheson replied that aid would not be effective and would be detrimental to the American position in East Asia. Smith asked if the fall of Formosa to the Communists was inevitable. Acheson replied, "My own judgment is that it is."[31]

The pressure on Acheson did not disappear in the months that followed, but he was unmoved. In February, reacting angrily to the bombing of Shanghai by Chiang's forces, he asked whether the rude response to his protest presented the opportunity to get out of Formosa and end the last dribble of aid to a regime he abhorred. The moment was apparently not ripe, however, for the "complete freedom of maneuver and disassociation" from the Kuomintang.[32]

---

[30] Acheson memorandum of meeting with Joint Chiefs of Staff, December 29, 1949, ibid., pp. 463–67; NSC 48/2, Declassified Documents Reference System (75) 269B.

[31] Rusk memorandum of conversation, January 2, 1950, Acheson memorandum of conversation, January 5, 1950, FR, 1950, 6:256–63; U.S. Senate, Executive Session of the Committee on Foreign Relations, January 13, 1950, Historical Series, 81st Congress, p. 184.

[32] FR, 1950, 6:313n.4, 314n.6.

In March Acheson decided that Butterworth had endured enough abuse as assistant secretary for Far Eastern affairs and accepted Rusk's offer to take the post. Rusk was extraordinarily successful where the secretary was weakest—on the Hill. In the months ahead, when Formosa was expected to fall, it would be important to have a fresh and skillful figure in the job. Rusk, however, was more intensely concerned than Acheson or Butterworth about constructing the containment line in East Asia. He was more receptive than Acheson or Butterworth to arguments about the strategic value of Formosa. He was troubled by a sense that both American and Asian opinion perceived the initiative in Asia to be with the Communists. He, Dulles (who had joined the department in March), Jessup, Kennan, and Davies thought it important for the United States to take a dramatic stand to demonstrate concern beyond the NATO area. Like Kennan, Rusk thought Formosa an advantageous place to act and, like Jessup, he thought a UN trusteeship might keep the United States out of reinvolvement in the Chinese civil war.

The scenario Rusk favored in late May 1950 called for Dulles to see Chiang and tell him that the fall of Formosa was inevitable and that the United States would do nothing to help him. His only recourse would be to appeal to the UN to establish a trusteeship over the island. If he did so, the United States would support him and would prevent an attack while the trusteeship action was pending. The goal, clearly, was to deny what was perceived as the otherwise inevitable fall of Formosa to the Communists. The means, once again, would be an independent regime with no claim to rule China. Acheson had always left the door open to the possibility of an independent Formosa's emerging as a showcase of liberal democracy. Rusk, in the weeks preceding the anticipated Communist attack, tried to drive Chiang and the American government toward agreement. Simultaneously, he and his colleagues moved in two other directions, both based on the assumption that Chiang would be as recalcitrant as ever. First, they sought a place of refuge for him, after the fall (the

Filipinos said he would not be welcome; if he came, they would give him twenty-four hours to get out). Second, they indicated to Chinese representatives that Chiang was the obstacle to American aid to Formosa. Koo and Hollington Tong came away from discussions with Rusk and Dulles persuaded that, however obliquely, the Americans were saying that Acheson might be won over to aiding a reformed, i.e. Chiangless, regime. American interest in seeing real power reside with K. C. Wu and Sun Li-jen had long been evident. In June the hints bore fruit: a report reached Rusk that a coup was imminent. Later that week, however, war began in Korea.[33]

Toward Accommodation with the People's Republic

The principal reason for Acheson's determination to cut off aid to Chiang and to acquiesce in the fall of Formosa was the desire to establish the best possible relationship with Mao's regime. The Communist victory posed dangers for the United States because of evident Soviet influence among Mao's colleagues. Acheson and his advisers were eager to lessen that influence and to develop among the Chinese Communist leaders a sense of a need for ties to the West.

The State Department considered trade, recognition, and Chinese representation on the UN Security Council as means of achieving tolerable relations with the Communists. Trade would be used as a weapon, to demonstrate the extent of Chinese dependence on the West. Eventual recognition was assumed, but it would not be automatic. Recognition, too, might be useful as a lever with which to gain advantage for the United States. Policy on the Security Council representation question would have to be more flexible. The People's Republic might well be seated without American approval. There would be no attempt to use the veto.

A variety of domestic restraints and Chinese Communist actions delayed recognition, but these were diminishing in

[33] Memorandum by W. Park Armstrong, May 31, 1950, ibid., pp. 347–51, 346n.2; Koo Diary, entry for June 4, 1950, box 217; Rusk interview.

importance. There were indications that the United States would grant recognition to the People's Republic after the elections of November 1950. "Formal, regularized relations . . . not intimate but proper" were anticipated.[34] The department assumed that Peking's representatives would represent China in the UN as early as February or March 1950. But Acheson's preparations for overcoming public and Congressional opposition to an accommodation with the Communists were halted by the coming of war in Korea and abandoned after Chinese intervention in that war.

Kennan and his staff set the tone for dealing with the Chinese Communists in November 1948. The Kuomintang government would soon disappear, and the United States should determine its policy on recognition when that happened. Aid to Chiang was useless, but American ends in China might be achieved by using economic bargaining power to exact concessions, presumably from the successor Communist regime.[35]

Butterworth reflected the same position in talks with British officials in January and February 1949. They agreed that trade and recognition provided opportunities for bargaining. Butterworth was also prepared to cut off all Economic Cooperation Administration (ECA) operations in Communist-controlled areas to make it "just as difficult for the Communists as possible, in order to force orientation to the West." On the other hand, he favored restoration of trade relations with Communist China as "the most feasible means of maintaining contact" and thought it desirable to allow the Communists to import petroleum products "in order that they might develop a sense of dependence on the West."[36]

The department's premises were detailed in NSC 41, drafted by the State Department in late February 1949. The goal was to prevent "Soviet domination of China for strategic

[34] The words are Butterworth's in Butterworth Oral History.

[35] PPS 39/1, November 23, 1948, *FR, 1948*, 8:208–11.

[36] Sprouse memoranda of conversations, January 6, 1949, and February 10, 1949, *FR, 1949*, 9:5–6, 823–26.

ends." The alternatives posed were political and economic warfare to isolate and intimidate the Chinese, or restoration of economic relations and efforts to divide the Chinese and Russian Communists. The department insisted that the first course would force Mao into complete subservience to the Soviet Union, was obviously undesirable, and should not be risked except in extremis. The second alternative might produce an independent regime and was the policy to be pursued.[37]

Reports from the field, from Moscow as well as from offices in China, reinforced hope of an independent Communist regime. There was evidence of tension between Russian and Chinese leaders. There was suspicion that Russian-controlled Chinese Communists were worried by Mao's apparent interest in mutually beneficial relations with the United States. John M. Cabot, consul-general at Shanghai after a tour in Yugoslavia, sent a number of thoughtful letters and cables indicating his belief that a Sino-Soviet split was inevitable. The critical question of *when* might be affected by American policy. In March Acheson authorized Ambassador J. Leighton Stuart to approach Communist leaders. He was cautioned to avoid any ultimatums and any publicity. Acheson was eager to explore issues with Mao and Chou En-lai, but reports of talks were to be sent "eyes only for the secretary." The American public and the president were not quite ready to acknowledge the conquerors.[38]

In April, as the People's Liberation Army poised to cross the Yangtze, Acheson advised diplomats in China not to demand recognition of their official consular status from the Communists. Such action would convey a sense of "de jure

[37] *Ibid.*, pp. 826–34.

[38] Cabot to Butterworth, December 30, 1948, *FR, 1948,* 7:707–18; memorandum by chief of Division of Commercial Affairs for Paul H. Nitze, January 7, 1949, Stuart to Acheson, January 27, 1949, Kohler (Moscow) to Acheson, April 19, 1949, Cabot to Stuart, April 20, 1949, Cabot to Acheson, May 31, 1949, Stuart to Acheson, March 10, 1949, Acheson to Stuart, April 6, 1949, *FR, 1949,* 8:16–19, 88–89, 249–51, 256–57, 355–57, 173–77, 230–31.

relations in which we [are] unable [to] reciprocate," presumably because the Kuomintang still controlled China south of the Yangtze. After the Yangtze defenses were breached, Acheson raised with Stuart the question of de facto recognition. He was concerned about Communist attitudes toward American officials and property. Was de facto recognition the best hope for protecting American interests, or would the Communists become more demanding? Would they immediately want de jure recognition "which the United States might be unprepared to grant in absence some sense of international responsibility?" Stuart conceded that de facto recognition would probably lead to a more correct attitude on the part of the Communists, but only if it were treated as tantamount to de jure recognition. Stuart clearly preferred sharper bargaining before dispensing what he saw as a reward for good behavior. Increasingly, discussions in the department on how to handle the Chinese Communists seemed liked a seminar on adolescent psychology.[39]

On June 1, O. Edmund Clubb, the consul-general at Peking, reported an unusual initiative attributed to Chou En-lai. Chou indicated, as Mao had on previous occasions, that he was interested in American trade and investment on terms of mutual advantage. But he also noted that there were party leaders opposed to friendly relations with the United States. A more forthcoming attitude would be welcome, timely, and mutually advantageous.[40]

Acheson was in Paris when the department received and formulated a response to Chou's message. Clubb and Stuart advised the acting secretary to be wary. Clubb suspected the Communists wanted the best of both worlds, to obtain American aid while supporting the Soviet Union. Stuart wanted the Chinese to demonstrate their desire for good relations by their actions. The president agreed emphatically: there was

[39] Acheson to various consular offices in China, April 6, 1949; Acheson to Stuart, May 13, 1949, Stuart to Acheson, May 17, 1949, ibid., pp. 926–27, 21–25.

[40] Clubb to Acheson, June 1, 1949, ibid., pp. 357–60.

to be no indication of any softening toward the Communists. Nothing came of Chou's demarche.[41]

In May and June Stuart met several times with Huang Hua, his former student who was serving as chief of the Communists' Office of Alien Affairs. These meetings culminated in an invitation for Stuart to visit Yenching University in Peking, where he could expect to be welcomed by Mao and Chou. Word of the invitation generated excitement within the Department of State, but Butterworth and Davies feared an adverse public reaction. Davies thought Stuart should accept the opportunity to berate Mao and Chou about proper behavior and believed the public would approve a trip for that purpose. Butterworth devised an elaborate scheme for disguising the trip as a mission to rescue the staff of the Mukden consulate-general. The president would have none of it; "under no circumstances" was Stuart to visit Peking. An extraordinary opportunity to explore terms of accommodation was brushed aside, apparently because the president did not wish to be held responsible for applying the *coup de grâce* to the Kuomintang. But this was only one of several times Truman resisted department recommendations designed to improve relations with the Communists. Indeed it was only with great difficulty that Acheson was able to dissuade Truman from ordering Stuart to visit Kuomintang headquarters at Canton instead of Peking.[42]

---

[41]Clubb to Acheson, June 2, 1949, Stuart to Acheson, June 7, 1949, Webb (acting secretary) to Clubb, June 14, 1949, memorandum by Webb, June 16, 1949, Clubb to Acheson, June 27, 1949, *ibid.*, pp. 363–64, 372–73, 384–85, 388, 398–99. See also Robert M. Blum, "The Peiping Cable: A Drama of 1949," *New York Times Magazine,* August 13, 1978.

[42] Stuart to Acheson, June 30, 1949, Davies memorandum for Kennan, June 30, 1949, Acheson to Stuart, July 1, 1949, *FR, 1949,* 8:766–69. See also Robert Blum's study for the Senate Foreign Relations Committee, "The United States and Communist China in 1949 and 1950: The Question of Rapprochement and Recognition," U.S. Senate, 93rd Congress, January 1973, pp. 7–10. On the proposed Canton trip, see Acheson memorandum of conversation with Truman, July 11, 1949, Stuart to Acheson, July 18, 1949, Acheson memorandum of conversation with Truman, July 18, 1949, Clark to Acheson, July 19, 1949, Acheson to Stuart, July 20, 1949, *FR, 1949,* 8:780–81, 791, 793–94.

In an unrelated action on the day Acheson informed Stuart of the president's decision, Mao contributed to the difficulty of reaching an accommodation. He denounced the United States and declared that China would lean to the side of the Soviet Union; it would not allow itself to become dependent on the West. Acheson expected such rhetoric and had tried to prepare Congress and the president for it. In mid-March he had predicted to the Senate Foreign Relations Committee that Chinese Communist leaders, as they gained control of China, would "go out of their way to show their sympathetic attitude of cooperation with the Russians. I think they are going to show a considerable amount of hostility to us and to the West." [43] As Sino-Soviet tensions developed, he expected the Chinese to become even more insistent on their kinship with the Russians. He would be patient. But if Acheson was unperturbed by Mao's speech, it nevertheless increased his problems in persuading the president, Congress, and the public of the wisdom of his course.

The equanimity with which Acheson approached policy toward China was not shared by most of his advisers. Kennan, Davies, Rusk, and Jessup feared that the apparent inaction of the United States in East Asia was upsetting to Americans and Asians. In July Kennan called for a "change of climate" in policy toward East and South Asia. Rusk converted Kennan's idea into a forty-seven-point "action program" that included a "declaration of nonrecognition" of Communist China, continued support for Kuomintang China in the UN, and assistance to "non-Communist China." In August Kennan, Davies, and Jessup devised a twenty-one-point program containing a call for a policy of "frank hostility to the Chinese Communists." They wanted to demonstrate American willingness to use force, to react with strength, "with majesty and greatness." A week later Davies suggested bombing a few installations in Manchuria to demonstrate

[43] U.S. Senate, Executive Session of the Committee on Foreign Relations, March 18, 1949, Historical Series, 81st Congress, p. 34.

that the United States would not tolerate the Chinese behaving like "bandits and blackmailers."[44]

Acheson refused to encourage Truman to play Teddy Roosevelt and continued preparing the country for the accommodation with the People's Republic that he assumed was inevitable. Nonetheless his aides persisted in efforts to manipulate trade and recognition policies in order to reform Chinese Communist behavior and appease public, Congressional, and presidential opinion. In September a high-level department meeting concluded that the British were eager to normalize relations with China. Rusk and Butterworth urged delay, and Acheson agreed to ask Bevin to exact satisfactory performance on China's international obligations. He indicated to Bevin that it was of great importance to the United States to let the dust settle, to let events rather than an act of the West proclaim a Communist victory. Clearly, Acheson was prepared to wait until after the annihilation of Chiang Kai-shek and his forces, another inevitability he did not wish to delay.[45]

A number of remarks attributed to the president in the summer and fall of 1949 indicated his preference for more active opposition to the Chinese Communists than Acheson was advocating. At least once there was a suggestion in his remarks of doubt that the department was following his wishes. Several weeks after denying permission for Stuart to go to Peking, Truman began pressing for revision of NSC 41, which had precluded economic warfare against the new regime. On October 1 he "indicated strongly" his desire that the department do nothing to subvert the Kuomintang blockade of mainland ports. Acting Secretary James E. Webb reported that "the President stressed again the fact that his policy was to permit the blockade to work effectively, to which

[44] Rusk memorandum for Secretary, July 16, 1949, 890.00/7–1649, and Jessup memorandum, August 18, 1949, 890.00/8–1849, National Archives; Davies for Kennan, August 24, 1949, FR, 1949, 9:536–40.

[45] 890.00/9–1349, National Archives; Acheson memorandum of conversation with Bevin, September 13, 1949, FR, 1949, 9:81–85.

policy he expected strict adherence." Two days later he remarked that the United States should be in no hurry to recognize the People's Republic, noting that the country had
waited many years to recognize the Russian regime. Not long
afterward, when Consul-General Angus Ward was im-
prisoned in Manchuria, Truman contemplated using force to
liberate the consular staff.[46]

In these circumstances, Acheson's failure to respond to
the Chinese interest in recognition was less remarkable than
his success in restraining his colleagues and the president
from more aggressive action. He delayed two months before
responding to the president's call for revision of NSC 41, and
then argued against a change of policy. No recommendation
for a show of force against the People's Republic went forward from the department. Instead, Acheson had a study
prepared on recognition policy, lectured congressmen on the
meaning of recognition, and used Jessup as choreographer
for a series of elaborate dances that consumed approximately
six months, their only significant result. He was confident
that time was on the side of sensible policy and that his opponents understood precisely what he was doing. Wellington
Koo complained bitterly as Jessup and outside consultants
studied policy and as Jessup embarked on a sea voyage to examine conditions in East Asia. Koo realized that the department was stalling until everyone agreed it was too late to
help Kuomintang China.[47]

Keeping the door open for recognition of the People's
Republic was a more difficult, and ultimately impossible,
task. Nonetheless, the record of Acheson's efforts is clear.
Throughout 1949 and the first half of 1950 he persisted in his

---

[46] Merchant memorandum for Sprouse, August 24, 1949, Acheson memorandum
of conversation with Truman, September 16, 1949, Webb memorandum of conversations with Truman, October 1 and 31, 1949, *ibid.*, pp. 870–71, 878, 1141, 1355;
Webb memorandum of conversation with Truman, October 3, 1949, PPS Records,
box 13, "China 1949" file.

[47] Acheson to National Security Council, November 4, 1949, *FR, 1949,* 9:890–96;
Jessup to Bernard Noble, October 9, 1949, box 47, Philip C. Jessup Papers, Library of
Congress; Jessup interview; Koo Diary, entry for November 18, 1949, box 217.

attempt to persuade Truman that efforts to detach the Peking regime from Moscow did not constitute appeasement, that harassment would be a mistake. No doubt reluctantly, apprehensively, Truman stayed with him. When confronted with outrageous Chinese behavior, Acheson argued that vital American interests had not been affected, that policies likely to drive Mao closer to Stalin were not warranted. In May 1949, before the Ward case came to a head, he argued that it be viewed as a special situation. In November, as Ward was brought to trial and public outrage verged toward explosion, Acheson stressed the fact that no Americans had been killed in Communist-controlled areas. He argued that, considering the circumstances of revolution and civil war and the refusal of the United States to recognize the regime, American consular posts had "on the whole not fared badly." The public explosion came, but the torrents of abuse did not move him and he held the president's support.[48]

In January 1950 both the department and the Communist regime misplayed a minor problem in Peking to the benefit of opponents of Sino-American accommodation. Acheson thought he had given the Communists a clear signal of American intent to establish formal relations as soon as practicable. But the Chinese were impatient and pressed the United States and other regimes that still withheld recognition, threatening to requisition their property in Peking, including the consular premises of the governments involved. Acheson devised a compromise that seemed sensible. The Communists were informed that they could take a large part of the area, but not the building the United States planned to use for its chancellery. Such an arrangement might give the Communists face without creating an uproar in the United States. The Peking regime was warned, however, that seizure of the building in question would be unacceptable and result in the withdrawal of all American diplomatic personnel in

---

[48] Acheson memorandum of conversation with Truman, November 17, 1949, PPS Records, box 13, "China 1949" file; Acheson to Consul-General, Shanghai, May 3, 1949, and to Souers, November 4, 1949, FR, 1949, 9:936–38, 891–92.

China. The Chinese seized the building and American officials were ordered out of China. Each side apparently thought the other was bluffing. The results were unfortunate, but neither Edmund Clubb in Peking nor Acheson perceived the action as a final break. Indeed, withdrawal had long been advocated by Jessup and others in the department as a means of avoiding incidents that would inflame public opinion against the Chinese.[49]

A few weeks after the incident Trygve Lie, secretary general of the UN, met with Acheson to express his fear about the consequences. Acheson's "let the dust settle" speech of January 12 had reassured him about American intentions, but he feared Peking's action might complicate and delay a settlement. He feared the United States might try to keep the People's Republic out of the UN, resulting in a permanent Russian withdrawal. Rusk, who was present, indicated his expectation that "in a matter of several weeks seven members of the Security Council will have recognized the communist regime and when that happens a communist representative will be seated on a procedural vote." Rusk left no doubt that the United States regarded the issue as procedural and that "we would neither ourselves exercise the veto nor acquiesce in a veto by anyone else."[50]

Rather than being distraught about the prospects for normalization of relations with the People's Republic, Acheson was anticipating better opportunities when Mao returned from his protracted negotiations with Stalin. He planted rumors of Stalin's attempts at extortion with Cyrus Sulzberger, Paris-based correspondent for the New York Times. But the alliance Mao and Stalin signed in February was clearly a setback. In April Clubb's informants gave him little

---

[49] Butterworth Oral History; "Situation in the Far East," U.S. Senate, Executive Session of the Committee on Foreign Relations, January 24, 1950, Historical Series, 81st Congress, pp. 205–6; Clubb to Secretary of State, January 20, 1950, FR, 1950, 6:286–89; Jessup for Acheson, July 28, 1949, PPS Records, box 13, "China 1949" file.

[50] Memorandum of meeting, January 21, 1950 (obtained through mandatory review request).

hope for an early open break between Peking and Moscow. There appeared to be but a slight chance for a more conciliatory attitude toward the United States for several years. Still Acheson was in no hurry. Kuomintang resistance on the mainland had been virtually eliminated. Chiang's flight to Formosa was another complication, but the CIA estimated that the problem would disappear before the end of the year. Perhaps the president would be ready to act after the November elections. In the interim, nonrecognition might please the French, who were worried about Chinese support for Ho Chi Minh in Indochina. So long as Chiang was destroyed, so long as there was no chance of further involving the United States in the Chinese civil war, Acheson could wait. There was no compelling reason for more immediate action.[51]

War in Korea

The war in Korea brought an end to Acheson's complacency about East Asia. His position on Formosa was immediately undermined and his efforts to hold course on recognition, UN representation, and aid to the Kuomintang ended in failure after the Chinese intervened.

At their first meeting after the North Korean attack, Acheson advised Truman to order the navy to prevent the People's Republic from invading Formosa and Chiang's forces from attacking the Chinese mainland. With war in Korea, the strategic importance of Formosa was obviously greater than Acheson would have conceded earlier. Until Russian and Chinese Communist intentions were revealed and the aggression in Korea repelled, Formosa would have to be protected. Moreover, if Korea was to be defended, inaction

[51] Acheson to Bruce (Paris), January 25, and February 11, 1950, Clubb memorandum, April 9, 1950, FR, 1950, 6:294–96, 308–11, 327–28; for the British assumption that recognition would follow the election of 1950, see memorandum of conversation between Jessup and Sir Oliver Franks, August 28, 1950, and Ambassador, India, to Officer-in-Charge, India-Nepal, December 30, 1950, ibid., pp. 164–66, 613–16.

on Formosa could not easily be justified. Ordering the fleet to the Formosa Straits would mute criticism without committing the United States to Chiang's cause. The president accepted the recommendation and declared publicly that "determination of the future status of Formosa must await the restoration of security in the Pacific, a peaceful settlement with Japan, or consideration by the United Nations."

In the months that followed, Acheson fiercely resisted efforts by Louis Johnson and MacArthur to ally the United States with Chiang's regime. He fought to prevent Chiang from using the United States Navy as a cover for offensive operations against the mainland and won a presidential directive to MacArthur, warning him not to encourage any such action. Instead, Acheson persuaded the president to accept the Jessup-Rusk-Dulles idea of working through the UN toward a one-China, one-Formosa policy. At least temporarily, he could not acquiesce in the Communist conquest of the island. The United States would seek a UN-supervised plebiscite in which it was assumed the people of the island would vote to be free of any form of mainlander control. Chiang was furious, understanding full well American intent to undermine his regime. Acheson was determined not to allow the Korean conflict to draw the United States any deeper into the Chinese civil war. He and the president anxiously signaled Mao that whatever they did, they were not attempting to prepare Chiang for a counterattack on the mainland. Even after the People's Liberation Army intervened in Korea, Acheson was unwilling to work with Chiang. Even when he despaired of any accommodation with the Peking regime and contemplated its overthrow, there was no place in his fantasy for Chiang.[52]

[52] Acheson to Karl Rankin, July 21, 1950, Secretary of Defense to Secretary of State, July 29, 1950, Secretary of State to Secretary of Defense, July 31, 1950, Secretary of Defense to General MacArthur, August 4, 1950, memorandum of Acheson-Franks conversation, August 31, 1950, Acheson to Ambassador, India, September 1 and 19, 1950, Webb to Rankin, September 13, 1950, FR, 1950, 6:385, 401–5, 423, 473–76, 478–80, 514, 497–98; Koo memorandum of conversation with Rusk, September 19, 1950, Koo Papers, box 180.

Rusk, in his talks with Koo and other Chinese leaders, left no doubt that the prerequisite to any greater American commitment to Formosa was its conversion into an independent, liberal democracy. In July he spent two hours trying to persuade Hu Shih to lead a liberal anti-Chiang movement. He explained to Koo that America's friends were hostile to the Kuomintang regime. Its continued existence and its claim to be the government of China caused problems for the United States. But he also held out the hopes that democratic reforms and restraint in operations against the mainland would result in increased American aid.[53]

The best analysis of American policy was prepared for Koo by a member of his staff. Its author argued that while American resistance to communism was universal, the application was selective. In East Asia the United States hoped to prevent the spread of communism with as little aid as possible. Specifically, the Korean War had not brought a change of policy. The Americans fought in Korea with an eye on Yugoslavia and Iran. They hoped their resistance would deter Communist action elsewhere: "To save South Korea is only incidental." Nor did the operations of the navy indicate a change of policy toward China. Truman and Acheson were more interested in Communist China than in "our Government," more interested in Formosa than in the Kuomintang regime: "To save our Government is also incidental."[54]

The Kuomintang analyst outlined American intentions: 1) to recognize Communist China at the first sign of friendliness; 2) to divide the Chinese Communist leadership if Titoism proved impossible; 3) to maintain Formosa as a symbol of resistance to communism to keep up the hopes of anti-Communist elements on the mainland; 4) to use Formosa as a bargaining chip with the Communists; 5) to build up a group of liberal elements in Formosa who could participate in any

[53] Koo Diary, entry for July 24, 1950, box 218; memoranda of conversations with Rusk, July 25 and August 31, 1950, Koo Papers, box 180.

[54] "The United States Policy in China," Koo Papers, box 175 ("from file 6–3").

coalition government formed by the Communists after recognition. If no compromise with the Communists proved possible, the United States would seek to use Formosa as a citadel of defense against communism and have a UN plebiscite conducted to see if the Formosans wanted independence.

Koo's aide appears to have been closely attuned to the arguments of Rusk and Dulles. In mid-August Rusk outlined American policy for Karl Rankin, an American diplomat extraordinarily sympathetic to Chiang. Without compromising its freedom of action, the United States would "continue" its policy of denying Formosa to the Communists. It would give the Kuomintang regime the supplies it needed. Temporarily, economic and military assistance would be available, to be used only for the purpose given and not "subject to racketeering." (Truman exclaimed that all the money the United States had given Kuomintang leaders was invested in American real estate.) The ECA was not to engage in joint operations with the Kuomintang which might symbolize an American commitment to underwrite the economy of the island. "We do not wish to make any commitment to Chinese authorities as to how long this relationship will extend into the future." Aid, recognition, Chinese representation in the UN were all matters of American policy and would not be made the subject of any commitment to the Chinese government. In September Koo asked Rusk if the United States was simply playing for time until Soviet intentions were clear, and recorded in his diary that Rusk blushed![55]

As UN forces repelled the invaders and approached the 38th parallel, the lines of America's interim policy toward China were evident. There would be no commitment to the Kuomintang regime and every obstacle would be put in the way of its offensive operations against the mainland. Quite strikingly, Acheson referred to Chiang's attacks on the Peo-

[55]Rusk to Rankin, August 14, 1950, *FR, 1950,* 6:434–38; Truman remark in memorandum "Korean Situation," June 26, 1950, Dean Acheson Papers, box 65, Truman Library; memorandum of conversation with Rusk, September 19, 1950, Koo Papers, box 180.

ple's Republic as acts of aggression to which the United States refused to be a party.[56] The possibility of allowing the Communists to take Formosa at some later time remained, although Acheson was again willing to work toward a separatist Formosan regime. The possibility of recognition of the People's Republic remained, postponed at least until after the election and the end of the Korean War, resting largely on whether the People's Republic intervened in Korea or attacked Formosa. Efforts were made to assure Peking of Washington's benign intentions, in the hope the Chinese Communists would continue quiescent despite air force overflights, attacks on Manchuria, and MacArthur's blatant machinations with Chiang. Finally, the United States was still willing to accept the People's Republic in the United Nations, notwithstanding its negative vote.

Perhaps the Korean War and the momentary confluence of American and Kuomintang interests would have passed without consequence, nothing more than what Clubb called a "strange interlude." But Rusk, Jessup, Davies, and others in the department had early concluded that it would be important for UN forces to cross the 38th parallel and unite all of Korea. Davies insisted that there should be no "signs of hesitation" lest they be exploited by the Russians. Rusk was unwilling to determine Soviet terms for ending hostilities while the UN forces were doing so well. Rapid success brought greater ambitions, and Acheson was persuaded that the Chinese would not intervene in Korea. Despite Chinese threats and staff warnings that they were not bluffing, Acheson and Rusk chose to accept estimates that the Chinese would not come to the rescue of the North Koreans. They were wrong, the results were disastrous, and they responded by blaming the Chinese instead of themselves. Rusk briefly considered the possibility that the Chinese had been provoked by the

---

[56] Acheson to Louis Johnson, July 31, 1950, and to Ambassador, India, September 1, 1950, *FR, 1950*, 6:404, 478–80.

march of American troops toward their borders, but neither he nor Acheson dwelled long on that thought.[57]

Direct confrontation between American and Chinese troops in Korea ended the possibility for the normalization of relations. Twenty years passed before that possibility emerged again. The American position on Chinese representation on the Security Council changed. Now the United States opposed vehemently any arrangements that might allow the seating of Peking: there could be no reward for "aggression." Rusk even implied that seating the Chinese Communists would lead to American withdrawal from the UN—although Dulles warned Koo the United States would still be receptive to a face-saving formula.[58]

American policy toward Formosa remained ambivalent. While Americans were fighting Chinese Communists in Korea, they could not allow them to take Formosa. The hope that by abandoning Chiang and Formosa the administration could mute Mao's hostility and keep him from Stalin's embrace was surrendered. Chinese actions indicated that Peking expected the worst from the United States and Mao's sensibilities were no longer a central concern. Nonetheless, Acheson and his advisers had a difficult time developing a friendlier policy toward the Kuomintang regime. They never gave up their hope of getting rid of Chiang and his coterie. Walter Judd, Koo, and several Chinese missions were struck by Rusk's interest in political figures who might serve as alternatives to Chiang. Even as CIA operatives moved across

[57] Memorandum of conversation, October 11, 1950, ibid., pp. 524–28; memorandum by John Allison for Rusk, July 1, 1950, PPS draft memorandum, in consultation with Jessup, July 25, 1950, draft memorandum by Davies, September 22, 1950, memorandum by Harding Bancroft, September 23, 1950, Clubb to Rusk, September 27, 1950, Merchant and U. Alexis Johnson memoranda for Rusk, October 30, 1950, memorandum of conversation between Rusk and Franks, November 29, 1950, FR, 1950, 7:272, 469–73, 753–55, 759–63, 795–96, 848–49, 1252–53.

[58] Rusk memorandum of conversation with Belgian ambassador, November 30, 1950, ibid., pp. 1265–67; memorandum of conversation with Dulles, December 19, 1950, Koo Papers, box 180.

the Pacific with supplies for anti-Communist guerrilla operations on the mainland, Rusk refused to accept Chiang's leadership. Similarly, Rusk consistently rejected offers of military
assistance from Formosa, continuing to deprecate the ability
or will of Kuomintang forces to fight. A little aid to
strengthen the island's defenses would be forthcoming, but
nothing more—nothing for the recovery of the mainland.[59]

And yet, there were important changes in policy. The
quest for a UN resolution on Formosa was dropped. Dulles
and friendly senators had warned Acheson that if the General
Assembly passed anything that might allow surrender of the
island to the Communists, the domestic political consequences would be intolerable. Acheson still opposed ties to
Chiang, but he agreed that the situation had changed with
Chinese intervention and that the General Assembly was unpredictable. It was best to defer the discussion of Formosa
and the idea of Formosan independence. The administration
also resumed military assistance to the Kuomintang regime.
The result, as Clubb warned, was to create the impression
that the United States was no longer agreeable to UN consideration of the Formosa question "and that we intend come
what may to follow an intimate power relationship with the
Nationalists on Formosa."[60]

Conclusion
Careful study of the working papers of the Department of
State reveals that the policies advocated by the secretary
often did not reflect the opinions of his advisers. Analysis of
Acheson's response to information and recommendations
suggests that he selected ideas without regard to source, pro-
vided they were in keeping with his strong conviction that
American interests on the Asian mainland would be served

[59] Memoranda of conversations with Rusk, January 18 and March 23, 1951, Koo
Papers, box 184; and Koo Diary, entries for March 23, May 9 and 15, 1951, box 218.

[60] Dulles to Acheson, November 15, 1950, and Clubb to Rusk, December 1, 1950,
FR, 1950, 6:572–73, 585–86.

best by a policy of salutary neglect. One important ingredient in American policy toward China in 1949 and 1950 was the willingness of the secretary of state to ignore the advice of his subordinates as well as the pressures of the Pentagon, antiadministration forces in Congress, and Americans who lobbied on behalf of Chiang Kai-shek. Sir Oliver Franks, the British ambassador, in whose judgment Acheson had supreme confidence, reinforced his approach consistently.

Acheson's principal advisers, with the exception of Butterworth, advocated more aggressive policies in East Asia. Butterworth, even more than Jessup, seemed in harmony with Acheson's approach to China. Rusk's ideas were farthest removed from those of the secretary. He labored unendingly to change Acheson's mind about the defense of Formosa and to create a Formosa Acheson might find attractive. His ideas had little influence on the secretary, but he was a good soldier, intensely loyal, and extremely useful at keeping Chiang's friends at bay.

Acheson was utterly contemptuous of Chiang and the Kuomintang government. Chiang's lobbying activities and the support for them from crude politicians and vulgar journalists only intensified his disgust. The image of a corrupt and inept Kuomintang leadership pervaded the department. Chiang's cohort had forfeited its claim to further American support. When he examined analyses of the Chinese Communist movement, Acheson seized upon references to strong nationalist currents, to the determination of men like Mao and Chou to preserve China's independence and territorial integrity. Such an image of the Communists justified his desire to waste nothing more on Chiang.

Acheson's goal was to reach an accommodation with the People's Republic under the most advantageous terms for the United States. He hoped to encourage the Peking regime to distance itself from the Soviet Union and to recognize the importance of its historic ties to the West. The quest for advantage doubtless contributed to delay, and ultimately to failure. But Acheson saw no reason to be eager about the normalization of relations with the new regime. His determination to proceed deliberately was strengthened when Mao and Chou indicated a desire for American aid and voiced the doctrinaire assumption that American capitalism required trade with China to avoid depression. He assumed that the Russians could not provide the economic and technical assistance China needed and that it would be useful for the People's Republic to perceive that it needed the United States more than the United States needed it. Such an awareness might prompt good behavior.

He opposed overt involvement with Formosa because the aim of American policy was to separate the People's Republic from Moscow's control, in part by focusing on Soviet imperialism. It was essential not to provide the Communists with a concrete anti-American issue. His interest in even covert operations to save Formosa vanished when he realized that Chiang would soon be ensconced there, that the native independence movement lacked the power to throw out the Kuomintang.

Acheson's confidence in his passive policy toward Asia was founded on his indifference to the region. He was not persuaded that much of consequence to the United States could happen on the Asian mainland. He was much more interested in British and French opinion, in pacifying major allies, than in the fate of Chiang Kai-shek or Southeast Asia. When his advisers became frantic in their concern over his disinterest, he agreed to exercises in political theater—invitations to Asian leaders, statements of the importance of Asia, and Jessup's extended tour. When Jessup reported that no major expenditure of American power or resources was required, only a little aid and a little psychological warfare, he was telling the secretary precisely what he wanted to hear.

Acheson was also certain of his ability to cope with Congressional and public opinion. Indeed, public opinion polls showed a low regard for Chiang and little inclination to aid him—before the Korean War. The polls did indicate opposition to recognition of the Communist regime or a place for it in the UN, but it was reasonable to assume these reservations would disappear when Chiang did. Republican opposition to his policies and attacks by McCarthyites irritated Acheson, but he was not apprehensive. He had worked with Vandenberg and Dulles to surmount such problems in the past, and he assumed "the primitives" were still manageable.

The second important ingredient in American policy toward China appears to have been Truman's greater responsiveness to domestic pressures. Congressional leaders feared the disruptive influence of the China bloc, and Democrats concerned about reelection in 1950 were uneasy. Truman delayed the termination of aid to the Kuomintang and prevented steps that might have led to an early normalization of relations with the Communists. Acheson and Truman thought they had time, that foreign policy goals would not be jeopardized by obeisance to temporary domestic political needs.

In the spring of 1950 there seemed to be a race between Rusk's efforts to change policy and the tolling of the bells that would sound Chiang's doom. Delays caused by the inability to get the desired responses from Mao, by Truman, perhaps also by French apprehension about Peking's intentions in Southeast Asia allowed a third ingredient—war in Korea—to win a reprieve for Chiang. But even the coming of war in Asia did not preclude accommodation with the People's Republic. Acheson worked desperately to keep that option retrievable, and he might well have succeeded had it not been for the decision to send UN forces across the 38th parallel. Even then Acheson tried to stave off an association with Chiang that would prevent a settlement with the Chinese Communists.

Acheson's performance was not perfect, but it was perfectly creditable until the decision to cross the 38th parallel. Conceivably Rusk understated the danger of Chinese intervention. Perhaps Acheson deferred to a Pentagon led by Marshall and Deputy Defense Secretary Robert A. Lovett, two of the few men he respected. Or, most obviously, the temptation to disarm domestic critics by "liberating" Korea proved irresistible. But Acheson's response to Chinese intervention was senseless. He knew full well that the United States, thanks to MacArthur, was sending confusing signals to Peking. In the heat of battle and bearing a burden of guilt as Americans died at Chinese hands, he blamed the Chinese for their anger at the United States. He assumed it would take too long for the Sino-Soviet split to manifest itself. Mao might be independent, but he was intensely anti-American and his hostility had to be reciprocated, had to be the basis of policy. Nonetheless, Acheson refused alliance with Kuomintang China, leaving that mistake for the succeeding administration.

In 1951 Acheson and the Truman administration squared off against the plague of McCarthyism, a kind of public constraint he could never have imagined and could not ignore. By its disastrous decision to cross the 38th parallel the administration had rearmed the "primitives"—and it spent its last years staggering under McCarthy's attack.

SUMMARY OF DISCUSSION
Waldo Heinrichs

WARREN COHEN'S paper offered a new interpretation of
United States policy toward China. It opened up the possibility that, contrary to conventional interpretation, policy had
considerable flexibility on the question of reaching accommodation with the emerging People's Republic of China.
This was a fresh, vigorously argued thesis arousing lively
debate.

Cohen's argument in a nutshell was that by the end of
1948 a radical change had occurred in State Department
thinking from the view that the Chinese Communists and the
Soviet Union were identical to the view that a Titoist China
was possible and that a wedge might be driven between Moscow and Peking. This required pursuit of an accommodation
with the Chinese Communists. Relentlessly, and increasingly
against the advice of his subordinates, Dean Acheson pursued that policy through 1949 and 1950 until the decision
was made to cross the 38th parallel during the Korean War.
The United States must accept the fact, he held, that soon the
Chinese Communists would be the only Chinese left to deal
with. He did not presume friendliness, but rather the formal
relations that existed with adversaries such as Hitler's Germany in the 1930s and currently with the Soviet Union.
Acheson sought desperately to tie the president to this policy, but Truman intervened at critical points with contrary
decisions. But for those interventions, Cohen believed, accommodation with the People's Republic of China might
have been achieved before June 1950. Acheson was the focal

point of Cohen's thesis. China itself was unimportant to
Acheson. Detachment of China from the Soviet orbit as a
means of pursuing containment of the Soviet Union *was* important.

Most of the discussants accepted the argument that
Acheson sought accommodation. The outstanding exception
was Ronald Steel, Cohen's principal commentator, who was
skeptical of the thesis as a whole. Steel saw American rather
than Soviet expansion as the key. Hostility to any form of nationalism not subject to United States control seemed to him
the one unifying factor in American foreign policy, then as
now. A China not subservient to American interests was a
China hostile to American interests. These guiding assumptions made him dubious of what he termed Cohen's sympathetic portrait of Acheson as the victim of a hostile domestic
climate and honest misjudgments in the heat of war.

The evidence, Steel felt, would sustain a different conclusion. He wondered how Acheson could possibly have
convinced Peking of his desire to reach an accommodation
when, for example, he told the Senate Foreign Relations
Committee in October 1949 that "the fundamental starting
point in our relations with China" was the fact that the new
Chinese government was "really a tool of Russian imperialism in Asia." Further, he noted the contradiction between
Acheson's warning in January 1950 that the United States
should not aid governments lacking public support and his
instruction to Philip Jessup to make absolutely certain that
no opportunity was neglected to halt the spread of communism. Had Acheson been committed to accommodation with
Peking he would not have tolerated schemes devised by his
subordinates for a separate Taiwan, and he would actively
have sought to build public support for a new departure.

The fact that Chiang was an embarrassment to Acheson,
who preferred compliant, "clean" puppet governments like
that of Bao Dai in Indochina, did not, in Steel's opinion,
mean the secretary was prepared to switch to Peking. Acheson and his colleagues were in a quandary over the rump Na-

tionalist regime. They did not really want to confront the choice of abandoning Chiang, whom they regarded as doomed, or taking over his government. Indecisiveness about the leftover China rather than decisiveness about the new China characterized the American government.

Steel argued in conclusion that, given an interpretation such as he had outlined, the decisions taken after June 25, 1950, reflected, or at the least were in no way out of line with, Acheson's established views. Interposition of the fleet in the Taiwan Straits was already in the cards. The temptation to roll back communism across the 38th parallel was stronger than any desire for accommodation with Peking. Acheson's dismissal of the warnings conveyed by the Indian ambassador as the mere vaporings of a panicky Panikkar suggested that opening relations with Communist China was far from his mind. Altogether, Acheson impressed Steel not as an independent, farsighted statesman, but as typical of consistently misguided postwar American foreign policy making.

A number of remarks in the ensuing discussion tended to reinforce Cohen's thesis by showing how the politics of policy making could explain Acheson's apparent inconsistencies. Discrepancies in public statements might well arise, it was suggested, from the fact that Acheson was addressing different audiences: one should consider when and to whom he spoke. Ernest May directed attention to the different roles a secretary of state might play. Besides representing positions developed in his department, though shaped somewhat by himself, Acheson may also have thought of himself as the president's lawyer, concerned with a broader set of issues his "client" had entered into with Congress and the public. Here again inconsistencies would undoubtedly result. Participants differed in assessing Acheson's performance in bureaucratic politics. On the positive side, Cohen saw Acheson successfully manipulating the military, conceding a phrase here and there to satisfy them, to the end that no action was taken on Taiwan, at least before the Korean War, that would obstruct recognition of Peking. In the same manner Acheson occasionally gave play to divergent views of his advisers. As one commentator noted, it is impolitic for any secretary to squelch dissent within his department. With respect to public opinion formation, several discussants argued that Acheson had made a substantial effort to pave the way for a new policy, the China White Paper and briefings by Jessup serving as examples.

On the other hand, several conferees raised questions about the intensity and singlemindedness of Acheson's commitment to a policy of splitting the Chinese Communists from Moscow. To Robert Blum, Acheson seemed undecided. China policy was inconsistent and experimental, moving on several tracks at once. He detected three phases in 1949 alone: a probing of the possibilities of Chinese Titoism in the spring; a hardening against the Chinese Communists after Mao Tse-tung's "lean to one side" speech of July 1; and quiescence from September onward when Acheson decided to "hunker down" and wait for the long-term development of a Sino-Soviet split. That split, Allen Whiting noted, by Acheson's own estimate might not occur for as long as twelve years. Whiting emphasized the vital importance of the Sino-Soviet alliance in fundamentally altering the context of Acheson's diplomacy. Relevant here was Thomas Paterson's comment in a later session that American policy moved only very slowly and cautiously to accommodate Titoism in its original form in Yugoslavia.

Several discussants noted that domestic pressures were rising: the American political atmosphere became increasingly poisoned and official thinking, as reflected in NSC 68, was more and more obsessed with Soviet menace and inclined to militarize and dichotomize world politics. As Bruce Cumings said, the bells were tolling not only for the Kuomintang but for Acheson's policy as well. These tendencies are obvious from hindsight, but the conferees were by no means sure how much weight the actors attached to them before the Korean War. Acheson at least, Cohen insisted, was convinced that time was on his side.

Some also questioned the viability of Acheson's policy, given the negative impact of his public statements on the Chinese Communist leaders. Whiting cited as illustration the China White Paper's letter of transmittal, which in the most authoritative manner depicted the Chinese Communists as puppets of Moscow, and the absence in the White Paper itself of any record of the conversations between the American foreign service officers and the Communists at Yenan during the war. Mao and Chou En-lai knew that at Yenan they had not presented themselves as subservient to Moscow, Whiting continued. Indeed Chou had bluntly stated to General Marshall in 1946 that how far they inclined toward Moscow depended upon the United States. Under these circumstances, Peking's instantaneous, vituperative, and emotionally charged reaction to the White Paper seemed understandable to Whiting; it pulled the rug out from under those responsible for probing the American position as late as May 1949.

Why Acheson went to such lengths to project an image contrary to the one on which his policy was based was a difficult question. One possible answer put forward in Cohen's paper was that Acheson was following John Davies' advice to scold (ma) the Chinese into a more nationalistic posture. Whatever the explanation, Whiting concluded, Acheson totally underestimated the effect on the other side of what he perhaps regarded as superficial aspects of his policy, with the result of reducing whatever chances existed for accommodation.

Acheson's willingness to agree to the crossing of the 38th parallel was inevitably a point of major interest. Why, asked Robert Messer, had Acheson abandoned his consistent policy of "almost fatalistic realism" regarding accommodation with the Chinese Communists and acquiesced in the decision to unify Korea by force?

As so often in dealing with the elusive question of motivation, the conferees had a wide variety of responses which, however, were not necessarily mutually exclusive. Messer himself suggested that the most plausible explanation might be that Acheson succumbed to the temptation of total victory because of his patronizing attitude to the Chinese, based on his fatal underestimation of them, perhaps as a race, certainly as a military power. Warner Schilling felt that if Acheson was in fact deeply committed to accommodation, he would be the last person to see himself as others did and regard the crossing into North Korea as an encroachment on China. Cumings noted that war in General MacArthur's bailiwick diminished State Department influence over events there. He also found Acheson's reversal fairly typical: having been bloodied in the first phase of the war, Americans sought revenge.

Cohen himself said that the best explanation he could give of Acheson's decision concerning the crossing of the 38th parallel was the same he had advanced ten years earlier in *America's Response to China*: it was "a case of political opportunism; it looked like an easy thing to do under the circumstances and so it was done." As several discussants noted, the administration's troubles with Congress and in domestic policy generally created a powerful need to present an image of toughness in Korea. The perplexing point was how Acheson could have believed his reassurances to Peking were adequate when he knew of raids from Taiwan and a bombing run into Manchuria. Up until the Korean War, Cohen stated, Acheson could make the argument that his signals to the Chinese were fairly clear, which made it all the harder to understand his failure to recognize how confused the American signals became after the war started.

Messer put the value of Cohen's paper most succinctly in saying that what was new and revealing to him was that, given the picture in its entirety, Acheson was "so determined, so deliberate, so sophisticated" in his pursuit of accommodation. He had not given him that much credit, especially in light of Acheson's public pronouncements and later writings. To a number of those willing to accept Cohen's thesis, Acheson's goal of accommodation seemed less stark and commanding than Cohen pictured and increasingly elusive, remote, and vulnerable to external contingencies and domestic pressures. Underlying this concern was the further question of whether the Acheson policy had sufficient weight to have led to continued pursuit of accommodation with the People's Republic if the 38th parallel had not been crossed.

The Strategic Perspective: The Rise and Fall of the "Defensive Perimeter" Concept, 1947–1951

John Lewis Gaddis

ONE OF the frustrations of being a statesman is that one's speeches are not always remembered for the reasons one wants them to be. Few have had better cause to acknowledge this difficulty than Dean Acheson, whose National Press Club speech of January 12, 1950, intended as the enunciation of a new Far Eastern strategy in the wake of China's "fall" to communism, has more often been recalled as having invited the North Korean attack on South Korea through its exclusion of that latter country from the American "defensive perimeter" in the Pacific. Acheson always insisted that his speech only reflected established policy and could not have had the effect attributed to it; still one wonders whether privately he may not have felt, as General J. Lawton Collins later suggested, "like a batter swinging at a bad ball [who] would have liked to have had that swing back again."[1]

I am indebted for suggestions on this topic to Thomas H. Etzold, whose own somewhat different treatment of it appears as "The Far East in American Strategy, 1948–1951," in Etzold, ed., *Aspects of Sino-American Relations Since 1784* (New York: 1978), pp. 102–26.

[1] J. Lawton Collins, *War in Peacetime: The History and Lessons of Korea* (Boston: Houghton Mifflin, 1969), p. 31. Acheson's speech, entitled "Crisis in Asia—An Examination of U.S. Policy," is printed in the *Department of State Bulletin* (January

Given presently available evidence, it is impossible to confirm or refute charges that Acheson's speech encouraged the North Korean attack.[2] Sufficient evidence does exist, though, to demonstrate that there was nothing casual or inadvertent about his proclaimed strategy of defending offshore islands, while by implication avoiding direct commitments on the Asian mainland. By the time Acheson spoke, this "defensive perimeter" concept had received endorsements from the commander in chief, Far East, the Joint Chiefs of Staff, the National Security Council, and the president of the United States. The product of no single individual or agency within the government, it had nonetheless been generally acknowledged by early 1950 as representing the most appropriate strategic posture for the United States in East Asia.

But this consensus in support of the defensive perimeter proved to be remarkably brief. It is also now possible to explain how the Truman administration came to reverse its own strategy within six months of its proclamation, by which time it had decided to commit air, naval, and ground forces to the defense of South Korea, accelerate military aid to the French in Indochina, and, by sending the Seventh Fleet to patrol the Taiwan Strait, involve the United States directly in the Chinese civil war. This abrupt turnabout reveals much about shifting American perceptions of interests and threats in East Asia; it is as well an illuminating commentary, as was Acheson's Press Club speech, on the gap between the intentions of statesmen and the consequences of their actions.

"Today, so far as I can learn, we are operating without any over-all strategic concept for the entire western Pacific

---

23, 1950), 22:111–18; see also Dean Acheson, *Present at the Creation: My Years in the State Department* (New York: Norton, 1969), pp. 358, 691.

[2] For the best available evidence on this question, see Robert R. Simmons, *The Strained Allliance: Peking, P'yŏngyang, Moscow and the Politics of the Korean Civil War* (New York: Free Press, 1975); and Masao Okonogi, "The Domestic Roots of the Korean War," in Yonosuke Nagai and Akira Iriye, eds., *The Origins of the Cold War in Asia* (New York: Columbia University Press, 1977), pp. 299–320.

area." This warning, contained in a March 1948 letter from George F. Kennan, director of the State Department's Policy Planning Staff, to Secretary of State George C. Marshall, did much to stimulate thinking within the government on the concept of a defensive perimeter. With his recipient's background obviously in mind, Kennan apologized "for being so bold, as a civilian, to offer suggestions on matters which are largely military; but it is essential that *some* over-all pattern including military as well as the political factors be evolved." Kennan then went on to propose the following as "the most desirable political-strategic concept for the western Pacific area":

1. While we would endeavor to influence events on the mainland of Asia in ways favorable to our security, we would not regard any mainland areas as vital to us. Korea would accordingly be evacuated as soon as possible.

2. Okinawa would be made the center of our offensive striking power in the western Pacific area. It would constitute the central and most advanced point of a U-shaped U.S. security zone embracing the Aleutians, the Ryukyus, the former Japanese mandated islands, and of course Guam. We would then rely on Okinawa-based air power, plus our advance naval power, to prevent the assembling and launching [of] any amphibious force from any mainland port in the east-central or northeast Asia.

3. Japan and the Philippines would remain outside this security area, and we would not attempt to keep bases or forces on their territory, *provided* that they remained entirely demilitarized and that no other power made any effort to obtain strategic facilities on them. They would thus remain neutralized areas, enjoying complete political independence, situated on the immediate flank of our security zone.

If Washington could accept this concept, then "we would have firm points of orientation for our short-term policies in this area." Without some such concept, "we cannot move at all." Kennan concluded: "I need hardly stress the desirability of an early clarification of our policy in this area in view of the trend of world events and the necessity of having all our hatches battened down for the coming period."[3]

Kennan found few objections to these views when he met in Tokyo that same month with General Douglas MacArthur; indeed, from Kennan's account, it is difficult to determine who influenced whom.[4] MacArthur outlined a defensive line including the Aleutians, Midway, the former Japanese mandated islands, Okinawa, the Philippines, Australia, New Zealand, and the British and Dutch islands in the southwest Pacific. Okinawa, he stressed, was the strongpoint; from it he could control each of the ports in northern Asia from which an amphibious operation could be launched. He also agreed with Kennan regarding the desirability of not retaining U.S. troops permanently in Japan, although he did consider it necessary to hold on to Clark Field in the Philippines.[5] For the next year and a half MacArthur repeatedly expressed in official cables, newspaper interviews, and personal correspondence the idea that as a result of World War II the American strategic frontier had shifted from the West Coast to the Asian offshore island chain, and that the security of the United States depended on keeping those islands out of hostile hands.[6]

[3]Kennan to Marshall, March 14, 1948, U.S. Department of State, Foreign Relations of the United States (hereafter FR), 1948, 1:531–38.

[4]Kennan had outlined an earlier version of the defensive perimeter concept before leaving on his Far Eastern trip: "We should make a careful study to see what parts of the Pacific and Far Eastern world are absolutely vital to our security, and we should concentrate our policy on seeing to it that those areas remain in hands which we can control or rely on. It is my guess . . . that Japan and the Philippines will be found to be the corner-stones of such a Pacific security system and that if we can contrive to retain effective control over these areas there can be no serious threat to our security from the East within our time." PPS/23, "Review of Current Trends: U.S. Foreign Policy," February 24, 1948, FR, 1948, 1:525.

[5]Kennan notes, conversations with MacArthur, March 5 and 21, 1948, enclosed in PPS/28, "Recommendations with Respect to U.S. Policy toward Japan," March 25, 1948, ibid., 6:700–1, 709.

[6]See MacArthur to Albert C. Wedemeyer, C-65590, November 20, 1948, Joint Chiefs of Staff Records (hereafter JCS Records), William D. Leahy Papers, File 9, "China—1948" folder, Record Group (hereafter RG) 218, Modern Military Records Division, National Archives; Fayette J. Flexner notes, conversation with MacArthur, December 6, 1948, FR, 1949, 9:263–65; New York Times, March 2, 1949; Max W.

By the summer of 1949 the concept of a defensive perimeter had become widely accepted in Washington. A Central Intelligence Agency study in May stressed the importance of the offshore islands in facilitating access to the strategic raw materials of India and Southeast Asia, especially if the Suez route should be closed. The Joint Chiefs of Staff informed the National Security Council in June that "from the military point of view, the ultimate minimum United States position in the Far East vis-à-vis the USSR, one to which we are rapidly being forced, requires at least our present degree of control of the Asian offshore chain." In November an internal State Department memorandum concluded, citing U.S. military authorities, that "our position is not directly jeopardized by the loss of China as long as the security of the islands continues to be maintained." A draft National Security Council paper asserted the following month that "the United States must maintain a minimum position in Asia if a successful defense is to be achieved against future Soviet aggression. This minimum position is considered to consist of at least our present military position in the Asian offshore island chain, and in the event of war its denial to the Communists."[7]

Acheson was hardly breaking new ground, then, when

Bishop to W. Walton Butterworth, April 1, 1949, FR, 1949, 7:695; William R. Mathews account of interview with MacArthur, August 5, 1949, enclosed in Mathews to John Foster Dulles, June 5, 1950, John Foster Dulles Papers, box 49, "Mathews" folder, Mudd Library, Princeton University; William J. Sebald to Acheson, September 9, 1949, FR, 1949, 7:857; H. Alexander Smith Diary, October 10, 1949, H. Alexander Smith Papers, box 282, Mudd Library, Princeton University; MacArthur to Arthur Hayes Sulzberger, October 28, 1949, Douglas MacArthur Papers, RG 5, box 1A, file #4, MacArthur Memorial, Norfolk, Va.

[7] CIA ORE 17–49, "The Strategic Importance of the Far East to the US and the USSR," May 4, 1949, Army Staff Records, P&O 350.05 TS 4 May 49, RG 319, Modern Military Records Division, National Archives; NSC 49, "Strategic Evaluation of United States Security Needs in Japan," June 9, 1949, FR, 1949, 7:774–75; State Department Consultants Report, "Outline of Far Eastern and Asian Policy for Review with the President," November 14, 1949, ibid., pp. 1211–12; NSC 48/1, "The Position of the United States with Respect to Asia," December 23, 1949, U.S. Department of Defense, United States-Vietnam Relations, 1945–67 (Washington, D.C., 1971), 8:257 (hereafter cited as Pentagon Papers).

he told the National Press Club that "this defensive perimeter runs along the Aleutians to Japan and then goes to the Ryukyus . . . [and] from the Ryukyus to the Philippine Islands." As he later recalled, "with the authority of the Joint Chiefs of Staff and General MacArthur behind me, it did not occur to me that I should be charged with innovating policy or political heresy."[8] But an examination of the assumptions that led the State Department, the Joint Chiefs, and MacArthur to agree on this concept reveals striking disparities; these in turn suggest the fragile nature of the consensus upon which the defensive perimeter concept rested and help to account for its untimely demise.

The State Department based its support of the defensive perimeter concept in part on a strong sense of pessimism regarding the ability of the United States to influence events on the Asian mainland. The frustrating outcome of the Marshall mission did much to generate this sense of detachment; Marshall's own influence as secretary of state clearly reinforced it.[9] The department did yield to Congressional pressures for a limited program of economic and military aid to Nationalist China in 1948. But it did this more for the purpose of defusing opposition to the European Recovery Program than from any conviction that aid to China might actually be effective.[10] Acheson, upon becoming secretary of

[8]*Department of State Bulletin* (January 23, 1950), 22:116; Acheson, *Present at the Creation*, p. 357.

[9] See, for example, Marshall to John Leighton Stuart, February 9, 1948, *FR, 1948*, 8:13–14; and Butterworth to Lewis Clark, March 8, 1948, *ibid.*, pp. 30–31. Marshall told the Senate Foreign Relations Committee on February 26, 1948: "I am trying to do my best to see that we act where there is some chance of popular result of action, and 'hat we carefully avoid procedures which will draw us into things which will be tremendously, I think, to our disadvantage, and weaken us in the future." U.S. Senate Committee on Foreign Relations, *Foreign Relief Assistance Act of 1948*, Historical Series (Washington, D.C., 1973), p. 362.

[10] See, on this point, Tang Tsou, *America's Failure in China, 1941–50* (Chicago: University of Chicago Press, 1963), p. 446; and Warren I. Cohen, *America's Response to China* (New York: Columbia University Press, 1971), p. 196.

state, made no effort to conceal his own views. In his August 1949 letter transmitting the China White Paper to the president he argued bluntly, with reference to Chiang Kai-shek's impending defeat, that "nothing that this country did or could have done within the reasonable limits of its capabilities could have changed that result; nothing that was left undone by this country has contributed to it." United States assistance could be effective if it was the missing component in the situation in question, he noted in his National Press Club speech, but "the United States cannot furnish all these components to solve the question. It can not furnish determination, it can not furnish the will, and it can not furnish the loyalty of a people to its government." [11]

Related to the department's pessimism regarding opportunities for shaping events on the mainland was the conviction that China was not vital to the security of the United States in any event. This conclusion stemmed in part from a sharp awareness of the limits of American power and of the need, as a result, to distinguish vital from peripheral interests. [12] It also grew out of a tendency to define vital interests primarily in terms of industrial war-making capacity. Hence, Kennan's conclusion in the summer of 1948 that there were only five vital power centers in the world—the United States, the Soviet Union, Great Britain, the Rhine valley, and Japan—and that the task of containment was to see to it that the four not then under Soviet control remained so. [13] "If this

[11] U.S. Department of State, United States Relations with China, with Special Reference to the Period 1944–1949 (Washington, D.C., 1949), p. xvi (hereafter cited as China White Paper); Department of State Bulletin (January 23, 1950), 22:116–17. See also Acheson's speeches to the Commonwealth Club, San Francisco, March 15, 1950, and to the Harvard Alumni Association, Cambridge, Mass., June 22, 1950, ibid., March 27, 1950, pp. 470–71, and July 3, 1950, 23:16.

[12] Cohen, America's Response, pp. 193–94; John Lewis Gaddis, "Was the Truman Doctrine a Real Turning Point?" Foreign Affairs (January 1974), 52:391–92.

[13] Kennan National War College lecture, "Contemporary Problems of Foreign Policy," September 17, 1948, George F. Kennan Papers, box 17, Mudd Library, Princeton University. See also George F. Kennan, Memoirs: 1925–1950 (New York: Norton, 1967), p. 359.

is true," Kennan told an audience at the Naval War College in October,

> . . . you do not need to hold land positions on the Eurasian land mass to protect our national security. If that is true, you can theoretically content yourself with permitting most of these land areas to be in the hands of people who are hostile to ourselves as long as you exercise that power of inhibiting the assembling and launching of amphibious forces from many Asian ports.[14]

Acheson set out the implications of this line of reasoning in secret testimony before the Senate Foreign Relations Committee in May 1950: "I think we have to start out with the realization that the main center of our activity at present has got to be in Europe. We cannot scatter our shots equally all over the world. We just haven't got enough shots to do that."[15]

Still another persistent theme in the State Department's thinking had to do with the need to be selective about allies. Progressive nationalism was the wave of the future in Asia, department Far Eastern specialists believed; the United States, if it expected to retain influence in that part of the world, would have to accommodate itself to that trend.[16] This obviously meant avoiding commitments to support colonialism, as in the case of the French in Indochina or the Dutch in Indonesia; it also meant putting distance between the United States and what were perceived to be the reactionary nationalist regimes of Chiang Kai-shek in China and

[14] Kennan Naval War College lecture, October 11, 1948, Kennan Papers, box 17. For other expressions of this point of view, see CIA ORE 17–49, May 4, 1949, Army Staff Records, P&O 350.05 TS 4 May 49; and NSC 48/1, December 23, 1949, *Pentagon Papers*, 8:228–39.

[15] Acheson executive session testimony, May 1, 1950, U.S. Senate Committee on Foreign Relations, *Reviews of the World Situation, 1949–1950*, Historical Series (Washington, D.C., 1974), p. 292 (hereafter cited as *Senate Reviews*).

[16] This theme was a prominent feature of Acheson's National Press Club speech; see the *Department of State Bulletin* (January 23, 1950), 22:112–13. See also Acheson's testimony before the Senate Foreign Relations Committee on October 12, 1949, and May 1, 1950, *Senate Reviews*, pp. 87, 291–92; and NSC 48/1, December 23, 1949, *Pentagon Papers*, 8:226–27.

Syngman Rhee in South Korea.[17] Departures from this principle ran the risk not only of opposing irreversible forces in
Asia but also of losing the strategic initiative by associating
the United States with unpredictable clients whose interests,
however impeccably anti-Communist, did not always parallel
its own.

Finally, there existed within the State Department the
conviction that even if China should become a Communist
state, the Russians would not necessarily be able to control it.
In his National Press Club speech and other public pronouncements early in 1950, Acheson had hinted broadly at
the possibility of differences between the Russians and the
Chinese Communists.[18] Only with the opening of the State
Department archives, however, has it become clear to what
extent United States Far Eastern policy from 1947 on had
been based on that expectation.[19] As a department memoran-

[17] See, for example, two memoranda by O. Edmund Clubb, August 3 and 28,
1947, FR, 1947, 7:266, 701; Joseph E. Jacobs to Marshall, September 19, 1947, ibid.,
6:803–7; and PPS/13, "Resume of World Situation," November 6, 1947, ibid., 1:776.

[18] Department of State Bulletin (January 23, 1950), 22:115. See also Acheson
remarks to the Advertising Council, White House, February 16, 1950, and his Commonwealth Club speech, San Francisco, March 15, 1950, ibid., March 20 and 27,
1950, pp. 428, 468, 472.

[19] See, for example, John Carter Vincent to Marshall, June 20, 1947, FR, 1947,
7:849; Clubb to Marshall, August 28, 1947, ibid., pp. 264–65; George H. Butler memorandum, July 27, 1948, FR, 1948, 8:123; PPS/39, "United States Policy toward
China," September 7, 1948, ibid., pp. 147–49; circular instruction on "Pattern of Soviet Policy in Far East and Southeast Asia," October 13, 1948, ibid., 1:639; "U.S. Policy toward China," February 28, 1949, FR, 1949, 9:492–95; Acheson memorandum,
conversation with Ernest Bevin, September 13, 1949, ibid., p. 83; Kennan lecture to
Fourth Joint Orientation Conference, Pentagon, September 19, 1949, Kennan Papers,
box 17; Dean Rusk speech to Boston Conference on Distribution, October 10, 1949,
Department of State Bulletin (October 1949), 21:630–31; NSC 48/1, December 23,
1949, Pentagon Papers, 8:243–44; NSC 48/2, "The Position of the United States with
Respect to Asia," December 30, 1949, ibid., p. 270; Paul Nitze memorandum, "Re-
cent Soviet Moves," FR, 1950, 1:146. See also Acheson's executive session testimony
before the Senate Foreign Relations Committee, March 18, 1949, U.S. Senate, Com-
mittee on Foreign Relations, Economic Assistance to China and Korea, Historical
Series (Washington, D.C., 1974), pp. 30–31; and October 12, 1949, January 13, 1950,
March 29, 1950, Senate Reviews, pp. 97, 177, 272–74. The Central Intelligence
Agency took a similar view (CIA ORE 27–48, November 3, 1948, copy in Army Staff
Records, P&O Division, Dec. File, 1946–48 [TS] 091 China), as did President Truman
(see The Journals of David E. Lilienthal: The Atomic Energy Years, 1945–1950 [New
York: Harper & Row, 1964], p. 525; and Arthur H. Vandenberg, Jr., ed., The Private
Papers of Senator Vandenberg [Boston: Houghton Mifflin, 1952], pp. 559–60).

dum put it in November 1949: "We anticipate the possibility that great strains will develop between Peiping and Moscow. These strains would not only work to our advantage but would contribute to the desired end of permitting China to develop its own life independently rather than as a Russian satellite."[20] It was not always clear whether the Chinese people themselves would overthrow the Communists once their ties to the Russians became apparent, or whether the Communists would follow Tito's example and repudiate Moscow's leadership. But since the Russians would control China in neither case, there was general agreement within the department that the "loss" of that mainland area to communism was no irreparable disaster for American security interests and hence did not merit remedial action.

The Joint Chiefs of Staff also came to support the defensive perimeter concept, but by a different route. Unlike the State Department, the Chiefs and their subordinates consistently took the position that the United States could influence events on the mainland through a selective and well-coordinated program of military aid. "The latent resources and manpower of China are such," the Chiefs argued in the spring of 1947, "that even small amounts of United States assistance to the National Government will materially strengthen its morale and at the same time weaken the morale of the Chinese communists."[21] Similar assumptions lay behind Lieutenant General Albert C. Wedemeyer's September 1947 recommendation that the United States furnish the Na-

[20] Charlton Ogburn, Jr., memorandum, "Decisions Reached by Consensus at the Meetings with the Secretary and the Consultants on the Far East," November 2, 1949, FR, 1949, 9:160–61.

[21] SM–8388, June 9, 1947, "Study of the Military Aspects of United States Policy toward China," FR, 1947, 7:843. See also JCS 1721/5, "United States Policy toward China," June 9, 1947, JCS Records, CCS 452 China (4-3-45), sec. 7, pt. 1; NSC 6, "The Position of the United States Regarding Short-Term Assistance to China," March 26, 1948, FR, 1948, 8:47–50; William D. Leahy to James V. Forrestal, April 1, 1948, JCS Records, CCS 452 China (4-3-45), sec. 7, pt. 2; NSC 22, "Possible Courses of Action for the U.S. with Respect to the Critical Situation in China," July 26, 1948, FR, 1948, 8:118–22.

tionalists with the material support necessary to prevent Manchuria from becoming a Soviet satellite, and Vice Admiral Oscar C. Badger's advocacy during 1948 of limited military aid to anti-Communist regional warlords once it became apparent that Chiang Kai-shek's government was on the verge of collapse.[22]

The Joint Chiefs found it difficult as well to accept the view that significant differences could exist between the Chinese Communists and the Russians. "It is believed," a June 1947 study observed, "that the Chinese communists, as all others, are Moscow inspired and thus motivated by the same basic totalitarian and anti-democratic policies as are the communist parties in other countries of the world. Accordingly, they should be regarded as tools of Soviet policy."[23] A victory for communism in China would, therefore, significantly affect the world balance of power, since it would make that country a satellite of the Soviet Union.[24] The Chiefs concluded:

> The United States must seek to prevent the growth of any single power or coalition to a position of such strength as to constitute a threat to the Western Hemisphere. A Soviet position of dominance over Asia, Western Europe, or both, would constitute a major threat to United States security.
>
> United States security interests require that China be kept free

[22] Wedemeyer to Truman, September 19, 1947, pt. 2, annex D, *China White Paper*, p. 814; Badger to Louis Denfeld, July 16, 1948, *FR, 1948*, 8:171–72. See also Badger's testimony before the Senate Foreign Relations and Armed Services Committees, September 8, 1949, U.S. Senate, Committee on Foreign Relations, *Military Assistance Program, 1949*, Historical Series (Washington, D.C., 1974), p. 541.

[23] SM-8388, June 9, 1947, *FR, 1947*, 7:840. See also Robert P. Patterson to Marshall, February 26, 1947, *ibid.*, p. 800. For evidence that Admiral Badger may not have shared this view, see DeWitt C. Ramsey to Denfeld, February 18, 1949, Records of the Immediate Office of the Chief of Naval Operations (hereafter CNO Immediate Office Records), box 1, folder A8-2, RG 11, Operational Archives, Naval Historical Center, Washington, D.C.

[24] See Wedemeyer's report to Truman, September 19, 1947, pt. 2, annex D, printed in *China White Paper*, pp. 809–10; also Wedemeyer to Forrestal, March 29, 1948, JCS Records, CCS 452 China (4-3-45), sec. 7, pt. 2.

from Soviet domination; otherwise all of Asia will in all probability pass into the sphere of the USSR.[25]

Hence, the importance of a program of limited military aid to the Nationalist government.

But whatever the Chiefs' perception of the interests at stake in China, they shared with the State Department a keen sense of the limits on American resources and of the need to rank interests accordingly. It is significant that in 1947 they placed China thirteenth on a list of countries whose defense was considered important to the national security of the United States.[26] By mid-1948 China had dropped to seventeenth place on a list of military aid priorities approved by the State-Army-Navy-Air Force Coordinating Committee.[27] "[C]urrent United States commitments involving the use or distinctly possible use of armed forces are very greatly in excess of our present ability to fulfill them either promptly or effectively," the Joint Chiefs warned Secretary of Defense James Forrestal in November 1948. In March 1949 they noted that "aid spread too thin may not be adequate anywhere, whereas concentrated aid where it will best serve the ultimate objective of our own security may be all or even more than we can provide."[28] During the MacArthur hearings in 1951 General Marshall recalled that "we would literally have [had] to take over control of the country in order to insure that the [Chinese Nationalist] armies functioned with efficiency. . . . At that time

[25] NSC 22/1, "Possible Courses of Action for the U.S. with Respect to the Critical Situation in China," August 6, 1948, FR, 1948, 8:133. This language also appears in SM-8388, June 9, 1947, FR, 1947, 7:844.

[26] JCS 1769/1, "United States Assistance to Other Countries from the Standpoint of National Security," April 29, 1947, ibid., 1:746.

[27] SANACC 360/11, August 18, 1948, enclosed in Rusk to Acheson, March 16, 1949, FR, 1949, 1:262.

[28] Joint Chiefs of Staff to Forrestal, November 2, 1948, enclosed in NSC 35, "Existing Commitments Involving the Possible Use of Armed Forces," November 17, 1948, FR, 1948, 1:661; JCS undated comment, enclosed in SANA-6333, March 16, 1949, FR, 1949, 1:258.

. . . we had one and a third divisions in the entire United States."[29]

Moreover, mainland China did not appear to provide favorable terrain upon which to fight if war with the Soviet Union came. As early as July 1945, a Joint Chiefs of Staff examination of postwar strategic requirements had defined as among "potentially critical operational zones" the offshore island chain, but no points on the Asian mainland.[30] "[In] the case of warfare with our ideological opponents," another study concluded in April 1947, "China could be a valuable ally only if we diverted to her great quantities of food and equipment manufactured in this country. It is extremely doubtful that the end result would be any great assistance to our war effort."[31] The Joint War Plans Committee concluded two months later that while it might be desirable to hold certain areas around Tsingtao for the purpose of aiding Chinese Nationalist forces and conducting strategic air strikes against the Soviet Union, "this course of action would be beyond Allied capabilities during the first phases of the war and . . . any U. S. forces in the area on D-Day should be withdrawn when their positions become untenable." The Far East itself, because of its distance from the centers of Soviet warmaking capability, was not "a feasible avenue of approach to the USSR."[32]

Nor did American strategic planners believe that control of the Asian mainland would offer the Russians significant advantages in time of war. "Soviet conquest of . . . Asia," the Joint War Plans Committee concluded in August 1947,

[29] Marshall testimony, May 10, 1951, U.S. Senate, Committees on Armed Services and Foreign Relations, *Military Situation in the Far East* (Washington, D.C., 1951), p. 465.

[30] JPS 633/4, "United States Post-War Military Policy and Strategic Plan," Army Staff Records, ABC 092 (18 July 45), sec. 1-A.

[31] JCS 1769/1, April 29, 1947, *FR*, 1947, 1:745.

[32] JWPC 476/1, "The Soviet Threat in the Far East and the Means Required to Oppose It: Short Title, MOONRISE," June 16, 1947, JCS Records, 381 USSR (3-2-46), sec. 5; JWPC 476/2, August 29, 1947, *ibid.*, sec. 6.

"would provide few military advantages and would not substantially increase their over-all military capability."[33] The Joint Staff Planners reiterated this conclusion in September 1949: "The inability of the USSR to rapidly extend lines of communications, base development operations, and military and political control through the vast areas of Siberia and into Communist-dominated China appears to preclude military exploitation of this area, to our detriment, in the immediate future."[34] A comprehensive National Security Council study of Asian policy determined later that year that neither primary strategic interests nor the means to achieve its objectives in case of war existed for the United States in Asia. Accordingly, "the current basic concept of strategy in the event of war with the USSR is to conduct a strategic offensive in the 'West' and a strategic defense in the 'East.'" This meant, in the Far East, the "minimum expenditure of military manpower and material" in such areas as would show "the most results in return for the United States effort expended." Such a strategy required defense of the offshore island chain.[35]

But the Joint Chiefs of Staff and the State Department were not the only significant shapers of strategy in the Far East. Of almost equal importance was the position of General of the Army Douglas MacArthur, commander in chief of U. S. Forces, Far East, and supreme commander, Allied Powers, Japan. MacArthur, like the Joint Chiefs, saw possibilities for effective military aid to China, provided the United States concentrated on the issue of military security and put aside its concern for internal reform. "Desirable as such reform may be," he wrote in March 1948, "its importance is but secondary to the issue of civil strife now engulfing the land, and the two issues are as impossible of synchronization as it

[33] *Ibid.*

[34] JSPC 877/72, "The Impact of Current Far Eastern Developments on Emergency War Planning," September 14, 1949, Army Staff Records, P&O 1949–50 381 TS, sec. 3, case 56.

[35] NSC 48/1, December 23, 1949, *Pentagon Papers,* 8:256–57.

would be to alter the structural design of a house while the same was being consumed by flame." Chiang Kai-shek might be on his way out, MacArthur commented in August 1949, "but as long as he will fight I believe in helping him, as I would help anyone else who would fight the Communists."[36]

But MacArthur came to this position by a process of reasoning very different from that of the Joint Chiefs of Staff or the Department of State. Unlike them, he regarded American strategic interests in the world as undifferentiated: "[I]f we embark upon a general policy to bulwark the frontiers of freedom against the assaults of political despotism, one major frontier is no less important than another, and a decisive breach of any will inevitably threaten to engulf all." For MacArthur, victories of communism in China were those of the Soviet Union; the dangers they posed to U.S. security were no less than those created by the expansion of communism elsewhere in the world. As Senator H. Alexander Smith noted following a conversation with MacArthur in September 1949: "He is violently against any form of communism wherever it shows itself and would back any of the anticommunist forces everywhere in the world."[37]

MacArthur's well-known conviction that the Far East was being neglected in favor of Europe grew logically out of this perception of undifferentiated interests. "It no longer appears realistic to consider the Far East as a static and secure flank in the military contest with Communism," he cabled General Wedemeyer in November 1948.[38] By 1949 he was complaining vigorously about a "Europe first" mentality in Washington and a corresponding inclination to "scuttle the

[36] MacArthur to Charles A. Eaton, March 3, 1948, MacArthur Papers, RG 6, box 2, "FECOM: Formosa" file; Mathews account, interview with MacArthur, August 5, 1949, Dulles Papers, box 49, "Mathews" folder. See also Kennan's notes of a conversation with MacArthur, March 21, 1948, FR, 1948, 6:711–12.

[37] MacArthur to Eaton, March 3, 1948, MacArthur Papers, RG 6, box 2, "FECOM: Formosa" file; Smith notes of conversation with MacArthur, September 27, 1949, Smith Papers, box 98, "Far East Trip, 1949" folder.

[38] MacArthur to Wedemeyer, C-65590, November 20, 1948, Leahy Papers, file 9, "China—1948" folder.

Pacific." He attributed these tendencies to the influence of General Marshall and the "bright young men" around him, and to the inability of the Joint Chiefs to "understand" the Far East, a failing stemming from their concentration on European affairs during and since World War II.[39] What Washington failed to see, a study prepared by MacArthur's staff argued, was that the Soviet offensive had shifted from the European theater to the Far East, partly as the result of the success of containment in Europe. United States military planning had not shifted accordingly, though; as a result, utilization by the Soviet Union of the resources of the Far East, if linked with the industrial machine of Japan, "might prove ultimately decisive."[40]

MacArthur was much less clear on how the United States should go about dealing with this threat. He was fond of insisting that "anyone in favor of sending American ground troops to fight on Chinese soil should have his head examined,"[41] a point of view that would appear to have ruled out direct military assistance to Chiang Kai-shek. Moreover, MacArthur was extraordinarily sensitive to the self-defeating effects of prolonged military occupations (a characteristic he shared with Kennan). One of his chief priorities after 1948 was to end the American occupation of Japan;[42] it

[39] Max W. Bishop memorandum, conversation with MacArthur, February 16, 1949, FR, 1949, 7:656; Ramsey to Denfeld, February 18, 1949, CNO Immediate Office Records, box 1, folder A8-2; MacArthur to Kennan, June 16, 1949, MacArthur Papers, RG 5, box 1A, file 5; Jessup memorandum, conversation with MacArthur, January 8, 1950, FR, 1950, 6:1111; MacArthur to Robert C. Richardson, June 9, 1950, MacArthur Papers, RG 5, box 49. MacArthur was not alone in his conviction that Europe was getting a disproportionate share of resources at the expense of the Far East. See Wedemeyer to MacArthur, October 20, 1947, ibid., RG 10, box 10; Arthur W. Radford to MacArthur, June 15, 1949, ibid., box 8; and Bishop to MacArthur, May 22, 1950, ibid.

[40] Briefing by Maj. Gen. Charles A. Willoughby, "Relation of World-Wide Political Situation to CINCFE Missions," October 1, 1949, MacArthur Papers, RG 6, box 83, "RMAP" folder.

[41] Douglas MacArthur, Reminiscences (New York: McGraw-Hill, 1964), p. 389. See also a memorandum by John Foster Dulles of a conversation with MacArthur, July 1, 1950, Dulles Papers, box 47, "Acheson" folder.

[42] MacArthur to Roy Howard, April 24, 1947, and to Robert A. Taft, March 23, 1950, MacArthur Papers, RG 5, boxes 28 and 56. MacArthur called, in October 1950, for the early withdrawal of U.S. forces from Korea once military operations had been

seems unlikely that he would have welcomed similar responsibilities elsewhere. Given these circumstances, given the
limited resources made available by Washington, it made
sense from MacArthur's perspective to endorse the island perimeter concept as the most efficient way to retain a military
presence in Asia without getting bogged down either in protracted war or in protracted occupation.

Hence, though the State Department, the Joint Chiefs of
Staff, and MacArthur all came to support the defensive perimeter concept, they did so for very different reasons. State
saw the offshore island chain as a detached position from
which to encourage Asian nationalism as a bulwark against
Soviet expansionism. The Chiefs regarded it as a line capable
of being held at minimal cost, should war come, while the
strategic offensive proceeded elsewhere. MacArthur saw it as
the nation's first line of defense and, more distantly, as a
series of bases from which to launch offensive operations
aimed at regaining the mainland, though the nature and precise objectives of those operations were never made clear.
These differences in priorities and expectations became painfully clear as the administration sought to apply the defensive perimeter concept in three areas that did not easily fit it:
Taiwan, Indochina, and Korea.

There was never any question, whether in the Pentagon,
the State Department, or the Far East Command, as to the
strategic importance of Taiwan once it became apparent that
Chiang Kai-shek was not going to be able to retain control of
the mainland. The implications of a Taiwan dominated by
"Kremlin-directed Communists," the Joint Chiefs concluded
late in 1948, would be "very seriously detrimental to our national security," since it would give the Communists the capability of dominating sea lines of communication between
Japan and Malaya and of threatening the Philippines, the

---

completed "to the end that we may save . . . the Korean people from the undue impact of American troops upon the peaceful settlement of their internal affairs."
MacArthur to Truman, October 30, 1950, ibid., box 1A, file 5.

Ryukyus, and ultimately Japan.[43] A State Department draft report to the National Security Council early in 1949 argued that "the basic aim of the U.S. should be to deny Formosa and the Pescadores to the Communists."[44] MacArthur was particularly emphatic on this point. He told Max W. Bishop, chief of the State Department's Division of Northeast Asian Affairs, that "if Formosa went to the Chinese Communists our whole defensive position in the Far East was definitely lost; that it could only result eventually in putting our defensive line back to the west coast of the continental United States."[45]

It is interesting to note, however, that neither the State Department, the Joint Chiefs, nor MacArthur initially favored using American forces to deny Taiwan to the Chinese Communists. The Chiefs, citing "the current disparity between our military strength and our many global obligations," opposed military involvement on the grounds that "this might . . . lead to the necessity for relatively major effort there, thus making it impossible then to meet more important emergencies elsewhere."[46] MacArthur repeatedly made it clear that he did not favor the creation of American military bases on Taiwan; the important thing was to deny the island to potential adversaries, while retaining the use of such other more easily controlled strongpoints as Okinawa and the Philippines.[47] The State Department opposed military action on

[43] Leahy to Forrestal, November 24, 1948, enclosed in NSC 37, "The Strategic Importance of Formosa," December 1, 1948, FR, 1949, 9:261–62. See also Denfeld to Forrestal, February 10, 1949, enclosed in NSC 37/3, February 11, 1949, ibid., p. 285.

[44] State Department draft report, NSC 37/1, "The Position of the United States with Respect to Formosa," January 19, 1949, ibid., p. 274. See also Lovett to Truman, January 14, 1949, ibid., p. 266.

[45] Bishop memorandum, conversation with MacArthur, February 16, 1949, ibid., 7:656–57. See also Flexner notes, conversation with MacArthur, December 6, 1948, ibid., 9:263–64.

[46] Denfeld to Forrestal, February 10, 1949, enclosed in NSC 37/3, February 11, 1949, ibid., p. 285.

[47] Flexner notes, conversation with MacArthur, December 6, 1948, ibid., p. 265; Kenneth Krentz to Butterworth, April 25, 1949, ibid., p. 317. MacArthur did not in these conversations make clear his reasons for opposing direct U.S. military involve-

the grounds that overt attempts to detach Taiwan from China would risk offending Chinese nationalism and might undermine the department's strategy of attempting to drive a wedge between the Chinese Communists and the Russians. As Acheson put it: "We are most anxious to avoid raising the spectre of an American-created irredentist issue just at the time we shall be seeking to exploit the genuinely Soviet-created irredentist issue in Manchuria and Sinkiang."[48]

The State Department's preferred solution, approved in February 1949 by both the National Security Council and the president, was to deny the island to *both* the Chinese Communists and the Chinese Nationalists by discreetly promoting development of a Taiwan autonomy movement.[49] To this end, Acheson assigned Livingston Merchant, then counselor at the U.S. embassy in Nanking, to make contact with the governor of Taiwan, Ch'en Ch'eng, with a view to discouraging the further influx of refugees from the mainland, encouraging Taiwanese participation in the government, and, upon receipt of assurances that action had been taken in these two areas, promising American economic aid. Acheson stressed the need for secrecy: "It is a cardinal point in our thinking that if our present policy is to have any hope of success in Formosa, we must carefully conceal our wish to separate the island from mainland control."[50] Merchant soon reported back that the Taiwanese autonomy movements were poorly

---

ment on Taiwan, but it seems reasonable to speculate that his often expressed concern about both manpower shortages and the counterproductive effects of prolonged occupations played some role in his thinking.

[48] Acheson statement at National Security Council meeting, March 1, 1949, *ibid.*, p. 295. See also NSC 11/2, December 14, 1948, FR, *1948*, 8:341; NSC 37/1, January 19, 1949, FR, *1949*, 9:272–73; and Livingston Merchant to Acheson, March 23, 1949, *ibid.*, pp. 302–3.

[49] NSC 37/2, "The Current Position of the United States with Respect to Formosa," February 3, 1949, *ibid.*, pp. 280–82. See also Lovett to Truman, January 14, 1949, *ibid.*, pp. 265–67.

[50] Acheson to Merchant, February 14, 1949, *ibid.*, pp. 287–88; NSC 37/4, "The Current Position of the United States with Respect to Formosa," February 18, 1949, *ibid.*, pp. 288–89; Acheson statement at National Security Council meeting, March 1, 1949, *ibid.*, p. 295.

organized and that if an autonomous Taiwan could be established, the United States would still run the risk of offending Chinese nationalism if it sent military forces to defend
the island. Other reports indicated that Taiwan was "packed
with troops" loyal to Chiang Kai-shek and that "as time goes
on, we will discover that we cannot any more do business
successfully with these people in Formosa than we could do
on the mainland." By May Merchant was advising Acheson
that the strategy of promoting Taiwan's autonomy had failed.[51]

Acheson had anticipated the possibility that even with a
successful Taiwan autonomy movement the United States ultimately might find it necessary to send troops to defend the
island. In a National Security Council meeting on March 1 he
had urged the military not to exclude from its thinking "the
possibility that it might later be called upon to employ modest military strength in Formosa in collaboration with other
friendly forces."[52] Whether in response to this suggestion or
not, the Joint Chiefs advised the secretary of defense on
March 22 that, while they did not favor overt military action
with regard to Taiwan at that time, "there can be no categori-

[51] Merchant to Acheson, March 23, 1949, ibid., pp. 302–3; Allen Griffith to
Harlan Cleveland, April 14, 1949, enclosed in Cleveland to Butterworth, April 29,
1949, ibid., p. 319; Merchant to Acheson, May 4, 1949, ibid., pp. 324–25; Merchant
to Butterworth, May 24, 1949, ibid., pp. 346–50. In a Policy Planning Staff paper
drafted early in July 1949 but immediately canceled, Kennan argued that "Formosan
separatism is the only concept which has sufficient grass-roots appeal to resist communism." This could now be achieved only by persuading other Far Eastern powers
to intervene in Taiwan, obviously an unlikely prospect, or through unilateral United
States action to eject Chiang Kai-shek's forces from the island. "I personally feel that
if the second course were to be adopted and to be carried through with sufficient resolution, speed, ruthlessness and self-assurance, the way Theodore Roosevelt might
have done it, it would not only be successful but would have an electrifying effect in
this country and throughout the Far East." Kennan argued that if the president and
the National Security Council were willing to act on this basis, "then my personal
view is that we should take the plunge." If not, efforts should be made to prepare
U.S. and world opinion for a Chinese Communist takeover of the island. PPS/53,
"United States Policy toward Formosa and the Pescadores," drafted by Kennan, July
6, 1949, but canceled the same day, ibid., pp. 356–59. See also George F. Kennan,
Memoirs: 1950–1963 (Boston: Little, Brown, 1972), p. 54.

[52] Acheson statement to National Security Council, March 1, 1949, FR, 1949,
9:296.

cal assurance, however, that other future circumstances, extending to war itself, might not make overt military action eventually advisable from the over-all standpoint of our national security." [53] Later that spring the Joint Staff Planners worked out a new emergency war plan specifying that, in case of war with the Soviet Union, provision would be made for "denial to the Soviets of the use of Formosa as a base for offensive operations." [54] It is not clear to what extent the State Department was aware of this plan, which gained the final approval of the Joint Chiefs of Staff on December 8, 1949. Its general direction, though, was not inconsistent with the position Acheson had taken in the National Security Council the previous March.

Meanwhile the question of Taiwan had become embroiled in American domestic politics. Congressional supporters of Chiang Kai-shek had already demonstrated their power by forcing on the administration a continued program of limited military aid to the Nationalists; they also managed to provoke angry debates in August over the China White Paper and in September over W. Walton Butterworth's nomination to be assistant secretary of state for Far Eastern affairs. [55] In October Senator H. Alexander Smith, an influential Republican member of the Senate Foreign Relations Com-

[53] JCS 1966/11, "The Strategic Importance of Formosa," March 22, 1949, JCS Records, 381 Formosa (11-8-48), sec. 1. See also Louis Johnson to Sidney Souers, April 2, 1949, FR, 1949, 9:307–8; and Omar Bradley to Johnson, August 17, 1949, enclosed in NSC 37/7, "The Position of the United States with Respect to Formosa," August 22, 1949, ibid., pp. 377–78.

[54] JCS 1844/46, "Joint Outline Emergency War Plan OFFTACKLE," approved December 8, 1949, JCS Records, 381 USSR (3-2-46), sec. 41. For preliminary versions of this plan, see JSPC 877/58, May 10, 1949, JSPC 877/59, May 29, 1949, and JSPC 877/66, August 2, 1949, all in ibid., secs. 32 and 36. The Joint Strategic Plans Committee had concluded in September 1949, before OFFTACKLE had been formally approved, that "the future of Formosa is a critical factor, for should this strategic island come under active Communist control, and should its relations with the USSR be close enough to extend base rights or permit Soviet development in the area, a revision of our war plans would be required." JSPC 877/72, September 14, 1949, Army Staff Records, P&O 1949–50, 381 TS, sec. 3, case 56.

[55] Tsou, America's Failure, pp. 498–504, 507–10.

mittee, traveled to Taiwan over the objections of the State Department;[56] he returned convinced that the United States should under no circumstances allow the island to fall into the hands of the Chinese Communists and repeatedly urged this position on administration officials.[57] Senator William F. Knowland, upon his return from a similar trip in December, called for the dispatch of a military mission to Taiwan, and during the first week in January 1950 both Senator Robert A. Taft and former President Herbert Hoover endorsed the use of military force if necessary to deny the island to the Communists.[58]

These views found some sympathy within the military establishment. MacArthur had continued to stress both the strategic importance of Taiwan and the ease of defending it; all that would be necessary, he argued, would be the dispatch of a military mission and the provision of limited military aid.[59] By December 1949 the Joint Chiefs had also come

[56] Smith Diary, October 13–18, 1949, box 282. Smith's diary and correspondence for 1949 provide detailed information about his decision to concentrate on the issue of Taiwan. There is strong evidence that the Moral Re-Armament movement played an important role in shaping Smith's views on this subject through the activities of John Roots, a member of Smith's staff, and H. Kenaston Twitchell, Smith's son-in-law. Roots and Twitchell in turn maintained close contacts with high officials of the Chinese Nationalist government who were also active in Moral Re-Armament. See especially the Smith Diary for April 7, 8, 27, and 29, 1949; also Roots to Smith, April 12 and August 4 and 27, 1949, Twitchell to Smith, July 9 and 23, 1949, and Smith to Twitchell, August 13, 1949, all in Smith Papers, box 98.

[57] Smith vacillated on the question of just how the United States should go about denying Taiwan to the Communists. At times he seemed to favor direct military occupation, at other times neutralization through blockade or a UN trusteeship (the latter to be justified on the grounds that Taiwan was still part of the Japanese empire). See Jack McFall memorandum, Smith conversation with Acheson, November 30, 1949, FR, 1949, 9:205–8; Smith Diary, December 2, 10, and 20, 1949, box 282; Smith to Bradley, December 6, 1949, Smith to Herbert W. Wheeler, December 21, 1949, Smith to Thomas C. Hart, December 23, 1949, and Smith to Acheson, December 27, 1949, all in Smith Papers, box 98.

[58] Tsou, America's Failure, pp. 529–30.

[59] Sebald to Acheson, September 9, 1949, FR, 1949, 7:857; Willoughby briefing, "Relation of World-Wide Political Situation to CINCFE Missions," October 1, 1949, MacArthur Papers, RG 6, box 83, "RMAP" folder; MacArthur to Sulzberger, October 28, 1949, ibid., RG 5, box 1A, file 4; Magruder summary of MacArthur views, November 2, 1949, FR, 1949, 7:894; Trace Voorhees to Johnson, December 14, 1950, copy in MacArthur Papers, RG 6, box 2, "Formosa" folder. In these last two docu-

to the conclusion that "a modest, well-directed, and closely supervised program of military aid to the anti-communist government of Taiwan would be in the security interest of the United States."[60] But the State Department continued to resist efforts to deny Taiwan to the Chinese Communists by anything other than political or economic means. As one department memorandum put it, any attempt to detach the island from mainland control either through the use of force or through some trusteeship arrangement on behalf of Taiwanese self-government "would outrage all Chinese elements and as a resort to naked expediency would destroy our standing with the smaller countries of the world."[61]

Pessimistic about the efficacy of political and economic measures, the department began taking steps in December to prepare American and world opinion for Chinese Communist takeover of the island, which it expected to occur sometime in 1950.[62] And after an extensive series of discussions in the

---

ments, MacArthur was quoted as arguing that aid to Taiwan could be defended on the grounds that until the Japanese peace treaty was signed, the island was still part of the Japanese empire.

[60] Bradley to Johnson, December 23, 1949, enclosed in NSC 37/9, "Possible United States Military Action toward Taiwan Not Involving Major Military Forces," December 27, 1949, FR, 1949, 9:460–61. See also J. Lawton Collins to the Joint Chiefs of Staff, JCS 1966/22, December 7, 1949, JCS Records, 381 Formosa (11-8-48), sec. 2. In a draft letter prepared for Secretary of Defense Johnson to send to President Truman, Assistant Secretary of the Army Tracy Voorhees noted: "Generally speaking, the staffs agree that efforts should be continued and perhaps increased to deny Formosa to the Communists. . . . They include political and economic aid, and also military advice and assistance short of overt military action." Voorhees draft, Johnson to Truman, December 15, 1949, copy in MacArthur Papers, RG 6, box 2, "Formosa" folder.

[61] Ogburn memorandum, November 2, 1949, FR, 1949, 9:161. See also NSC 37/8, "The Position of the United States with Respect to Formosa," October 6, 1949, ibid., pp. 392–97; and Acheson to John J. MacDonald, November 18, 1949, ibid., pp. 428–29.

[62] Merchant to Butterworth, December 1, 1949, ibid., pp. 431–33; "Policy Information Paper—Formosa," December 23, 1949, printed in U.S. Senate, Military Situation in the Far East, pp. 667–69. A CIA intelligence estimate of October 1949 had concluded that "failing U.S. military occupation and control, a non-communist regime on Taiwan probably will succumb to the Chinese communists by the end of 1950." (CIA ORE 76-49, October 19, 1949, quoted in NSC 48/1, December 23, 1949, Pentagon Papers, 8:245.) In an executive session of the Senate Foreign Relations Committee on January 13, 1950, Senator Smith asked Acheson, "Is it inevitable,

National Security Council during the last week in December, the department was able to secure Truman's endorsement of a statement that, while the United States could continue to attempt to deny Taiwan to the Chinese Communists by non-military means, it should at the same time recognize that such a policy might not succeed and "should make every effort to strengthen the overall U.S. position with respect to the Philippines, the Ryukyus, and Japan." [63] Truman made this policy public on January 5, 1950, in a statement reaffirming the Cairo Declaration's commitment to return Taiwan to China and disavowing any intention of using American troops to defend the island or to furnish military aid and advice. [64]

Needless to say, the administration's strategy of excluding Taiwan from the American defensive perimeter was not popular with supporters of Chiang Kai-shek. Senator Knowland warned Acheson that the department was following "a fatal policy . . . which we would live to rue and regret." "I cannot get over the feeling," Senator Arthur H. Vandenberg snapped, in a sarcastic reference to the Cairo Declaration, "that the final fate of six million people in Formosa should be conclusively and forever settled by a mimeograph on the porch of Shepherd's Hotel in Cairo on a Sunday afternoon." Senator Smith noted in his diary: "We believe that Acheson misjudged the cause of China's deterioration and defeat—that he did not understand that it is not a civil war but a conquest by Russia and that the State Department has completely missed the significance of Formosa." John Foster Dulles at-

---

then, that the island will fall to the Communists?" Acheson replied, "My own judgement is that it is." *Senate Reviews*, p. 184.

[63] NSC 48/2, December 30, 1949, *FR, 1949*, 7:1219–20. See also NSC 48/1, December 23, 1949, *Pentagon Papers*, 8:244–46; Butterworth to Acheson, December 28, 1949, *FR, 1949*, 9:461–63; and Acheson's memorandum of a conversation with the Joint Chiefs of Staff, December 29, 1949, *ibid.*, pp. 463–67.

[64] *Public Papers of the Presidents: Harry S. Truman: 1950* (Washington, D.C.; U.S. Government Printing Office, 1965), pp. 11–12 (hereafter cited as *Truman Public Papers*). See also Acheson's press conference statement, *Department of State Bulletin* (January 16, 1950), 22:80–81.

tacked the whole idea of a defensive perimeter strategy in a public speech late in January: "If we renounce all goals beyond the reach of our military and economic grasp, that means abandoning about 1,800,000,000 people. That, in turn, invites the encirclement which Soviet Communism has long and openly planned against us."[65]

In fact, the administration had not written off Taiwan *in the event of war with the Soviet Union.* Acheson hinted at this in a press conference on January 5, when he was asked the significance of Truman's statement that day that "the United States has no desire to obtain special rights or privileges or to establish military bases on Formosa at this time." The phrase "at this time," Acheson explained, "is a recognition of the fact that, in the unlikely and unhappy event that our forces might be attacked in the Far East, the United States must be completely free to take whatever action in whatever area is necessary for its own security."[66] General Omar Bradley, in off-the-record testimony before the Senate Foreign Relations Committee on January 25, indicated that the Joint Chiefs were fully aware of the dangers control of Taiwan by a potential enemy would pose to the American position in the Pacific.[67] The next day the Joint Chiefs concluded that the

[65] Acheson memorandum, meeting with Knowland and Smith, January 5, 1950, *FR, 1950,* 6:263; Senate Foreign Relations Committee executive session, January 13, 1950, *Senate Reviews,* pp. 184–85; Smith Diary, January 20, 1950, box 282; Dulles speech, "The Importance of Spiritual Resources," January 27, 1950, Cold Spring Harbor, Long Island, copy in Dulles Papers, box 48, "Liberation Policy" folder. See also Dulles to Vandenberg, January 6, 1950, *ibid.,* "Formosa" folder.

[66] Acheson press conference statement, January 5, 1950, *Department of State Bulletin* (January 16, 1950), 22:81.

[67] Bradley's on-the-record executive session testimony is in *Senate Reviews,* pp. 239–45. Senator Smith later noted with reference to this session that the Joint Chiefs' position seemed to be "that while we do not need Formosa as a base of our own from which to carry on any aggressive warfare, it would necessarily be strategically serious if Formosa were in the hands of a potential enemy. This simply means that if the Chinese Communists took Formosa, Russia could establish bases there and threaten our whole lifeline which extends from Japan through Okinawa and the Philippines in the Pacific." Smith went on to add: "It is very clear that the recommendations of the Joint Chiefs were disregarded by the President and the State Department in arriving at the decision to give no further aid to Formosa." Smith to John McWilliams, January 30, 1950, Smith Papers, box 100. See also Smith Diary, January 26, 1950, box 282.

emergency war plan providing for the denial of Taiwan to the Russians in case of war should remain in effect through the middle of 1951.[68] It is significant also that General Mac-Arthur, after a meeting with the Joint Chiefs in Tokyo early in February, told them "that he had agreed completely with the Joint Chiefs of Staff point of view with respect to Formosa."[69]

But war plans, of course, could not be revealed; as a result the administration continued to project the image, as retired General William J. Donovan put it, of "an ineffectual angel beating in the void his luminous wings in vain."[70] Nor did Republican efforts to change administration policy let up. Senator Smith sent his son-in-law and an aide to Taiwan late in April 1950; he then saw to it that their report, advocating a United States commitment to defend the island, gained wide circulation within Congress, the State Department, and the Pentagon.[71] Knowland, in a letter to Secretary of Defense Johnson in May, argued that the situation had changed since Truman's January statement: the Chinese Communist regime was now aligned with and receiving military assistance from the Soviet Union; moreover it had seized American property. "Time is rapidly running out."[72] Meanwhile, Republicans had gained an advocate in the State Department with the appointment of John Foster Dulles as a special consultant with responsibility for the Japanese peace treaty. Dulles favored finding a formula to "neutralize" Taiwan; at a meeting with

[68] JCS 1844/53, January 26, 1950, JCS Records, 381 USSR (3-2-46), sec. 44. See also James F. Schnabel, *Policy and Direction: The First Year* (United States Army in the Korean War series) (Washington, D.C.: Office of the Chief of Military History, Department of the Army, 1972), pp. 50–51.

[69] JCS 2106, "Notes on Visit of the Joint Chiefs of Staff to Alaska, the Far East, and the Pacific," March 13, 1950, JCS Records, 333.1 Far East (1-13-50).

[70] Donovan address, New York City, February 16, 1950, copy in Dwight D. Eisenhower Papers, 1916–52 file, box 32, Dwight D. Eisenhower Library, Abilene, Kansas.

[71] "Report on Formosa," May 1950, copy in Smith Papers, box 100, "Twitchell Report" folder. See also Smith to H. Kenaston Twitchell, June 3, 1950, *ibid.*

[72] Knowland to Louis Johnson, May 15, 1950, copy in Smith Papers, box 100, "Foreign Relations Committee" folder.

Republican senatorial leaders on May 23 it was agreed, as Smith put it, "that we would start no 'fireworks' until Dulles has a chance to move in on this with Acheson." [73]

Dulles already had such an effort well underway. On May 18 he had prepared a memorandum warning of dire consequences for the American position in the world "if our conduct indicates a continuing disposition to fall back and allow doubtful areas to fall under Soviet Communist control." This prospect could be avoided "if at some doubtful point we quickly take a dramatic and strong stand that shows our confidence and resolution. . . . Of all the doubtful areas where such a stand might be taken, Formosa has advantages superior to any other."

If the United States were to announce that it would neutralize Formosa, not permitting it either to be taken by the Communists or to be used as a base of military operations against the mainland, that is a decision which we could certainly maintain, short of open war by the Soviet Union. Everyone knows that that is the case. If we do not act, it will be everywhere interpreted that we are making another retreat because we do not dare risk war. [74]

Dulles submitted this document to Assistant Secretary of State for Far Eastern Affairs Dean Rusk, who was already leaning toward a revision of policy on Taiwan. [75] One week later Rusk told Pentagon officials that he expected to be able to obtain a broadening of existing policy regarding military assistance to the island; [76] on May 30 he observed at a meet-

[73] Smith Diary, May 24, 1950, box 282. For the circumstances surrounding Dulles's appointment, see Townsend Hoopes, *The Devil and John Foster Dulles* (Boston: Little, Brown, 1973), pp. 85–91.

[74] Dulles memorandum of May 18, 1950, FR, *1950*, 1:314–16. Dulles also submitted copies of this document to Paul Nitze, director of the Policy Planning Staff, and to Undersecretary of State James E. Webb.

[75] Senator Smith noted in his diary after lunching with Rusk and Dulles on May 13 that "the Formosa prospects look better. . . . [T]he State Department at least seems willing to take a new look at the whole Formosa situation." Smith Diary, May 14, 1950, box 282

[76] J. H. Burns to Director, Joint Staff, and others, May 29, 1950, JCS Records, 381 Formosa (11-8-48), sec. 3. See also Burns to Rusk, May 29, 1950, FR, *1950*, 6:346–47.

ing of State Department Far Eastern specialists that world and domestic opinion were unhappy at the lack of forthright American action in the Far East, that Formosa was a plausible place to "draw the line," and that it was important politically if not strategically as an example of continuing Communist expansion. That same day Rusk prepared for Acheson a draft memorandum incorporating word for word Dulles's observations of May 18.[77]

Simultaneously, pressures were building within the Pentagon for a reconsideration of policy on Taiwan. Retired Admiral Charles M. Cooke, then living on the island, repeatedly bombarded MacArthur and Admiral Forrest P. Sherman, chief of Naval Operations, with warnings about a Soviet air buildup on the Chinese mainland: "If Formosa is lost to the Communists, which means to the Russians, which means further the setting up of a Russian jet plane air strength in Formosa, World War III sooner or later becomes inevitable."[78] These views received powerful reinforcement on May 29, when MacArthur sent the Joint Chiefs a list of the reinforcements he would need to hold the defensive perimeter line if Taiwan should fall under the control of a hostile power. "The time has passed," he noted pointedly, "when this situation can be considered by the United States from a detached or an academic viewpoint."

[77] W. Park Armstrong memorandum of Rusk-Nitze-Jessup-Merchant-Sprouse conversation, May 31, 1950, ibid., pp. 347–49; Rusk draft memorandum to Acheson, May 30, 1950, ibid., pp. 349–51. There is no indication whether this memorandum was actually sent or not.

[78] Cooke to MacArthur, May 2, 1950, MacArthur Papers, RG 10, box 3. See also Cooke to Knowland, April 10, 1950, copy in Smith Papers, box 100, "Foreign Relations Committee" folder; Cooke to Sherman, April 14, 1950, Forrest P. Sherman Papers, folder 1, in CNO Immediate Office Records; Cooke to MacArthur, April 27, 1950, MacArthur Papers, RG 10, box 3; Cooke to Sherman, May 23, 1950, Sherman Papers, folder 1. Cooke claimed at one point to be working for the International News Service on Taiwan, at another to be affiliated with Commerce International China. He emphatically disclaimed any connection with the Chinese Nationalist government, but not before receiving a warning from Sherman on the impropriety of retired naval officers' receiving emoluments from foreign governments. See Cooke to Sherman, April 14, 1950, Sherman to Cooke, May 29, 1950, and Cooke to Sherman, undated but probably mid-June 1950, all in Sherman Papers, folder 1.

In the event of war between the United States and the USSR, Formosa's value to the Communists is the equivalent of an unsinkable aircraft carrier and submarine tender, ideally located to accomplish Soviet strategy as well as to checkmate the offensive capabilities of the central and southern positions of the FEC [Far Eastern Command] front line.[79]

On June 9 Secretary of Defense Louis Johnson asked the opinions of the Joint Chiefs on the proposition that "the United States should make every effort to keep the Communists out of Formosa even though this might entail holding Formosa with the aid of U.S. military forces."[80] And on June 14 MacArthur dispatched another lengthy memorandum emphasizing that "[u]nless the United States' political-military strategic position in the Far East is to be abandoned, it is obvious that the time must come in the foreseeable future when a line must be drawn beyond which Communist expansion will be stopped."[81]

As of June 25, though, no decision on a revision of policy had been made. The outbreak of fighting in Korea on that date obviously placed the Taiwan situation in a dramatically different strategic context. General Bradley suggested to the Joint Chiefs of Staff that "if Korea falls, we may want to recommend even stronger action in the case of Formosa."[82] That night he read MacArthur's June 14 memorandum on the island at a meeting with Truman and his top advisers at Blair House. Acheson rejected MacArthur's suggestion that a mili-

[79] MacArthur to Department of the Army, C56410, May 29, 1950, MacArthur Papers, RG 6, box 2, "Formosa" folder. Bradley forwarded this message to Johnson with the suggestion that it was "of sufficient importance to be brought to the personal attention of the President." Bradley to Johnson, May 31, 1950, JCS Records, CJCS 091 China (31 May 50).

[80] S. G. Kelly to Vice Admiral Duncan, June 9, 1950, JCS Records, 381 Formosa (11-8-48), sec. 3.

[81] MacArthur "Memorandum on Formosa," June 14, 1950, FR, 1950, 7:161–65. MacArthur incorporated much of the language of his May 29 message into this memorandum, including reference to Taiwan as an "unsinkable aircraft carrier."

[82] Bradley to the Joint Chiefs of Staff, June 25, 1950, JCS Records, 381 Formosa (11-8-48), sec. 3. See also Bradley draft memorandum for Johnson to Truman, June 25, 1950, ibid.

tary mission be sent to Taiwan, but he did recommend dispatching the Seventh Fleet to the Taiwan Strait to prevent either an attack on the island by the Chinese Communists or an attack on the mainland by Chiang Kai-shek. Truman approved this action and announced it publicly on June 27. "It was all very wonderful and an answer to prayer," Senator Smith noted in his diary. "The saving of Formosa was clearly God guided." [83]

But the administration did not regard its action with respect to Taiwan as constituting intervention on behalf of the Nationalists in the Chinese civil war. What it hoped to do instead was to forestall the seizure of the island by hostile forces, while making no commitments as to its ultimate political disposition. American officials repeatedly emphasized the even-handedness of their action; the dispatch of the Seventh Fleet, they argued, had been aimed as much at containing Chiang's aspirations to return to the mainland as those of the Communists to seize Taiwan. [84] The administration's rejection of Chiang's offer of 33,000 Nationalist troops for use in Korea reflected its concern not to associate itself too closely with his regime; so too did Truman's order to MacArthur to withdraw his message to the Veterans of Foreign Wars, a communication which repeated the general's familiar views regarding the strategic importance of Taiwan but which also condemned "the threadbare argument by those who advocate appeasement and defeatism in the Pacific that if we defend

---

[83] Jessup minutes, Blair House meetings of June 25 and 26, FR, 1950, 7:157–58, 179–80; Truman Public Papers: 1950, p. 492; Smith Diary, June 28, 1950, box 282.

[84] Joint Chiefs of Staff to MacArthur, JCS 84681, June 29, 1950, FR, 1950, 7:240–41; Acheson to U.S. UN mission, ibid., p. 276; Acheson to Lewis Douglas, July 28, 1950, ibid., 6:397; Rusk to Karl L. Rankin, August 14, 1950, ibid., p. 438; Truman radio-television address, September 1, 1950, Truman Public Papers: 1950, p. 613; Acheson to Loy Henderson, September 1, 1950, FR, 1950, 6:478–80; and Acheson's executive session testimony before the Senate Foreign Relations Committee, July 24 and September 11, 1950, Senate Reviews, pp. 316, 354. The minutes of the Blair House meeting of June 26, 1950, record Truman as commenting, with characteristic pungency, "that we were not going to give the Chinese 'a nickel' for any purpose whatsoever. He said that all the money we had given them is now invested in United States real estate." Jessup minutes, FR, 1950, 7:180.

Formosa we alienate continental Asia."[85] The Chinese Nationalist government's conviction that it represented the only legal government in China "was not held by rest of world," Acheson reminded the American minister in Taipei in September; "Chi Govt wld therefore be well advised to appreciate realities of tenuous position it now occupies."[86]

As might be expected, efforts to maintain neutrality in the Chinese civil war and still deny Taiwan to the Communists proved difficult. As early as July 27, 1950, the Joint Chiefs had recommended that the United States continue to defend Taiwan from attack regardless of what happened in Korea. In August the president approved the dispatch of a mission to survey Nationalist military needs; later that month he authorized the allocation of over $14 million for military aid to the island.[87] Acheson and Dulles agreed in October on the desirability of working through the United Nations for the permanent neutralization of Taiwan. At that time they took the view that such an arrangement would not allow for the use of the island as a base for military operations against the mainland;[88] but by November, following initial indications of Chinese Communist intervention in Korea, Acheson was refusing to rule out the use of Taiwan by UN forces for just this purpose.[89] Later that month the State Department abandoned its plan for UN-sanctioned neutralization, partly because the continued domestic political sensitivity of the

[85]FR, 1950, 6:453. For the events surrounding Truman's decision to order MacArthur to withdraw his message, see a memorandum by Lucius W. Battle, August 26, 1950, ibid., pp. 453–60; and two memoranda by George M. Elsey, August 26 and October 2, 1950, George M. Elsey Papers, box 72, Harry S. Truman Library, Independence, Mo. The Chinese troop offer and its subsequent rejection are documented in FR, 1950, 7:239, 262–63, 269, 276–77.

[86]Acheson to Rankin, September 4, 1950, FR, 1950, 6:485.

[87]Joint Chiefs of Staff to Johnson, July 27, 1950, ibid., p. 392; NSC 37/10, "Immediate United States Courses of Action with Respect to Formosa," August 3, 1950, ibid., pp. 413–14; Truman to Acheson, August 25, 1950, cited in ibid., p. 414n.

[88]John Allison memorandum, Dulles-Acheson conversation, October 23, 1950, ibid., pp. 534–36; see also Dulles memorandum of a conversation with Tingfu F. Tsiang, October 27, 1950, ibid., pp. 542–44.

[89]Acheson to Marshall, November 11, 1950, ibid., p. 555.

issue remained a problem, partly because of the administration's failure to rally support from its allies for its policy on Taiwan.[90]

Great Britain was one such ally, and the Taiwan issue figured prominently in the conversations among President Truman, Prime Minister Clement Attlee, and their respective advisers in Washington during the first week in December. In response to an observation by British Ambassador Sir Oliver Franks questioning the wisdom of continuing to recognize Chiang Kai-shek, Acheson admitted that

there was a lot of trouble wrapped up in this problem, and he did not know the answer. If one starts with the proposition that we want to deny Formosa to the mainland, there is no question that Chiang is a factor in this denial. He is on the spot. While we do not like the situation any better than the British do, it is dangerous to talk about the point Sir Oliver raised.

One might be able to render the American position consistent with the Cairo Declaration, Acheson noted, but "such arguments were not worthy of this discussion." The facts were that while the United States and its allies lacked the power to ensure that Korea remained both free and united, "we do not have to accept a communistic Formosa; we have the power to prevent that." Truman pointed out that the Cairo Declaration had been made at a time when Japan was the hostile power in the Pacific, not China or the Soviet Union. "When we thought that Formosa was not strategically important to us, we never considered that the Chinese Government would be one which would be very hostile to the United States. There is no question now that it is very hostile to us."[91]

Truman's observation reflects an underlying element of consistency in American policy on the Taiwan question: the

[90] Dulles to Acheson, November 15, 1950, *ibid.*, pp. 572–73. See also minutes of discussions of the Taiwan issue in the U.S. delegation to the UN, November 14 and 15, 1950, *ibid.*, pp. 556–72.

[91] Jessup minutes, Acheson-Franks conversation, December 7, 1950, *ibid.*, 7:1437; minutes, Truman-Attlee meeting, December 7, 1950, *ibid.*, pp. 1452–53, 1455–56.

fact that at no point during 1949 and 1950 was Washington prepared to acquiesce in control of the island by forces hostile to the United States *and* capable of taking military action against other links in the offshore island chain. The problem was to achieve this objective without getting further involved in the Chinese civil war. The United States was willing to install an autonomous regime on the island if that could be done without driving the Chinese Communists and the Russians together. When it became apparent that autonomy was not feasible, Washington resigned itself to the prospect of Chinese Communist control over the island as long as this did not involve a Soviet military presence as well. That possibility too had begun to appear increasingly unlikely by the spring of 1950; as a result, a revision of the administration's "hands-off" policy was well under way at the time the Korean War broke out. Korea brought about the decision to "neutralize" Taiwan for military reasons, but with the hope that there might still remain some chance for a political *modus vivendi* with the Chinese Communist government. Peking's intervention in the Korean conflict destroyed that prospect; hence, by the end of 1950 the Truman administration found itself in precisely the position it had sought to avoid: yoked, as it were, for better or for worse, to Chiang Kai-shek.

Just as Taiwan represented an anomaly as an island strongpoint excluded from the original defensive perimeter concept, so French Indochina, as a mainland area included within it, constituted another. Certainly there was little promising about the situation there, with an unpopular colonial government waging an increasingly costly and ineffective war against a guerrilla movement that was both communist and nationalist. Nevertheless, the United States had come, by 1950, to regard the defense of Indochina as an interest more vital than the denial to the Communists of either Taiwan or South Korea. As early as March 1949 a Policy

Planning Staff study had recommended that "we should . . . view the SEA [Southeast Asian] region as an integral part of that great crescent formed by the Indian Peninsula, Australia, and Japan."[92] NSC 48/1, a comprehensive review of Far Eastern policy submitted to the National Security Council in December 1949, concluded that if Southeast Asia were to be swept by communism, "we shall have suffered a major political rout the repercussions of which will be felt throughout the rest of the world."[93] And in April 1950 the Joint Chiefs of Staff proclaimed that "the mainland states of Southeast Asia . . . are . . . of critical strategic importance to the United States."[94]

This conviction regarding the significance of Indochina did not mean, of course, that the United States was willing to give uncritical support to the French there. "We will get nowhere by supporting the French as a colonial power against the Indochinese," Acheson told the Senate Foreign Relations Committee; "that is something which has very little future in it."[95] Nor did it extend to the point of being willing

[92] PPS/51, March 29, 1949, later circulated to the National Security Council as NSC 51, July 1, 1949, FR, 1949, 7:1129. Acheson shared the view that Indochina constituted part of an arc running from India to Japan but told the British ambassador in December 1949 that Southeast Asia was an area "of primary United Kingdom and Empire concern; that however was not to suggest that the U.S. was not prepared to play a helpful role." Acheson memorandum, conversation with Sir Oliver Franks, December 24, 1949, ibid., p. 930.

[93] NSC 48/1, December 23, 1949, Pentagon Papers, 8:248. At an executive session of the Senate Foreign Relations Committee on March 29, 1950, Senator Henry Cabot Lodge asked Philip Jessup: "Isn't the importance of keeping the Chinese Communists out of the Southeast greater than holding a little island like Formosa?" Jessup's reply: "I think so." Senate Reviews, p. 279.

[94] Joint Chiefs of Staff to Johnson, no date, enclosed in Johnson to Acheson, April 14, 1950, FR, 1950, 6:781.

[95] Acheson executive session testimony, October 12, 1949, Senate Reviews, p. 90. On the other hand, there were limits to how far the French could be pushed. As Acheson put it, "the thing that we have to be careful about is that we do not press the French to the point where they say, 'All right, take over the damned country. We don't want it,' and put their soldiers on ships and send them back to France." Executive session testimony, Senate Foreign Relations Committee, March 29, 1950, ibid., p. 267. See also Acheson's memorandum of a conversation with Carlos P. Romulo, March 10, 1950, FR, 1950, 6:753, and his Senate Foreign Relations Committee testimony of May 1, 1950, Senate Reviews, p. 306.

to promise American troops if Indochina was subjected to external attack.[96] But it did mean support for and, by February 1950, recognition of the Bao Dai government established by the French in an effort to encourage an anticommunist variety of nationalism in Indochina.[97] And it also meant approval by the president on April 24, 1950, of a directive that "the Departments of State and Defense should prepare as a matter of priority a program of all practicable measures designed to protect United States security interests in Indochina."[98]

American officials appear to have made an exception to their general rule of not regarding mainland areas as vital for several reasons: 1) the conviction that Ho Chi Minh was a more reliable instrument of the Kremlin than Mao Tse-tung; 2) the belief that the Soviet Union had designated Southeast Asia as a special target of opportunity; 3) concern over the importance of Southeast Asia as a source of food and strategic raw materials; and 4) in an early version of what came to be known as the "domino theory," fear of the strategic and psychological consequences for the rest of noncommunist Asia if Indochina should fall to communism.

Ho Chi Minh's Moscow connections had been the object of concern in the State Department since 1947.[99] Reports from Americans on the scene in Indochina stressing the na-

[96] "With regard to military assistance, the question is, what would be asked and what we could do. The French have a well-equipped and extremely good army on the border. I doubt very much whether we would employ forces of the United States in that area. The problem would hardly be one, or is unlikely to be one, of mass assault on a thing, but of subversion." Acheson executive session testimony, Senate Foreign Relations Committee, January 13, 1950, Senate Reviews, p. 181.

[97] See Acheson to Consulate General, Saigon, May 10, 1949, FR, 1949, 7:23–25; Butterworth to Jessup, January 20, 1950, FR, 1950, 6:698–700; Acheson to Truman, February 2, 1950, ibid., pp. 716–17.

[98] NSC 64, "The Position of the United States with Respect to Indochina," February 27, 1950, FR, 1950, 6:747; James S. Lay, Jr. to National Security Council, April 24, 1950, ibid., p. 787n.

[99] Marshall to U.S. Embassy, Paris, February 3, 1947, FR, 1947, 6:68; Acheson to U.S. Consulate, Hanoi, April 14, 1947, ibid., p. 85; Marshall to U.S. Consulate General, Saigon, July 17, 1947, ibid., pp. 117–18; Jefferson Caffery to Marshall, July 31, 1947, ibid., pp. 127–28; Marshall to U.S. Embassy, Nanking, July 7, 1948, FR, 1948, 6:28; Marshall to U.S. Embassy, Paris, July 3, 1948, ibid., p. 30.

tionalist character of Ho's movement and the apparent absence of direct support from Moscow made little impression.[100] "Question whether Ho as much nationalist as Commie is irrelevant," Acheson asserted in a terse May 1949 cable; "all Stalinists in colonial areas are nationalists. With achievement natl aims (i. e., independence) their objective necessarily becomes subordination state to Commie purposes." Eight months later, following the Soviet Union's recognition of Ho's movement, Acheson proclaimed that "the Soviet acknowledgement of this movement should remove any illusions as to the 'nationalist' character of Ho Chi Minh's aims and reveals Ho in his true colors as the mortal enemy of native independence in Indochina."[101] It is difficult to reconcile this position with Acheson's persistent optimism regarding prospects for nationalism in Communist China. One possible explanation—admittedly speculative—is that reports from Indochina were subject to comment by French and West European specialists in the State Department who tended to be more preoccupied with the Soviet "menace" than were the China experts who normally reported directly to the secretary.[102]

Related to concern about Ho's Moscow ties was the belief that the Russians regarded Southeast Asia as an especially promising area into which to attempt to project their influence. A State Department analysis in October 1948 had warned that Moscow was using its legation in Bangkok as a

[100]Charles S. Reed to Marshall, July 11, 1947, FR, 1947, 6:114; James L. O'Sullivan to Marshall, July 19, 1947, ibid., p. 120; O'Sullivan to Marshall, July 21, 1947, ibid., pp. 121–23; Reed to Marshall, July 24, 1947, ibid., pp. 123–27; O'Sullivan to Marshall, September 15, 1947, ibid, pp. 136–37; Department of State Policy Statement on Indochina, September 27, 1948, FR, 1948, 6:48; George M. Abbott to Marshall, November 5, 1948, ibid., pp. 54–55.

[101]Acheson to Consulate General, Hanoi, May 20, 1949, FR, 1949, 7:29; Acheson press conference statement, February 1, 1950, Department of State Bulletin (February 13, 1950), 22:244. See also Loy Henderson's address to the Indian Council on World Affairs, New Delhi, March 27, 1950, ibid., April 10, 1950, p. 565.

[102]I am indebted to Professor John Cady of the Ohio University History Department for this suggestion, based on his personal experiences in the State Department during the period in question.

center from which to direct communist movements in Southeast Asia previously coordinated through the Chinese Communists.[103] Soviet recognition of the Vietnamese Communists in January 1950 intensified this concern. As Charles Yost, director of the Office of East European Affairs, put it, "Indo-China may now be the focal point of the most intensive and determined Communist pressure."[104] An army intelligence report in March predicted that "Communist military measures in Korea will be held in abeyance pending the outcome of their program in other areas, particularly Southeast Asia." And in May 1950 Edmund Gullion, the American chargé in Saigon, urged that the very indefiniteness of the United States commitment in Indochina had encouraged the Soviets:

As Soviet power flows up to the margin, where it must be contained, key points are fewer and stand in bolder relief. Twilight zones in which we would not know what to do in case of attack (or what to propose to Congress) have either been eliminated by Soviet action or by decisions taken by American strategic planners. I fear that IC [Indochina] may still be in twilight zone and as long as it is it will remain temptation to Chinese Communists or Soviets.[105]

A third reason for considering Indochina more important than Taiwan or Korea had to do with the need to retain access to the food and strategic raw materials produced in the area, or at least to keep them out of the hands of the Russians. NSC 48/1 noted that neither Japan nor India could expect

---

[103] Department of State memorandum, "Basic Factors in Soviet Far Eastern Policy," enclosed in department circular telegram, October 12, 1948, FR, 1948, 1:644.

[104] Yost to George W. Perkins, January 31, 1950, FR, 1950, 6:710. Yost speculated that the Soviet recognition of Ho suggested that a competition for influence in Indochina was developing between the Russians and the Chinese Communists which "bodes well for the creation of friction between the two and the possible eventual development of Titoism in China, [but] its immediate effects are likely to be unfortunate in that the revolutionary time-table in that area may be speeded up by the maneuvers of each of the two partners to forestall the other." Ibid.

[105] Weekly Intelligence Report, Department of the Army, March 17, 1950, quoted in Schnabel, Policy and Direction, p. 63; Gullion to Acheson, May 6, 1950, FR, 1950, 6:803.

to be self-sufficient in food or cotton production without imports from Southeast Asia.[106] A study by the Joint Chiefs of Staff in April 1950 warned that Southeast Asia contained "major sources of certain strategic materials required for the completion of United States stock pile projects"; moreover, "Communist control of this area would alleviate considerably the food problem of China and would make available to the USSR important strategic materials." Soviet control of the major components of Asia's war-making potential, the study concluded, might in the long run "become a decisive factor affecting the balance of power between the United States and the USSR."[107]

Finally, and most important, American officials were convinced that if Indochina fell to the communists, other countries vital to the American position in the Far East would follow suit. "The choice confronting the United States is to support the French in Indochina or face the extension of Communism over the remainder of the continental area of Southeast Asia and, possibly, farther westward," a State Department working group noted in February 1950; "we would then be obliged to make staggering investments in those areas and in that part of Southeast Asia remaining outside Communist domination or withdraw to a much-contracted Pacific line."[108] Livingston Merchant, writing in March,

[106] NSC 48/1, December 23, 1949, Pentagon Papers, 7:258–59; see also CIA ORE 17–49, May 4, 1949, Army Staff Records, P&O 350.05 TS 4 May 49. It should be noted, though, that a major concern of U.S. planners during this period was to work out procedures whereby trade with mainland China could be maintained, both as a means of preventing China from becoming a Soviet satellite and as a means of providing raw materials and markets for the reviving Japanese economy. NSC 41, "United States Policy Regarding Trade with China," February 28, 1949, approved by Truman on March 3, 1949, FR, 1949, 9:826–34; Charles W. Yost memorandum, Acheson meeting with advisers, September 16, 1949, ibid., 7:1204–6; Acheson executive session testimony, Senate Foreign Relations Committee, October 12, 1949, Senate Reviews, pp. 97–98; NSC 48/1, December 23, 1949, Pentagon Papers, 8:262–64.

[107] Joint Chiefs of Staff to Johnson, as cited in n. 94. Livingston Merchant noted as well that if Indochina were to go communist, "the opening up to the Communist coalition of the raw materials of the Republic of the United States of Indonesia would be accelerated." Merchant to Butterworth, March 7, 1950, FR, 1950, 6:750.

[108] State Department working group paper, "Military Aid for Indochina," February 1, 1950, ibid., p. 714. See also Yost to Perkins, January 31, 1950, ibid., pp.

regarded it as a certainty "that the prestige of psychological results of another Communist triumph in Asia, following on the heels of China, would be felt beyond the immediate area and could be expected adversely to affect our interests in India, Pakistan and even the Philippines." The Joint Chiefs of Staff concluded in April that the loss of Indochina would mean the loss of other mainland states in Southeast Asia and a worsening of the internal security problems of the Philippines and Indonesia, which "would contribute to their probable eventual fall to the Communists"; this in turn would "result in virtually complete denial to the United States of the Pacific littoral of Asia."[109]

The outbreak of fighting in Korea on the one hand reemphasized the strategic importance of Indochina, but on the other imposed serious limitations on what the United States could actually do to help the French there. It is true that one of the decisions made at the Blair House meeting on June 26 was to accelerate military assistance to the French in Indochina;[110] statements stressing the critical significance of the region continued to circulate within the government through the remainder of the year. The Joint Chiefs of Staff put the matter bluntly in November, following Chinese Communist intervention in Korea: "The United States should take action, as a matter of urgency, by all means practicable short of the actual employment of United States military forces, to deny Indochina to communism."[111]

But short of employing American troops, there appeared to be few feasible means of accomplishing that objective.

710–11; NSC 64, February 27, 1950, *ibid.*, p. 747; and Johnson to Truman, March 6, 1950, *Pentagon Papers*, 2:A–17.

[109] Merchant to Butterworth, March 7, 1950, *FR, 1950*, 6:750; Joint Chiefs of Staff to Johnson, no date, enclosed in Johnson to Acheson, April 14, 1950, *ibid.*, p. 781.

[110] Jessup minutes, Blair House meeting, June 26, 1950, *FR, 1950*, 7:180. See also Truman's public announcement of June 27, *Truman Public Papers: 1950*, p. 492.

[111] Joint Chiefs of Staff to Marshall, November 28, 1950, enclosed in NSC 64/1, "The Position of the United States with Respect to Indochina," December 21, 1950, *FR, 1950*, 6:946. See also John F. Melby to Rusk and William S. B. Lacy, August 7, 1950, *FR, 1950*, 6:946. See also John F. Melby to Rusk and Asia Aid Policy Committee to the National Security Council, "Proposed Statement of U.S. Policy on Indo-China for NSC Consideration," October 11, 1950, *ibid.*, p. 888.

There was little confidence in Washington regarding the ability of the French either to pacify Indochina by military means or to make the kinds of political accommodations that would swing the forces of nationalism there away from Ho Chi Minh.[112] "The French, through their folly, . . . have left us with the choice of the following two ghastly courses of action," Charlton Ogburn, Jr., a Foreign Service officer with extensive experience in Southeast Asia, commented in August:

1. To wash our hands of the country and allow the Communists to overrun it; or,

2. To continue to pour treasure (and perhaps even ually lives) into a hopeless cause in which the French have already expended about a billion and a half dollars and about fifty thousand lives—and this at a cost of alienating vital segments of Asian public opinion.

Three months later, John H. Ohly, deputy director of the Mutual Defense Assistance Program, warned Acheson: "We have reached a point where the United States, because of limitations in resources, can no longer simultaneously pursue all of its objectives in all parts of the world and must realistically face the fact that certain objectives, even though they may be extremely valuable and important ones, may have to be abandoned if others of even greater value and importance are to be attained."[113]

There was a fundamental difference, the Joint Strategic

---

[112] See, for example, the covering letter to the report of the Melby-Erskine MDAP survey mission, August 6, 1950, *ibid.*, pp. 842–44; Melby to Rusk and Lacy, August 7, 1950, *ibid.*, pp. 845–48; Policy Planning Staff memorandum, "United States Policy toward Indochina in the Light of Recent Developments," August 16, 1950, *ibid.*, pp. 857–58. One factor further eroding confidence in the French was a report in August that they might seek to arrange a settlement of the Indochina question by working through the Chinese Communists. (See David Bruce to Acheson, August 12, 1950, *ibid.*, pp. 851–52; Acheson to Bruce, August 15, 1950, *ibid.*, pp. 854–56.) Confidence in Bao Dai, never high, had been shaken in October to the point that Acheson was willing to let him know "that US Govt does not regard him as indispensable to contd existence and growth in stability of legal Govt of Vietnam." Acheson to U.S. Legation, Saigon, October 30, 1950, *ibid.*, p. 913.

[113] Ogburn to Rusk, August 18, 1950, *ibid.*, p. 863; Ohly to Acheson, November 20, 1950, *ibid.*, pp. 929–30.

Survey Committee suggested that same month, between the strategic importance of Indochina in a global war with the Soviet Union and in a "cold war." War plans did not call for the retention of Indochina in the event of global war, since the main enemy in such a conflict would be the Soviet Union and the main theater of action would probably be Western Europe. But in any situation short of global war, the loss of Indochina would imperil the security of the other Southeast Asian states, the Philippines, Indonesia, even India and Pakistan. Moreover, "this loss would have widespread political and psychological repercussions upon other non-communist states throughout the world." Even minor commitments of military forces, while possibly sufficient to defeat the Viet Minh, would probably lead "to a major involvement of the United States in that area similar to that in Korea or even to global war." Accordingly, there was little alternative to continuing the existing military aid program, even though the French had failed thus far "to provide adequate political and military leadership, to develop sound military plans, and to utilize properly their military resources."[114]

But what would the United States response be in the event of Chinese Communist aggression not part of a global war? The Joint Chiefs took the position that the United States "should not permit itself to become engaged in a general war with Communist China but should, in concert with the United Kingdom, support France and the Associated States by all means short of the actual employment of United States military forces." It also recognized, though, that the French might bring the Indochina question before the United Nations General Assembly under the "Uniting for Peace" resolution, in which case "the United States would then probably be morally obligated to contribute its armed forces designated for service on behalf of the United Nations." Alarmed by this prospect, the Chiefs concluded: "It is, therefore, in the

[114] Joint Strategic Survey Committee analysis, November 17, 1950, enclosed in Joint Chiefs of Staff to Marshall, November 28, 1950, ibid., pp. 949–51.

interests of the United States to take such action in Indochina as would forestall the need for the General Assembly to invoke the provisions of the resolution, 'Uniting for Peace.' "[115]

By the end of 1950, then, the United States faced an apparently insoluble dilemma in Indochina. Administration officials were unanimous in their estimation of the region's strategic importance; nevertheless the burdens of military commitment in Korea, a country once thought less vital than Indochina, meant that the United States had to continue to rely for the defense of the territory on the French, whose very ineptitude had made their colony vulnerable in the first place. It took longer than expected to validate it, but the reluctant conclusion of an early 1951 National Security Council staff study proved, in the end, to be correct: "The United States cannot guarantee the denial of Southeast Asia to communism."[116]

Korea, of course, represented the most striking departure from the original defensive perimeter concept. In contrast to Taiwan and Indochina, here was an area in which United States troops had been stationed. After deliberations in Washington lasting almost two years, these troops were withdrawn in the spring of 1949, on the grounds that the defense of South Korea was not a vital strategic interest for the United States. Throughout this period American officials harbored serious reservations about both the intentions and capabilities of the South Korean government. And yet, when that country was attacked on June 25, 1950, the United States, with a rapidity that surprised both itself and its adversaries, committed air, naval, and ground forces to repel the in-

[115]Joint Chiefs of Staff to Marshall, November 28, 1950, ibid., pp. 947–48. Ironically, the "Uniting for Peace" resolution had been an American proposal, designed to circumvent the Soviet veto in the Security Council. See Acheson, Present at the Creation, p. 450.

[116]NSC Staff Study, enclosed in NSC 48/4, "United States Objectives, Policies and Courses of Action in Asia," May 17, 1951, Pentagon Papers, 8:442–43.

vasion. Five months later, Washington found itself in an un-declared war there with Communist China as well.

The initial decision to withdraw troops from southern Korea was made in the fall of 1947, primarily for strategic reasons: it appeared unwise to retain some 45,000 men in that area at a time of increasingly severe manpower shortages and proliferating commitments in Europe. The United States had occupied the southern half of Korea at the end of World War II to forestall a Soviet takeover, but it had never expected to have to keep troops there indefinitely, nor did it consider it strategically sound to do so.[117] As the Joint War Plans Com-mittee of the Joint Chiefs of Staff noted in June 1947, existing forces in southern Korea could not repel a Soviet attack if one should come; reinforcements from Japan would only weaken the security of that more vital and defensible position, while in no way matching force levels the Russians had the capa-bility to send in. "A withdrawal from Korea immediately after the outbreak of hostilities is indicated." By September the Joint Chiefs had concluded that "in the light of the present severe shortage of military manpower, the corps of two divisions . . . now maintained in south Korea, could well be used elsewhere."[118]

It is important to note, though, that Washington planners made a distinction between the American strategic interest in Korea, which they considered negligible, and the interest in terms of prestige and credibility. "This is the one country within which we alone have for almost two years carried on ideological warfare in direct contact with our ideological op-ponents," the Joint Strategic Survey Committee noted in April 1947, "so that to lose this battle would be gravely detri-mental to United States prestige, and therefore security, throughout the world." An analysis by the State-War-Navy Coordinating Committee concluded in August that "the U.S.

---

[117] See, on this point, John Lewis Gaddis, "Korea in American Politics, Strategy, and Diplomacy, 1945–50," in Nagai and Iriye, Origins of the Cold War, pp. 277–78.

[118] JWPC 476/1, June 16, 1947, JCS Records, 381 USSR (3-2-46), sec. 5; Forrestal to Marshall, September 29, 1947, FR, 1947, 6:818.

cannot at this time withdraw from Korea under circumstances which would inevitably lead to Communist domination of the entire country." General Wedemeyer, in his report to the president in September, argued that the withdrawal of American forces from southern Korea and the consequent occupation of the country by Soviet or northern Korean troops "would cost the United States an immense loss in moral prestige among the peoples of Asia."[119]

The compromise eventually reached was succinctly stated in the minutes of a meeting of State Department Far Eastern advisers held in Secretary of State Marshall's office on September 29, 1947:

It was agreed that (a) ultimately the US position in Korea is untenable even with expenditure of considerable US money and effort; (b) the US, however, cannot "scuttle" and run from Korea without considerable loss of prestige and political standing in the Far East and in the world at large; (c) that it should be the effort of the Government through all proper means to effect a settlement of the Korean problem which would enable the US to withdraw from Korea as soon as possible with the minimum of bad effects.[120]

An agreement with the Russians looking toward unification of the country having proven impossible to achieve, the United States fell back on a policy of providing military and economic assistance to the anticommunist government of Syngman Rhee, established under United Nations auspices in 1948, while gradually withdrawing American troops. This policy did not mean the abandonment of South Korea to Soviet domination, though, as two National Security Council papers on the subject made clear: "The overthrow by Soviet-dominated forces of a regime established in south Korea under the aegis of the UN would . . . constitute a severe

[119] JCS 1769/1, April 29, 1947, FR, 1947, 1:744; SWNCC 176/30, "United States Policy in Korea," August 4, 1947, ibid., 6:738; Wedemeyer report, September 19, 1947, pt. 3, app. E, ibid., p. 803. See also Francis B. Stevens to Kennan and John M. Allison, September 9, 1947, ibid., p. 784.

[120] Butterworth to Lovett, October 1, 1947, ibid., p. 820. See also PPS/13, "Resume of World Situation," November 6, 1947, ibid., 1:776.

blow to the prestige and influence of the UN; in this respect the interests of the U.S. are parallel to, if not identical with, those of the UN."[121]

Just what the United States would do to defend South Korea in case of attack, though, remained unclear. A Central Intelligence Agency report warned in February 1949 that "US troop withdrawal would probably result in a collapse of the US-supported Republic of Korea" and suggested that the continued presence of a moderate number of American forces in the area would discourage any invasion from the north while boosting morale in the south.[122] But MacArthur, the Joint Chiefs of Staff, and Secretary of Defense Johnson all advocated withdrawal, both because of the pressure of commitments elsewhere and because of the conviction that Korea would not provide favorable terrain upon which to fight if war should come.[123] Beneath the surface also was concern about the possibility that American troops might become involuntarily involved should Rhee make good on his frequent promises to "march north."[124] The State Department, originally inclined to favor the retention of American forces in

[121] NSC 8, "The Position of the United States with Respect to Korea," April 2, 1948, approved by Truman, April 8, 1948, FR, 1948, 6:1167; NSC 8/2, "The Position of the United States with Respect to Korea," March 22, 1949, approved by Truman, March 23, 1949, FR, 1949, 7:975.

[122] CIA ORE 3-49, "Consequences of US Troop Withdrawal from Korea in Spring, 1949," February 28, 1949, Army Staff Records, P&O 350.05 TS 28 Feb 49.

[123] Schnabel, Policy and Direction, pp. 30, 35, 50–51. See also Kenneth C. Royall to Acheson, January 25, 1949, FR, 1949, 7:945–46; Johnson to Acheson, May 4, 1949, ibid., p. 1007.

[124] Rhee told Secretary of the Army Kenneth C. Royall on February 8, 1949, of his desire to reinforce the South Korean army and move into North Korea. "I told the President that, of course, no invasion of North Korea could in any event take place while the United States had combat troops in Korea, and that his suggestion was in my opinion tantamount to a request that we should have all American combat troops removed." (Royall memorandum of conversation with Rhee, February 8, 1949, FR, 1949, 7:957.) For other expressions of concern regarding Rhee's intentions to "march north," see Everett F. Drumwright to Acheson, March 15, 1949, ibid., p. 966; Acheson to U.S. mission in Korea, April 13, 1949, ibid., pp. 987–88; John J. Muccio to Acheson, May 9, 1949, ibid., p. 1013; and two Acheson telegrams to the U.S. Embassy in Seoul, both dated May 9, 1949, ibid., pp. 1014–16. See also Schnabel, Policy and Direction, pp. 34–35.

Korea somewhat longer than planned, acquiesced, and the last American troops were withdrawn at the end of June 1949.[125] That same month an army study concluded that any "police action with U.N. sanction" in Korea including United States military units would "involve a militarily disproportionate expenditure of U.S. manpower, resources, and effort at a time when international relations in Europe are in precarious balance." Application of the Truman Doctrine to Korea "would require prodigious effort and vast expenditures far out of proportion to the benefits to be expected."[126]

Acheson's famous exclusion of South Korea from the American defensive perimeter was therefore, as he later claimed, consistent with existing policy. The secretary of state elaborated on his thinking three days after the Press Club speech, in executive session testimony before the Senate Foreign Relations Committee:

[T]he estimate that we have . . . is that South Korea could now take care of any trouble that was started solely by North Korea, but it could not take care of any invasion which was either started by the Chinese Communists or powerfully supported by them or by the Soviet Union.

Acheson added that should such an event occur, the United States would not undertake to resist it independently by military force. "Of course, if under the [UN] Charter action were taken, we would take our part in that, but probably it would not be taken because they [the Russians] would veto it."[127] Although military and economic aid continued to flow to the South Korean government during the first half of 1950, there

---

[125]Butterworth to Ray T. Maddocks, May 13, 1949, FR, 1949, 7:1022–23. See also Schnabel, Policy and Direction, p. 30.

[126]Department of the Army memorandum, "Implications of a Possible Full Scale Invasion from North Korea Subsequent to Withdrawal of United States Troops from South Korea," June 27, 1949, FR, 1949, 7:1054–56. This document was prepared in response to a last-minute request by General Bradley for yet another review of the decision to withdraw troops from South Korea. Schnabel, Policy and Direction, p. 50.

[127]Acheson testimony, January 13, 1950, Senate Reviews, p. 191. See also Acheson, Present at the Creation, p. 357.

was in Washington no sense of urgency about the situation there comparable to the concerns that had developed over Taiwan and Indochina.[128] As late as June 19 John Foster Dulles was warning Syngman Rhee that the United States could help to resist aggression only "if the governments threatened were themselves taking active steps to create conditions within their countries which would prohibit [the] growth of communism."[129]

The decision to come to the aid of South Korea following the June 25 attack was by no means a foregone conclusion. MacArthur's initial impression was that the invasion was not an all-out effort, that the Russians were probably not behind it, and that the South Koreans would win.[130] Secretary of the Army Frank Pace and Secretary of Defense Johnson initially opposed the commitment of ground combat forces, and the Joint Chiefs expressed concern about the impact such a decision would have in weakening the defenses of Japan and reducing the number of troops available for deployment to Western Europe, the area the Russians were thought most likely to attack.[131] Dulles supported the use of air and naval forces in Korea but warned that the Russians and the Chinese could indefinitely supply the North Koreans and that "it was hazardous for us to challenge communist power on the mainland." Secretary Pace replied that "the Defense Department's disposition to send divisions into Korea was not because of *their* desire to do so, but because they thought it necessary to support the political policies of the government."[132]

[128] See, on this point, Schnabel, *Policy and Direction*, pp. 35–36.

[129] Allison memorandum, Dulles-Rhee conversation, June 19, 1950, FR, *1950*, 7:108.

[130] Allison account, meetings with MacArthur on June 25 and 26, 1950, *ibid.*, pp. 140n., 141n.

[131] Jessup minutes, Blair House meetings, June 25 and 26, 1950, *ibid.*, pp. 159–60, 183; Charles L. Bolte to Pace, June 28, 1950, Army Staff Records, G-3, 091 Korea TS sec. 2, case 25. See also Schnabel, *Policy and Direction*, p. 79.

[132] Dulles memorandum of conversations with Acheson, Pace, and others, July 1, 1950, Dulles Papers, box 47, "Acheson" folder. "I had doubts as to the wisdom of engaging our land forces on the Continent of Asia as against any enemy that could be nourished from the vast reservoirs of the USSR. I expressed that doubt to the mili-

This was a perceptive comment, for in the end it was political and not strategic considerations that brought about American intervention in Korea. The blatant nature of the North Korean attack made resistance necessary, in the eyes of administration officials, not because South Korea was important in and of itself, but because any demonstration of aggression left unopposed would only encourage further aggressions elsewhere. "You may be sure," Charles Bohlen wrote to Kennan on June 26, "that all Europeans to say nothing of the Asiatics are watching to see what the United States will do." [133] Kennan himself believed that if the United States did not act, "there will scarcely be any theater of the east-west conflict which will not be adversely affected thereby, from our standpoint." [134] The fact that in attacking South Korea the North Koreans had directly challenged the United Nations made the argument even more compelling. Philip Jessup recalls Truman, at the Blair House meeting of June 25, repeating half to himself: "We can't let the UN down! We can't let the UN down!" [135]

The problem, once the inhibition about engaging in military operations on the mainland had been overcome, was to decide where to call a halt. "After all," Kennan noted in August, "when we start walking inland from the tip of Korea,

---

tary as soon as I returned and before our decision was made." (Dulles to Walter Lippmann, July 13, 1950, Dulles Papers, box 48, "Lippmann" folder.) Publicly, though, Dulles endorsed the decision. See his CBS radio interview, July 1, 1950, *Department of State Bulletin* (July 10, 1950), 23:50.

[133] Bohlen to Kennan, June 26, 1950, *FR, 1950,* 7:174–75. John D. Hickerson, assistant secretary of state for United Nations affairs, reflected administration thinking when he told a New York audience on September 17: "From the standpoint of military security, Korea is of no particular importance to the United States or, I suppose, to any of the other 52 members. But as a symbol, she is of tremendous significance—a symbol of the determination of all free nations that aggression will be firmly resisted, that an attack upon the United Nations will not be countenanced." *Department of State Bulletin* (October 2, 1950), 23:544.

[134] Kennan memorandum to Acheson, "Possible Further Communist Initiatives in the Light of the Korean Situation" (not sent), June 26, 1950, Kennan Papers, box 24.

[135] Philip C. Jessup, *The Birth of Nations* (New York: Columbia University Press, 1974), p. 10.

we have about a 10,000 mile walk if we keep on going, and we are going to have to stop somewhere." [136] Kennan himself and other Soviet specialists in the State Department favored limiting United Nations action solely to the liberation of South Korea. Others in State, together with the Joint Chiefs of Staff, argued that the 38th parallel had neither political nor military significance, that the United Nations should seize the opportunity to unify Korea while carefully avoiding any expansion of the conflict into Soviet or Chinese territory. General MacArthur and his supporters pressed for yet a third alternative: expansion of the conflict through the elimination of "privileged sanctuaries" north of the Yalu, and the use of Chinese Nationalist troops.

Kennan opposed crossing the parallel on the grounds that such a move would require the dispersal of United Nations forces while risking Soviet or Chinese intervention. "We must remember," he told a meeting at the State Department on July 21, "that what we were doing in Korea was, although for good political reasons, nevertheless an unsound thing, and that the further we were to advance up from the peninsula the more unsound it would become from a military standpoint." A month later he reminded an off-the-record press conference that

the Russians are terribly, terribly sensitive about places where foreign territory comes very close to their important centers. . . . I think you can see that if you put the shoe on the other foot and think how it would be with us if Soviet forces began to come within say seventeen miles of Southern California in fighting Mexico. [137]

[136] Kennan background press conference, Department of State, August 22, 1950, transcript in Kennan Papers, box 18.

[137] Kennan Diary, July 21, 1950, quoted in Kennan, Memoirs: 1925–1950, p. 488; transcript of Kennan press conference, August 22, 1950, Kennan Papers, box 18. Kennan's opposition to military operations north of the parallel did not extend to air and naval bombardment; indeed, during the first week of the conflict he suggested directing such actions against Chinese targets as well if Chinese Communist troops entered the fighting. Kennan notes on meeting in Acheson's office, June 28, 1950, quoted in Kennan, Memoirs: 1925–1950, p. 487; memorandum of National Security

Kennan's fellow Soviet specialist Charles Bohlen also warned of the Russians' sensitivity about borders and suggested that they might not even wait for UN forces to reach the parallel before taking action, possibly in coordination with the Chinese.[138] The State Department's Policy Planning Staff and the Central Intelligence Agency both shared these concerns, pointing as well to the difficulty Washington would have in generating support among its allies for any decision to unify Korea by force.[139]

But there were strong countervailing pressures on the question of the parallel within both the State and Defense departments. John M. Allison, director of the Office of Northeast Asian Affairs at State, was particularly vehement on the subject. "I believe that the time has come when we must be bold and willing to take even more risks than we have already," he argued in a memorandum to Dean Rusk on July 1.[140] Three weeks later he condemned the Policy Planning Staff's position as "a timid, half-hearted policy designed not to provoke the Soviets to war," adding:

We should recognize that there is grave danger of conflict with the USSR and the Chinese Communists whatever we do from now on—but I fail to see what advantage we gain by a compromise with clear moral principles and a shirking of our duty to make clear once and for all that aggression does not pay. . . . That this may mean war on a global scale is true—the American people should be

---

Council Consultants' meeting, June 29, 1950, FR, 1950, 1:328; Kennan draft memorandum, "Estimate: Possible Further Danger Points in Light of Korean Situation," June 30, 1950, Kennan Papers, box 24.

[138] Frederick E. Nolting minutes, Bohlen meeting with State Department officials, June 30, 1950, FR, 1950, 7:258; Kennan to Acheson, August 8, 1950, ibid., 1:363. See also two despatches from Alan G. Kirk, U.S. ambassador to the Soviet Union, to Acheson, July 27 and November 7, 1950, ibid., 7:483–85, 1085–87.

[139] George H. Butler draft, untitled Policy Planning Staff paper, July 22, 1950, ibid., pp. 449–54; Butler draft memorandum, July 25, 1950, ibid., pp. 469–73; Central Intelligence Agency memorandum, "Factors Affecting the Desirability of a UN Military Conquest of All of Korea," August 18, 1950, ibid., pp. 600–3.

[140] Allison to Rusk, July 1, 1950, ibid., 6:272. Rusk noted on his copy of this memorandum, "Agree DR."

told and told why and what it will mean to them. When all legal and moral right is in our side why should we hesitate?[141]

Dulles also favored crossing the parallel on the grounds that it had no legal standing and that aggressors ought to be punished; unlike Allison, however, he was unwilling to carry military operations to the point of provoking the Russians.[142] The Defense Department, reflecting the views of the Joint Chiefs of Staff, emphasized the military illogic of halting at the parallel and the difficulty of guaranteeing future South Korean security if that decision were made. It also advanced the interesting argument, later seconded by Allison, that a unified, noncommunist Korea might induce Manchuria to gravitate away from China and that that in turn might cause Peking to question its current alignment with Moscow.[143] Still other arguments stressed the unpopularity with both the South Koreans and the American public of any decision to stop at the parallel.[144]

On September 11 Truman approved a carefully worded compromise authorizing the invasion and occupation of North Korea *provided* Soviet or Chinese Communist intervention had neither taken place nor been threatened. Operations were in no circumstances to extend into Chinese or Russian territory, and only South Korean forces were to make

[141] Allison to Paul Nitze, July 24, 1950, *ibid.*, pp. 460–61. See also Allison to Rusk, July 15, 1950, *ibid.*, pp. 393–95. Allison's account of his position on the 38th parallel issue in his memoirs is, at best, misleading. See John M. Allison, *Ambassador from the Prairie* (Boston: Houghton Mifflin, 1973), p. 153.

[142] Dulles to Nitze, July 14, 1950, *FR, 1950,* 7:386–87; Dulles to William R. Mathews, July 24, 1950, Dulles Papers, box 49, "Matthews" folder; Dulles to Nitze, August 1, 1950, *FR, 1950,* 7:514.

[143] Defense Department draft memorandum, "U.S. Courses of Action in Korea," July 31, 1950, *FR, 1950,* 7:502–03, 506; revised version, same memorandum, August 7, 1950, *ibid.*, pp. 528–29, 532–33; Allison draft memorandum, "U.S. Courses of Action in Korea," August 12, 1950, *ibid.*, pp. 569–70.

[144] Allison to Rusk, July 13, 1950, *ibid.*, p. 373; Butler draft memorandum for Policy Planning Staff, July 25, 1950, *ibid.*, p. 472. Kennan was asked at his August 22 press conference whether public opinion might not be hard to satisfy if operations halted at the 38th parallel. His reply: "It is just one of those instances then when the people here will have to think very hard about what it is they are after." Press conference transcript, August 22, 1950, Kennan Papers, box 18.

the final approach to the Yalu. Should Soviet or Chinese intervention take place after the parallel had been crossed, efforts were to be made to stabilize the front at the most favorable possible position without risking escalation to general war.[145] This was, in essence, a kind of "floating perimeter" strategy, designed to allow the unification of Korea so long as enemy resistance remained manageable. As Dean Rusk explained it later that month, "the thinking in Washington is that we should let the Soviet make the decision for us as much as possible so that United Nations forces would carry on until we get some indication of Soviet reaction to their northward movement."[146]

As it turned out, it was the Chinese and not the Russians who determined the extent of the United Nations advance into North Korea. Confronted with this situation, MacArthur urged on Washington yet another strategic concept: a blockade of the mainland, the employment of Chinese Nationalist forces in Korea and elsewhere, the bombing of industrial facilities inside China and "privileged sanctuaries" along the Manchurian border, and, if necessary, the withdrawal of United Nations forces from Korea to more favorable terrain from which to carry on the struggle. MacArthur justified this expansion of the conflict on the grounds that the Chinese were already engaged in all-out war; the Russians, he maintained, would fight only in defense of their own interests, which did not necessarily parallel those of the Chinese. Failure to choose this course would mean United States involve-

[145] NSC 81/1, "United States Courses of Action with Respect to Korea," September 9, 1950, approved by Truman on September 11, 1950, FR, 1950, 7:712–21.

[146] Harding F. Bancroft minutes, Rusk meeting with Ambassador Warren R. Austin, September 23, 1950, ibid., p. 760. Dulles objected to the amount of freedom this strategy left for the military to make political decisions, but Acheson assured him that "at the present time we had good coordination between our political objectives and the conduct of our military affairs in Korea. If we were lucky and neither the Russians nor the Chinese intervened in North Korea, General MacArthur could act consistently with our overall political plans." (Minutes, meeting of U.S. delegation to the UN, September 21, 1950, ibid., pp. 745–46.) Acheson later sought to reassure the Chinese regarding Washington's intentions by calling attention to the U.S. record in the "brotherly development of border waters," citing the St. Lawrence and the Rio Grande. Department of State Bulletin (November 27, 1950), 23:855.

ment in "an indecisive campaign with the cost of holding a position in Korea becoming, in the long run, infinitely greater than were we to fight back along conventional lines."[147]

The administration rejected MacArthur's recommendation to widen the war, partly because it feared that an expanded Sino-American conflict would only serve Moscow's interests, partly because it could not count on support from allies, partly because it remained convinced, unlike MacArthur, that the decisive theater of action in the Cold War and in any future hot war as well would be Europe.[148] Accordingly, Washington reverted to the idea of attempting to stabilize a military line at or near the 38th parallel and, once this had been done, seeking an end to the fighting through negotiations. "Our purposes in Korea remain the same," Acheson assured Ernest Bevin late in November, "namely, to resist aggression, to localize the hostilities, and to wind up the Korean problem on a satisfactory UN basis and in such a way as not to commit US forces in large numbers indefinitely in that operation."[149] It was MacArthur's inability to accommodate himself to this strategy that led to his removal from command in April of 1951.[150]

[147]MacArthur to Robert C. Richardson, March 20, 1951, MacArthur Papers, RG 5, box 49. See also MacArthur to the Joint Chiefs of Staff, November 7 and 29, December 3 and 30, 1950, *FR, 1950,* 7:1077n., 1253n., 1320–22, 1630–33; and J. Lawton Collins to the Joint Chiefs, December 7, 1950, summarized in *ibid.,* p. 1469n.

[148]See, on these points, Jessup to Acheson, November 20, 1950, *FR, 1950,* 7:1193–96; Jessup speech to Philadelphia World Affairs Council, November 24, 1950, *Department of State Bulletin* (December 4, 1950), 23:885; Jessup notes, National Security Council meeting, White House, November 28, 1950, *FR, 1950,* 7:1242–49; Jessup notes, meeting of State Department, Defense Department, and Central Intelligence Agency representatives, Pentagon, December 1, 1950, *ibid.,* pp. 1276–81; Lucius W. Battle notes, Truman-Acheson-Marshall-Bradley meeting, White House, December 2, 1950, *ibid.,* pp. 1310–12; Jessup notes, Acheson-Marshall-Joint Chiefs of Staff meeting, Pentagon, December 3, 1950, *ibid.,* pp. 1323–34; Kennan, *Memoirs: 1950–1963,* pp. 32–33; minutes, Truman-Attlee meeting, White House, December 5, 1950, *FR, 1950,* 7:1395.

[149]Acheson to U.S. Embassy, London, November 28, 1950, *FR, 1950,* 7:1251.

[150]MacArthur complained to Carlos P. Romulo on December 26, 1950: "This group of Europhiles just will not recognize that it is Asia which has been selected for the test of Communist power and that if all Asia falls Europe would not have a

And yet the administration did not remain wholly unaffected by MacArthur's argument. Truman and his advisers did give serious consideration in November and December 1950 to authorizing "hot pursuit" by fighter planes across the Yalu and the bombing of Manchurian air fields and supply depots.[151] And in May 1951, one month after MacArthur's dismissal, Truman approved NSC 48/4, which provided:

In order to be prepared for Chinese aggression outside Korea, to protect the security of UN and U. S. forces, and to provide for appropriate military action in the event that UN forces are forced to evacuate Korea, [the United States should] expedite the development of plans for the following courses of action, if such action should later be deemed necessary:

(1) Imposing a blockade of the China coast by naval and air forces.

(2) Military action against selected targets held by Communist China outside Korea.

(3) Participation defensively or offensively of the Chinese Nationalist forces, and necessary operational assistance to make them effective.[152]

As it happened, armistice talks began in July, and the administration never had to put these plans into operation. But the fact that they were considered suggests that the administration and MacArthur were not so far apart at least in their conviction that the United States had no business attempting

---

chance—either with or without American assistance. In their blind and stupid effort to undermine public confidence in me as something of a symbol of the need for balanced thinking and action, they do Europe the gravest disservice and sow the seeds to its possible ultimate destruction." MacArthur Papers, RG 5, box 1A, file 5.

[151] See, on this point, Joint Chiefs of Staff to Marshall, November 9, 1950, *FR, 1950,* 7:1119–20; Marshall to Acheson, November 10, 1950, *ibid.,* p. 1126; Acheson to U.S. embassies in Great Britain, Australia, Canada, and France, November 13, 1950, *ibid.,* pp. 1144–45; Rusk briefing for ambassadors of nations contributing troops in Korea, November 30, 1950, *ibid.,* p. 1264; Battle memorandum, Acheson briefing on Truman statement at dinner with Attlee, December 6, 1950, *ibid.,* p. 1431.

[152] NSC 48/4, "United States Objectives, Policies, and Courses of Action in Asia," approved by Truman on May 17, 1951, *Pentagon Papers,* 8:432. Interestingly, the same document also called for efforts to "stimulate differences between the Peiping and Moscow regimes and create cleavages within the Peiping regime itself by ever practicable means." *Ibid.,* p. 431.

to fight Communist China with ground troops on the mainland of Asia, and in their determination to avoid in the future such costly departures from the original defensive perimeter concept.[153]

Ideally, a defensive perimeter strategy should seek to contain the expansive tendencies of potential adversaries without unnecessarily dispersing resources.[154] Such an approach assumes that because capabilities are finite, interests must be also; ends must be framed in such a way as to be consistent with means. Implicit also is the notion of selectivity, whether in the choice of terrain to be defended, instruments with which to carry out that defense, or allies to be enlisted in the effort. The overall objective is, or should be, to counter the other side's initiatives without restricting one's own.

At first glance, the concept of an American "defensive perimeter" in the Far East would appear to have met that standard. The primary interest involved was to ensure that East Asia did not come under the domination of a single hostile power. But because United States capabilities lay more in the area of technology than manpower and because of competing obligations in Europe, a region of even more vital interest, it made sense to confine the American presence in the Far East to islands capable of being defended by air and naval forces, thus avoiding the costs of operations against high manpower but low technology adversaries on the main-

---

[153] Significantly, NSC 124/1, approved by Truman on June 25, 1952, provided that in case of overt Chinese Communist aggression against Indochina, "the United States should take air and naval action in conjunction with at least France and the U.K. against all suitable military targets in China, avoiding insofar as practicable those targets in areas near the boundaries of the USSR in order not to increase the risk of direct Soviet involvement. In the event the concurrence of the United Kingdom and France to expanded military action against Communist China is not obtained, the United States should consider taking unilateral action." NSC 124/1, "United States Objectives and Courses of Action with Respect to Southeast Asia," *Pentagon Papers*, 8:534.

[154] See, on this point, Edward N. Luttwak, *The Grand Strategy of the Roman Empire* (Baltimore: Johns Hopkins, 1977), p. 61.

land. This was a realistic recognition both of global priorities and of existing asymmetries of power in the Far East.

As with most general concepts, application proved more difficult than articulation. It was all very well to relinquish commitments in mainland China, which was lost to the West anyway, but the problems of Taiwan, Indochina, and Korea defied such easy solution. Taiwan had been excluded from the perimeter for reasons of international politics—Acheson's desire to avoid further involvement in the Chinese civil war and to retain the option of exploiting Sino-Soviet tension. But domestic political pressures, together with concern over strategic implications should the island fall under Soviet control, quickly forced a reconsideration of that policy. Indochina was never really excluded from the perimeter, despite its mainland position, indigenous insurgency, and decaying colonial administration. South Korea was quite deliberately left out, only to be reincluded abruptly as a consequence of the North Korean attack. Indecision regarding the new perimeter on the Korean peninsula in turn provoked Chinese Communist intervention, with the result that the "defensive perimeter" at the end of 1950 looked very different from the way it had at the beginning of that year.

These anomalies suggest that while both the immediate *strategy* of maintaining a "defensive perimeter" and the long-range *interest* in preserving a nonhostile Asia were capable of eliciting agreement in Washington, no such consensus existed as to how to get from one point to the other. What, for example, was the threat to the balance of power—Soviet expansionism or international communism? Could the threat best be contained by encouraging resistance to it wherever it appeared or by opposing it selectively with a view to promoting fragmentation? What allies might appropriately be enlisted in these efforts? And what priorities should be assigned to them, given responsibilities in other parts of the world? Nor was there always sufficient coordination of political, economic, and military planning, with the result that actions taken in one field were not always thought out in terms of their implications for the other. There was also a failure to appreciate the psychological dimensions of strategy. It is significant that the decisions to defend Taiwan, Indochina, and South Korea were based as much on considerations of "prestige" and "credibility" as on the importance of these territories in and of themselves.[155] Finally, the Truman administration may have erred in delineating its strategy too precisely in public. Governments should never be ambiguous with themselves in defining vital interests, but a certain amount of public ambiguity in such matters can, at times, contribute toward the deterrence of adversaries, both foreign and domestic.[156]

By 1951 the defensive perimeter strategy was, to all intents and purposes, dead. Instead the Truman administration had backed into a strategy of resisting communist aggression wherever it occurred, but only at a corresponding level of violence. Almost immediately frustrations with the costs of this approach led the administration to seek ways of achieving its objectives less expensively. It was left to the Eisenhower administration, though, to articulate this concept in the form of the "New Look," a strategy designed quite deliberately to project ambiguity regarding possible responses to aggression in the interests of economy.[157] Two decades later, in reaction

[155]"There may be times when the army and the nation fully understand the reasons for withdrawing to the interior, when confidence and hope may even be fortified as a result; but they are very rare. As a rule, the people and the army cannot even tell the difference between a planned retreat and a backward stumble; still less can they be certain if a plan is a wise one, based on anticipation of positive advantages, or whether it has simply been dictated by fear of the enemy. There will be public concern and resentment at the fate of abandoned areas; the army will possibly lose confidence not only in its leaders but in itself, and never-ending rear guard actions will only tend to confirm its fears. *These consequences* of retreat should not be underrated." Carl von Clausewitz, *On War* (first published 1832), ed. and trans. by Peter Paret and Michael Howard (Princeton: Princeton University Press, 1976), p. 471.

[156]During the course of 1950 U.S. representatives in Taiwan, Indochina, and South Korea all warned separately of the unfortunate psychological consequences in their respective areas should Washington continue publicly to differentiate between regions of primary and secondary interest in the Far East. See Muccio to Rusk, May 25, 1950, *FR, 1950,* 7:88; Karl L. Rankin to Rusk, September 2, 1950, *ibid.,* 6:481; Donald R. Heath to Rusk and Jessup, October 15, 1950, *ibid.,* p. 896.

[157]See, on this point, Glenn H. Snyder, "The 'New Look' of 1953," in Warner R. Schilling, Paul Y. Hammond, and Glenn H. Snyder, *Strategy, Politics, and Defense Budgets* (New York, 1962), pp. 497–98.

to an even more costly flirtation with "flexible response" in Asia, the Nixon administration embarked on a strategy of encouraging Asian self-reliance while taking advantage of Sino-Soviet tension to move toward a rapprochement with Peking. It was an approach not too far removed from the original defensive perimeter concept as Acheson and his colleagues in the State Department understood it. Ironically, relics of the failure of that strategy—commitments to the defense of Taiwan, South Korea, and, one suspects South Vietnam as well had the events of 1975 not intervened—have prevented full implementation to this day.[158]

[158]Another irony is that of these three countries it was Indochina—the one never excluded from the "defensive perimeter"—that was in the end "lost."

SUMMARY OF DISCUSSION
Waldo Heinrichs

JOHN GADDIS provided a critical assessment of the strategic dimension of American East Asian policy. With the discussion of his paper, the spotlight shifted from diplomacy to war plans and capabilities, strategic estimates, and military influence on foreign policy. Gaddis's central proposition, the "defensive perimeter" concept, established the lowest common denominator in American strategic thinking about East Asia and served as a valuable point of departure in analyzing the American response to the rise of Communist China and the North Korean attack. Discussants probed the nature and limits of the original strategy, explored its context, and debated when and why shifts away from the perimeter strategy occurred.

In his opening remarks Gaddis summarized his thesis on the rise and fall of the defensive perimeter strategy. He emphasized how fragile the original consensus was. The offshore position set forth in Acheson's speech of January 12, 1950, had been extensively deliberated, but, as Gaddis had shown, it rested on contradictory perspectives. To the State Department the line represented the maximum reach of American vital interests; to various military agencies more hopeful of influencing events in Asia it was a minimum definition imposed by current constraints. Furthermore, the concept was almost immediately tested by circumstances and found wanting. In each of his three case studies—Taiwan, Indochina, and Korea—a reversal of attitudes occurred and the United States adopted a more forward position.

119

The history of this short-lived strategy suggested to Gaddis certain distinctive problems in American strategic thinking at the time. One was the tendency to compartmentalize military and political considerations, and the consequent failure to recognize the implications of each for the other. The study also raised for Gaddis the question whether it was wiser to define precisely and publicly what would be defended or instead to project some uncertainty and unpredictability. Specific delineation of a strategic frontier created an acute problem for American policy makers. In each of the three cases investigated, Gaddis pointed out, efforts to maintain American prestige and credibility contradicted the effort to differentiate between what was vital and what was peripheral. Dean Rusk put the dilemma this way, according to Thomas Paterson: If you do not pay attention to the periphery, the first you know, the periphery becomes the center. In the Gaddis view, American strategists never really worked out these problems in advance. Altogether, American strategic thinking in these years struck him as groping and immature. It was characterized by inconsistency rather than consistency.

As Gaddis made clear, East Asia was a strategic theater of secondary concern to the United States. His designated commentators, Samuel Wells and David Rosenberg, sketched in the primary strategic concerns. Europe remained, as always, the region of highest concern. Soviet armies sweeping across Europe seemed the principal threat. Another central concern, emerging since the war, was protection of the Mediterranean and the Arab oil states. Military policy advice, deployments, and war plans never wavered throughout this period in placing the utmost strategic importance on these transatlantic interests. Even after the start of the Korean War, Wells pointed out, the major threat was still assumed to be directed at Europe, and well over half the additional defense resources were allocated to Europe and its resupply in case of invasion.

Further preoccupying the military, according to Wells,

was service competition in two closely related contests: the struggles for strategic missions and for dollars. In 1948 American national security came to rest on atomic offensive capability, the only apparent means of offsetting Soviet superiority in conventional weapons. In the contest for that mission the air force held a commanding lead, the navy contended it, and the army trailed far behind. The navy rested its future, said Wells, on development of carrier planes capable of delivering atomic weapons and nuclear-powered ballistic missile submarines. The "battle for dollars" emerged from efforts beginning in 1947 to unify the service budgets and led to the so-called "revolt of the admirals" in 1949, culminating in the dismissal of the chief of Naval Operations, Admiral Louis Denfeld. For fiscal year 1950 (beginning July 1, 1949) the president imposed a defense budget ceiling of $15 billion. "Within these circumstances," said Wells, "each service felt it must strive to get part of the atomic offensive mission in order to survive as a viable military force." This sort of consideration, not China, was on the military mind.

Rosenberg presented a somewhat different picture with nearly the same implication for East Asian strategy. His researches in war plans suggested a three-stage evolution in American postwar strategic planning. In the first period, 1945–47, planning was activist, seeking forward bases and intervention where necessary to contain the Soviet Union. It was also somewhat rhetorical, designed to alert the American leadership to Soviet menace and American weakness. The second phase, 1947–49, was more cautious and discriminating, reflecting budgetary constraints and the ability and determination of the Joint Chiefs of Staff to establish priorities and relate military ends to modest means. War plans at this stage could not cope with the risk implicit in earlier forward containment strategy. In the third period, from the fall of 1949 to the Korean War, according to Rosenberg, planning began to turn full circle. Personnel shifts in the Joint Chiefs of Staff brought forward General J. Lawton Collins of the army and Admiral Forrest P. Sherman, service leaders more adept at bureaucratic politics and determined to circumvent budgetary restrictions. The navy now began searching for additional conventional war roles. The military was more inclined toward forward containment, with potential for a more active role in East Asia, but before the Korean War this was a disposition not a decision.

Dealing with such concepts as the defensive perimeter raised the question of how scholars should evaluate Policy Planning papers, National Security Council memoranda, and Joint Chiefs of Staff war plans. Wells asked to what extent they reflected objective analysis or institutional priorities or mere routine staff work. War plans of this period were largely guesswork, he suggested, based on projected weapons systems the capabilities of which were virtually unknown. NSC 68, often seen as a blueprint for an expanded Cold War, seemed to Wells little more than a planning exercise. The NSC imprint by no means implied a national decision. Some of these papers, Robert Blum pointed out, were information studies, others were interdepartmental negotiating instruments. NSC 48/2, though a significant document, represented a compilation of previous State Department positions rather than a new departure. To Roger Dingman, strategic planning of the period seemed "murky." He noted intense bureaucratic rivalry among the new planning groups, together with a curious lack of forcefulness of the military service in fighting for the means—deployments, bases, weapons—required for their war plans, due not only to budgetary constraints but also perhaps to uncertainty about what was important. To these discussants American strategic planning, beyond a few well-established transatlantic priorities, seemed even more inchoate than formal position papers suggested.

These remarks limned the context for discussions of East Asian strategy. They underscored the emphasis Gaddis placed on the tenuous nature of the defensive perimeter concept, as did subsequent remarks specifically bearing on the concept. To Warner Schilling, the perimeter concept meant "differing things to differing people" and nothing more. Dingman found the military more interested in points than in lines. In late 1945 and early 1946, he said, one could indeed detect a coalescence of war planners around the idea of defending the Pacific perimeter, the sea space, but this notion gave way to a search for positions that might assist strikes against the Soviet Union in the event of general war. Wells, who found the paper generally persuasive on high-level outcomes, suggested that the concept rested more on agreed indecision than any deliberate selection of a strategy.

Discussion of particular territories illustrated the difficulty of conceptualizing American strategic interests in the region. Indochina was in several respects different from the rest of the defensive perimeter, Bruce Cumings argued. Its importance derived not so much from its position in Asia as from American determination to support France for European reasons. Indochina differed too in lacking a domestic constituency like the China lobby.

Japan's initial exclusion from the perimeter also posed problems. Japan, Cumings observed, remained one of the four great industrial areas of the world which George Kennan insisted must be kept out of communist hands. Furthermore, as Dingman pointed out, despite American commitment to a neutralized and disarmed Japan, war planners in 1948 took note of its value as a possible base for launching immediate atomic attack in the event of general war. At Tokyo on the eve of the Korean War, Dingman added, the Joint Chiefs and MacArthur apparently agreed to proceeding with negotiations for a Japanese peace treaty, while MacArthur dropped his earlier opposition to permanent United States bases in Japan.

The question of defending Taiwan was the most puzzling of all. Gaddis had emphasized that the war plan for 1950 envisaged denial of the island to possible Russian use in the event of general war. Allen Whiting, commenting on Cohen's paper, had reinforced the point by noting that NSC documents of 1949 attached strategic significance to Taiwan

in the event of war. Both Gaddis and Cohen had shown that
the impulse to draw lines against the further spread of communism in Asia was rising in the State Department no less
than in the military. In the late spring of 1950 the threat
seemed pointed at Taiwan. As several discussants remarked,
the Chinese Communists easily took the island of Hainan and
were massing opposite Taiwan. Gaddis drew attention to reports at this time that the Soviets were transferring fighter
planes to the Chinese Communists. According to Whiting
and Nancy Tucker, observers generally agreed that a token
invasion of Taiwan would suffice, given the disarray of Nationalist forces on the island. Dingman added that just before
the North Korean attack Secretary of Defense Johnson and
General Bradley, chairman of the Joint Chiefs, returned from
Tokyo prepared to renew debate using MacArthur's arguments on the strategic importance of the island. Clearly a significant current of official thinking was setting in the direction of somehow denying Taiwan to the People's Republic.
These findings, in the judgment of Iriye, were among the
most important of the conference because they showed a fundamental departure in American thinking from the precept
established in World War II that Taiwan was part of China.

Nevertheless, as both Gaddis and Cohen agreed, national
policy as of June 25, 1950, remained what Acheson had consistently maintained it should be, that the United States
would not intervene in the Chinese civil conflict by using its
own forces to defend Taiwan. That determination Stephen
Pelz underlined in saying that in early June all three service
chiefs recommended against such a commitment. The underlying question, then, seemed to be not whether American
policy on Taiwan shifted before the Korean War, but to what
extent the rising preoccupation with Taiwan created a mindset that tended to predetermine the decision to interpose the
Seventh Fleet after June 25; to what extent, in other words,
the decision was a conditioned response, a knee-jerk reaction.

This was a line of argument pursued by Whiting. The

1949 NSC decisions assigning strategic importance to Taiwan in the event of war should be looked at as a bureaucratic compromise, he suggested. Acheson would not have felt he was making a concession of any importance in agreeing to them because the prospect of war originating in East Asia seemed so remote. With the Sino-Soviet alliance and then the North Korean attack, however, the compromise turned into a trap. Acheson and Truman would have found it difficult to argue that this was not the war they had been thinking about in 1949. A military alliance and a war theater existed; the conditions for defending Taiwan were fulfilled. Gaddis entirely agreed. Whiting's argument jibed with his own contention that such an understanding with the Joint Chiefs existed all along. He added that first perceptions of the Korean conflict as prelude to a general war with the Soviet Union would have given added incentive to preemptive action on Taiwan.

This was an intriguing and plausible line of argument. The problem was how much weight to assign it. Schilling remained unimpressed with the military factor in the Taiwan decision. It still puzzled him that Acheson would jeopardize all he hoped ultimately to accomplish with China by supporting the decision. The sort of advice he was getting from the military would surely not have seemed helpful. MacArthur's prediction of dire consequences from the fall of Taiwan, for example, was typical bureaucratic hyperbole designed to maximize the range of one's appeal. He asked what the difference would have been from a purely military point of view if the Russians had secured bases in Taiwan. Precisely what could they have done that they would otherwise have been unable to do? Interfere with American lines of communication in the Pacific–East Asian region, answered several discussants. Taiwan would then indeed be, said Gaddis, MacArthur's "unsinkable aircraft carrier." And the general would not be one to forget the lesson of 1941, when the Japanese bombed the Philippines from Formosa, Messer added. Schilling replied with this question: if Taiwan as a hostile base was so threatening, why had not the military considered the danger of South Korean bases to Japan when they discussed withdrawal in 1947–48? Gaddis agreed that this was an anomaly.

In Schilling's view the decision was primarily political. Acheson and Truman were less impressed with any military value in Taiwan than they were by the political strength and agitation of those who did value it, in Congress and the public. Incitement of the China lobby and further accusations of the "You lost China" variety were the last things they needed as they embarked on what must have seemed a perilous course in Korea. Gaddis accepted that Acheson was seeking to reduce friction in the domestic political context, but he was not prepared to discount military influence; both factors weighed in the Taiwan decision. Dispatch of the fleet was an expediency, designed to maintain a standstill in the Taiwan Strait until the Korean emergency subsided. That was expected to be soon if general war could be avoided. According to Gaddis, Acheson did not believe the decision was conclusive; he had "this curiously unrealistic view . . . that he could somehow get through to Peking, still establish some kind of special relationship, still bring about the split."

Discussion of the Taiwan decision suggested how deep if not definitive American concern with Taiwan was before the Korean War, how incremental and derivative United States involvement was, and how unwittingly it crossed a threshold of enormous consequence in ordering the fleet movement.

Discussion of the Korean intervention centered on the extent of the American commitment to South Korea. According to the Gaddis thesis no formal commitment existed. South Korea was excluded from the defensive perimeter and then rapidly reincluded upon being attacked. He offered two reasons, one historical, the other symbolic: the lesson of the 1930s that aggression must be resisted at the outset, and the need to maintain American prestige and credibility.

Schilling questioned the argument of credibility. If no commitment existed, he saw no reason why American credibility was at stake. Here Cumings took issue, arguing the

United States did indeed have a commitment to South Korea, implicit perhaps but no less determining. From 1947 to 1950, he maintained, the State Department had consistently warned of the political costs of losing South Korea. The Rhee regime was, after all, the only American-created government in East Asia. In Cumings' view, further commitment existed by way of the UN. He felt that Acheson was not shirking responsibility when he stated in his January 12, 1950, speech that local forces beyond the perimeter should look to the UN for their defense. Soviet-backed aggression, together with proof of South Korean will to resist but inadequate capability, created a decisive implicit obligation for the United States.

Several participants wondered whether it might not be possible to detect in the fall of the defensive perimeter strategy the rise of a new strategy, embracing and unifying the reversals of the original strategy illustrated by Gaddis. Blum offered for consideration a second perimeter, no less significant to containment policy, "a softer perimeter, one of political influence," embracing Korea, Taiwan, Indochina, Thailand, Burma, and India. This political perimeter would have the same instruments of American policy as the defensive perimeter—political support, military and economic aid, Point Four assistance—with one exception: there would be no use of American combat forces. Congressional appropriation in 1949 of $75 million for use in the general area of China "breathed life into this new containment line," according to Blum. It precipitated reexamination of Taiwan policy by the Joint Chiefs of Staff and State Department planning for use of the money elsewhere in the region.

Dingman too saw a second perimeter on the mainland but gave it a slightly more military cast. He found recognition in war plans that there were mainland positions that required the stationing of American military personnel not for defense but for "psychological deterrence." He noted a reversal in the spring of 1950 of the Joint Chiefs' position that East Asia was not an area of critical importance to the position that this was an area in which the United States could involve itself by sending military assistance groups for political and psychological reasons. In the December 1949 war plan a distinction was made between defense and deterrence, differentiating between offshore and mainland positions. Gaddis welcomed these suggestions.

No one questioned the existence of the defensive perimeter concept in strategic thinking, nor the value of it analytically as a point of departure. The concern of discussants lay with the centrality of the concept in American strategy and policy. The cumulative effect of discussion was to suggest that a more forward strategy of containment existed even before the Korean War. In the face of a perceived rise in Sino-Soviet power on the mainland, American policy makers looked beyond the offshore chain toward an independent Japan tied to the American security system, they intensified examination of the defense of Taiwan, and they initiated programs for maintaining the independence of small Asian states bordering China. Some commitments were less explicit and more conditional than others, some actions more symbolic than substantive. Altogether, however, they spelled increasing involvement and confrontation. The region as a whole seemed more inflammable before the spark was struck on June 25, 1950. How far East Asian circumstances and American regional policy prefigured the conflict after June 25 remained a question, but conferees agreed that one could not afford to neglect the regional background of the Korean War.

PART II
Chinese Nationalist Policy

Nationalist China's Decline and Its Impact on Sino-American Relations, 1949–1950

Nancy Bernkopf Tucker

AT THE beginning of 1949 the National Government of China was crumbling. After decades of almost constant warfare, Kuomintang attempts to exterminate the Chinese Communists were ending in bitter defeat. In Manchuria Chiang Kai-shek had futilely sacrificed some 400,000 of his best trained and equipped soldiers to a larger and logistically superior force. That same month, November 1948, overruling his advisers, Chiang had again engaged the Communists, this time in central China. The sixty-five-day Huai-hai battle along a 200-mile front, in which more than one million fighting men participated, saw ably commanded Communist legions encircle and destroy the government's troops. A Kuomintang relief column, overloaded with heavy arms and camp followers, was dispatched, but agile Communist units trapped this ponderous army behind rings of trenches. Then, after Generalissimo Chiang decided to bomb the column's valuable equipment rather than see it fall into enemy hands, the relief force, not surprisingly, surrendered.[1]

Military disaster was paralleled by diplomatic defeat. Madame Chiang Kai-shek's mission to the United States in the autumn of 1948 for urgently needed aid was proving

[1] Lucien Bianco, *Origins of the Chinese Revolution, 1915–1949*, translated by Muriel Bell (Stanford: Stanford University Press, 1967), pp. 177–78.

fruitless. Efforts by the Nationalists to cement an alliance in 1948 with presidential candidate Thomas E. Dewey and Republican Party stalwarts for a time appeared more promising. With a sympathetic White House, it was thought, the anti-Chiang bias in the State Department could be eliminated or at least circumvented. Truman's upset victory shattered these hopes. Thus the Nationalists were not surprised when the United States, along with France, Great Britain, and the Soviet Union, rebuffed their appeals to mediate the civil war in January 1949. Soon after, Mao Tse-tung denounced Chiang's proposed New Year's Day peace terms as hypocritical, countering with eight of his own that were equally unacceptable to the Generalissimo. Whereas Chiang demanded preservation of the Kuomintang constitution, government, and army, Mao disposed of all these "bogus" institutions and insisted upon land reform, abrogation of "treasonable" treaties, and punishment of a list of war criminals which, of course, included Chiang Kai-shek.[2]

Driven by mounting desperation, the badly shaken Nationalists sought frantically in the months that followed to escape from the catastrophe of Communist takeover. As time passed and alternatives lost promise, hope focused on the single source of support that might stem the quickening tide. Although the United States had been an increasingly reluctant benefactor, Kuomintang leaders came to believe, with a certitude born of despair, that salvation lay with American aid and that they could convince or coerce the Truman administration to cooperate. Pursuing this elusive goal, they fashioned ever more improbable stratagems to maneuver their restive ally into a firm commitment.

[2] See Lyman P. Van Slyke, ed., The China White Paper, August 1949 (Stanford: Stanford University Press, 1967), pp. 920–21; "Statement on the Present Situation by Mao Tse-tung, Chairman of the Communist Party of China, January 14, 1949," Selected Works of Mao Tse-tung (New York: International Publishers, n.d.), 5:315–19; Stuart, Nanking, to Secretary of State, in U.S. Department of State, Foreign Relations of the United States (hereafter FR), 1949, 8:22–23; memorandum of conversation by Director of the Office of Far Eastern Affairs (Butterworth) to the Acting Secretary of State, ibid., pp. 27–29; Acting Secretary of State to Stuart, Nanking, ibid., pp. 41–42.

As the country lurched from crisis to crisis, however, discord within the government hampered even this policy. While unity might not have preserved a non-Communist China, disunity simply ensured its demise. From the moment that illusions of possible victory dissolved at the close of 1948, the fiction of unified rule was abandoned.

Evidence of this decline appeared first in voices within Chiang Kai-shek's governing coalition that called stridently for his resignation. As in 1927, when military misfortune made him politically vulnerable, failures of leadership in late 1948 encouraged his opponents. The New Year's peace plan was, in fact, a final effort to preserve his formal governmental authority without acknowledging the enormity of Kuomintang losses. There were some in the party, however, who feared complete collapse and were willing, even anxious, to try to bargain with the Chinese Communists. On January 21, 1949, heeding at last the often-tendered demands of these dissidents, Chiang Kai-shek turned his fragile government over to Vice President Li Tsung-jen, his long-time rival.[3]

American Ambassador John Leighton Stuart had reported during 1948 that a growing number in the Chinese government and military considered a negotiated peace with the Communists and formation of a coalition government desirable and achievable through mediation by the Soviet Union.[4] As the Generalissimo was implacably opposed, advocates of this view were among those calling for Chiang's

[3] Bianco, *Origins*, pp. 177–78; and James P. Harrison, *The Long March to Power: A History of the Chinese Communist Party in Power, 1921–1972* (New York: Praeger, 1972), pp. 423–25. On Kuomintang members who desired Chiang's resignation, see *FR, 1948*, 7:625–27, and "Pai Chung-hsi Extends His Influence into the Nanking-Shanghai Area," *Hai ch'ao* (Tide Weekly) (Shanghai), February 11, 1949, quoted in *Chinese Press Survey* (Millard Publishing Co.), vol. 2, no. 6, February 21, 1949.

Over the next eighteen months events moved rapidly. In retrospect it is easy to see the glaring mistakes. Yet evidence of developments beneath the surface is harder to unearth, and much remains concealed in still inaccessible Kuomintang and Chinese Communist archives. In subsequent pages an effort is made to reconstruct the policies and actions of the Chinese National Government, but until the documents produced by the actors themselves are made available, historians must to an unfortunate extent wander in the dark.

[4] Stuart, Nanking, to Secretary of State, *FR, 1948*, 7:56–57 and 77.

retirement at the end of the year. Li Tsung-jen, upon assuming the presidency, immediately notified Soviet Ambassador N. V. Roschin that he would like to reopen discussions regarding Russian aid for a negotiated end to the civil war. At the same time Li authorized the pro-Soviet General Chang Chih-chung to conclude a commercial agreement with the USSR in Sinkiang. Later, when a new cabinet was formed under Ho Ying-ch'in, Li's chosen president of the Executive Yuan, a man with nine years' experience as Chinese ambassador to Moscow, was named foreign minister. Encouraged by the momentary support of Sun Fo, who proclaimed himself to be pro-Soviet, and by at least part of the influential Political Study Clique, Li went so far as to offer the Russians Chinese neutrality in a future world war. In response, Roschin demanded that Li also agree to form a genuinely cooperative relationship with Russia and to eliminate American influence from China.[5]

At this juncture developments took a most peculiar turn, or so it seemed. Li appealed to John Leighton Stuart for support in his talks with Roschin. Stuart got, and communicated to Secretary of State Dean Acheson, the impression that Li had tentatively agreed to a three-point accord incorporating the provision that China would cease to depend upon the United States. Yet here Li was in the "incredible" position (as the Department of State put it) of asking Americans to help him throw them out. Subsequently, Li's diplomatic spokesman Kan Chieh-hou denied that talks with the Russians had ever gone so far. The Chinese had agreed to neu-

[5] Discussion of factions in the Kuomintang follows. V. K. Wellington Koo Oral History Collection, vol I, sec. 4, p. 205, East Asian Institute, Columbia University (hereafter Koo Oral History); Shui Chieh-tan, "A Study of the Sino-Soviet Local Commercial Pact," Ta-kung pao (Shanghai), February 5, 1949, quoted in Chinese Press Survey, vol. 2, no. 5, February 11, 1949; "Says Pro-USSR Policy Is Bound to Be Changed If Peace Talks Break Down," Ta-kung pao, April 20, 1949, quoted in U.S. Consul-General, Shanghai, Chinese Press Review, no. 875, April 20, 1949; Joint Weeka no. 10, from State, Army, Navy, Air, Nanking, March 25, 1949, p. 2, file 350.2 Joint Weeka Reports, U.S. Consul-General, Hong Kong, China Post Files, Record Group (hereafter RG) 84, General Archives Division, Washington National Records Center, Suitland, Md.

trality because they needed time and hoped to delay Mao Tse-tung's advance. Stuart's help, it had been hoped, would strengthen Li against Roschin's demands, which were indeed finally refused.[6] In any case, the National Government, whether under the direct command of Chiang Kai-shek or the shaky leadership of Li Tsung-jen, could not bring itself to jettison the United States. Some factions might entertain the illusion that Soviet promises were reliable, but a history of unmet guarantees made the government unwilling to abandon its one stable, if inadequate, source of aid.

Moreover, the Russian connection did not and could not serve to soften Chinese Communist peace terms, which clearly amounted to unconditional surrender by the Nationalists. Soviet influence upon Chinese Communist Party (CCP) policies was, at best, tenuous, since Moscow had too often misjudged China's revolution and discouraged its leaders. Having cautioned them to discontinue military operations at the Yangtze River when success was within reach, the Russians were predictably ignored. The Nationalists' abiding belief in Soviet control over Communist activities in China testified to a prevailing misunderstanding of the Chinese Communist movement.[7]

Disagreement over negotiating directly with the CCP proved much more serious than that provoked by talks with the Soviet Union. Li Tsung-jen rapidly found himself confronted not only by adamant enemies, but also by uncompromising allies. Clinging to the idea of an "honorable

[6] 893.00/1-2349, no. 197, Stuart, Nanking, to Secretary of State, and 893.00/1-2349, no. 94, Acheson to Stuart, Decimal File, General Records of the Department of State, RG 59, National Archives, Washington, D.C.; statement by Kan Chieh-hou, August 24, 1949, V. K. Wellington Koo Papers, "U.S. White Paper on China 1949" folder 75.6, Butler Library, Columbia University (hereafter cited as Koo Papers). The British assistant undersecretary of state for foreign affairs (FE) believed the Chinese were trying to frighten the United States into intervention; see Holmes, UK, to Secretary of State, FR, 1949, 8:99–100.

[7] Chang Chih-chung told Philip Fugh on January 4, 1949, that the Soviets had advised the Chinese Communists to stop at the Yangtze River. John Leighton Stuart Diary, entry for January 4, 1949, Washington, D.C.; John Gittings, The World and China, 1922–1972 (New York: Harper & Row, 1974), p. 150.

peace," Sun Fo, who had been appointed president of the Executive Yuan by Chiang Kai-shek, moved the Executive Yuan away from the capital and charged Li with exceeding his authority in accepting Mao's eight points as a basis for talks.[8] Although Li did have the support of members of the Political Study Clique, as well as of his own Kwangsi faction and leftist elements such as the Kuomintang Revolutionary Committee, stubborn resistance on the part of traditionalists in the government and army made his task all the more difficult.[9] It was obvious that he could not command the Nationalist forces to stop fighting even if an agreement could be reached.

Li's impotence was all too apparent to the Communists. To them it seemed that Li was not sincere but was merely stalling for time while refurbishing his anti-Communist alliances.[10] Perhaps, too, the knowledge that disunity would

[8] Lu Ying-hua, "The Delicate Relations among Li Tsung-jen, Sun Fo, and Chang Chih-chung," *Niu shih* (Newsweek) (Shanghai), February 11, 1949, quoted in *Chinese Press Survey*, vol. 2, no. 6, February 21, 1949; "Peace Talks in Progress," *Ta-kung pao*, April 11, 1949, quoted in *Chinese Press Review*, no. 868, April 9–11, 1949. For Sun Fo's peace terms, see Joint Weeka No. 12, April 8, 1949, p. 3. Sun Fo was Sun Yat-sen's son by his first marriage. He served in a variety of government positions, including the presidency of the Legislative Yuan and, from November 1948 to March 1949, the presidency of the Executive Yuan (China's cabinet). Although he had opposed Chiang from time to time, in 1948 he was Chiang's candidate for the vice-presidency against Li. See Howard L. Boorman and Richard C. Howard, eds., *Biographical Dictionary of Republican China* (4 vols.; New York: Columbia University Press, 1967–71), 3:162–65.

[9] Editorials and news reports favorable to the concept of peace talks appeared frequently in the *Ta-kung pao*, the organ of the Political Study Clique. Comment hostile to a compromise peace was as prominent in the leading CC Clique newspaper *Shun pao*. See, for example, "Some Thoughts on the Peace Talks," *Ta-kung pao*, April 13, 1949, quoted in *Chinese Press Review*, no. 870, April 13, 1949; and "Surrender or Otherwise," *Shun pao* (Shanghai), April 19, 1949, *ibid.*, no. 874, April 19, 1949. On the affiliation of the *Ta-kung pao* with the Political Study Clique, see Han Ssu, *Kan! Cheng-hsueh hsi* (Look! The Political Study Clique) (Hong Kong, 1947), p. 14; and Suzanne Pepper, "The Politics of Civil War, China, 1945–1949" (Ph.D. diss., University of California, Berkeley, 1972), appendix A, pp. 572–76. On the *Shun pao*, see Walter Sullivan, "Chiang Aides Seen in New Maneuver," *New York Times*, February 11, 1949, p. 8.

[10] *Selected Works of Mao Tse-tung*, 5:341–45, 351–59, 383–85; "Feverish Kuomintang War Activity behind the 'Peace Front,'" North Shensi radio, February 9, 1949, in New China News Agency (hereafter NCNA) *Weekly Bulletin*, no. 89, February 15, 1949.

make Li's pledge hollow contributed to CCP intransigence. In any case, rejection of the demands for complete surrender led the very next day to a Communist assault on the Yangtze front. When the front collapsed and the People's Liberation Army rolled south almost unopposed, the Chinese Nationalists were, as in the past, left clutching at elusive American help, bereft of a viable alternative.

Li Tsung-jen, confronted with the failure of his peace proposals, struggled with scarcely more success to maintain the authority of his presidency. As he had quickly discovered, the Generalissimo's retirement partook more of fantasy than reality. Chiang Kai-shek viewed his departure from office as an opportunity to lay the onus of failure on someone else's shoulders. Retirement was never meant to be resignation.[11] Thus, whether in retreat at Fenghua or Shanghai or on Taiwan, the Generalissimo continued to direct government operations, continued to guide military campaigns, and continued to lose the Chinese mainland to communism.

Chiang Kai-shek's ability to rule from a semisecluded retirement hinged on two features of the Kuomintang political system: dictatorship and disunity. In 1924 the Kuomintang's founder and the nation's revolutionary father-figure, Sun Yat-sen, allowed Soviet advisers to reorganize his

---

[11] In Chiang's parting speech, he used the Chinese *yin-t'ui*, meaning withdrawal, instead of the stronger *tz'u-chih*, which would have meant resignation. See Koo Oral History, vol. I, sec. 1, p. 6. Philip Fugh, former secretary to John Leighton Stuart, United States ambassador to China, 1946–49, in an interview with the author, July 21, 1977, described the Generalissimo's action as asking Li to be his representative in charge of the presidency. Li Tsung-jen personally contended throughout 1949, and even after Chiang resumed the presidency on March 1, 1950, that Chiang was acting illegally. "The function of 'acting' is for the official position of the president and not for you as an individual. Furthermore, after your retirement you became a private citizen without any further concern with the function of the presidency. Without an election by the National Assembly you have no legal ground to become again the President of China." Open letter from Li Tsung-jen, New York City, to Chiang Kai-shek, Formosa, February 28, 1950, Koo Papers, box 221, "Li Tsung-jen 1949–51" folder; see also Li Tsung-jen Oral History Collection, vol. 4, pt. 7, ch. 52, pp. 52–53, Chinese Oral History Project, Butler Library, Columbia University (hereafter cited as Li Oral History). Li's memoirs have been published as *The Memoirs of Li Tsung-jen*, by Te-kong Tong and Li Tsung-jen (Boulder, Colo.: Westview Press, 1979).

following. Out of a weak political association, the advisers created a centralized party on the Bolshevik pattern. The new Kuomintang embarked on military unification and then announced the beginning of a period of political tutelage. At that point inclination and events interfered. Instead of emerging six years later into an age of democratic institutions as Sun had planned, China continued under the domination of a single authoritarian party. Moreover, the party fell under the domination of a single authoritarian leader—Chiang Kai-shek.

Chiang came to power by a somewhat circuitous route. Initially a minor military figure with disreputable underworld connections, he was, as Sun's protégé and president of the Whampoa Military Academy, in a position to take advantage of and occasionally help arrange misadventures of important contenders for party leadership. Although without government office through much of the 1930s, Chiang insinuated supporters into pivotal positions and increasingly exercised a dominant role in national affairs. By 1938 he had achieved the long-sought title of Kuomintang director-general (tsung-tsai), a recognition of his commanding, if not undisputed, status.[12]

Eleven years later, in 1949, the weight of habit and the dearth of compelling alternatives within the system had given Chiang an unbreakable grip on Nationalist fortunes. The interim had shown him to be tenacious. Throughout the bleak Chungking days of World War II, Chiang had led China's resistance to Japanese brutality. Although the Communists, with some cause, denounced his corruption, inefficiency, and incompetence and even suggested he might

---

[12] The title tsung-tsai was, for all practical purposes, the same as tsung-li, but the latter had been reserved in perpetuity to honor Sun Yat-sen. See William Tung, The Political Institutions of Modern China (The Hague: Martinus Nijhoff, 1968), p. 173; and Ch'ien Tuan-sheng, The Government and Politics of China (Cambridge, Mass.: Harvard University Press, 1950), p. 120. On Chiang's early career, see Brian Crozier, The Man Who Lost China (New York: Scribner, 1976), pp. 3–212; and Pi-chon P. Y. Loh, The Early Chiang Kai-shek: A Study of His Personality and Politics, 1887–1924 (New York: Columbia University Press, 1971).

sign a separate peace with Japan, the Generalissimo had hung on.[13] In 1945 he emerged from the Szechuan highlands to reimpose, however tenuously, Kuomintang rule over China.

Contrary to and yet coupled with this concentration of power, there was also chronic disunity in China. Though the Kuomintang had nominally united the nation in 1928, warlordism was never eliminated, regionalism flourished, and factions played havoc with internal party affairs. With an ancient, ofttimes scarlet history, factionalism in modern China splintered government leadership and rendered control of government policies a matter of personal relationship rather than official position. Destructive as they could be when major concerns were domestic and peaceful, the effects of factionalism on foreign policy for a government close to extinction were nothing less than disastrous.

Crowded into the framework of a single party, the Kuomintang, a multiplicity of alliances contended for influence.[14] The predominant groups were divided only roughly along the lines of China's most important governing units: the party, the army, and the government. The CC Clique, which was led by nephews of Chiang's revolutionary model, Ch'en Ch'i-mei, tended to dominate party affairs from its position in the Kuomintang's Organization Department. It also exerted significant control over the administrative bureaucracy through educational and cultural institutions, its own secret service network (called the Central Statistical Bureau), and its ability to assign party members to government posts

---

[13] The Hundred Regiments offensive, launched on August 20, 1940, by 400,000 troops of the Communist Eighth Route Army against Japanese forces in five northern provinces, was designed to keep the Sino-Japanese War alive and to prevent pessimistic or pro-Japanese elements in the Kuomintang from engineering a peace settlement. Chalmers A. Johnson, *Peasant Nationalism and Communist Power: The Emergence of Revolutionary China, 1937–1945* (Stanford: Stanford University Press, 1962), p. 57; and "Expose the Munich Plot in the Far East," *Selected Works of Mao Tse-tung,* (Bombay: People's Publishing House, 1956), 4:21–22.

[14] There were also minor political parties in Nationalist China, such as the Democratic League and the Young China Party, but they had little power and were generally insignificant. For a brief description of these organizations, see *The China Handbook, 1950* (New York: Rockport Press, 1950), pp. 254–59.

and supervise their performance. The Whampoa Clique was the strongest of the military groupings, deriving its preeminence from its tie with Chiang Kai-shek, who had been president of the Whampoa Military Academy during the 1920s. Finally, the Political Study Clique (sometimes referred to as the Political Science Clique) concentrated its energies in the governmental and financial spheres. Less formally organized than even the amorphous factions described above, the Political Study group provided Chiang with a pool of experienced bureaucrats, industrialists, and bankers.[15]

These cliques and their complex subdivisions exerted power through their links to Chiang Kai-shek. As one observer put it:

If we take the Kuomintang as a big Chinese family, then according to their respective positions, characteristics and styles, the Political Science Group may be compared to a middle-aged matron of great experience and worldly wisdom who, though only in the position of a concubine, still manages to make her weight felt within family circles by keeping the master of the house constantly under her control; the CC may be likened to the faithful wife of long standing who, though fundamentally well-beloved, nevertheless has to put up with the occasional whims and ill temper of the master; while the Fu Hsing Society [primarily Whampoa elements] is in the position of the unmarried daughter of the family who, though forced to adopt an attitude of coy reserve before the eyes of the world, still occupies a cozy corner in the heart of the old man.[16]

[15] Discussions of the cliques within the Kuomintang suffer from a lack of concrete data and a desire to fit a fluid situation into manageable static units. Chinese Communist intelligence agents, contemporary observers with an obvious need to understand the inner workings of the party, forewarned readers of their research that factional alignments among the Nationalists were too changeable and complex to be reliably reported. See the foreword to "Biographies of Kuomintang Leaders," mimeographed by the Committee on International and Regional Studies, Harvard University, February 1948, originally a confidential CCP publication entitled "A List of the Various Cliques among Members of Central Committees Elected by the Sixth Congress of the Kuomintang," August 31, 1945. Nevertheless, for a brief treatment of the subject, see Tien Hung-mao, Government and Politics in Kuomintang China, 1927–1937 (Stanford: Stanford University Press, 1972), pp. 45–72.

[16] Huang Pin, "Faction Strife in the Kuomintang," New Hope Weekly (Shanghai), no. 6, March 21, 1949, quoted in 893.00/4-149, no. 53, John M. Cabot, Consul-General, Shanghai, to Secretary of State, RG 59, National Archives. The New Hope

Chiang stood above all these alliances, utilizing the talents first of one and then another, keeping them constantly off-balance, never allowing any one to become strong enough to dominate the others or depose him. He dealt in much the same way with individuals, some of whom were attached to him directly and some of whom led independent followings and cooperated with him only sporadically. While Chiang exercised his control through a constellation of competing groups loyal to him, making his ouster difficult and his replacement impossible, others contested his authority through their own devoted factions. The foremost of these was the Kwangsi Clique, which in 1948, utilizing a temporary and unusually strong anti-Chiang alliance, put one of its own, Li Tsung-jen, into the vice-presidency against the wishes—and the chosen candidate—of Chiang Kai-shek.[17]

The precise impact of factionalism in the broader context of policy formulation, however, remains unclear.[18] Lloyd Eastman in *The Abortive Revolution* concludes that the many internecine rivalries were rarely disputes based on policy differences. Rather they were, as Liu Chien-ch'ün claimed, "struggle[s] for the rice bowl." [19]

There was not necessarily a conflict between the personal and impersonal goals of the faction members. But in Chinese society,

---

Weekly was controlled by the army, which goes far to explain the favorable way in which the Fu Hsing Society is described.

[17] For a detailed discussion of the background of the Kwangsi Clique, see Diana Lary, *Region and Nation* (New York: Cambridge University Press, 1974).

[18] Efforts to explain factionalism that have relied on generalizations about Chinese social traits and political behavior have stirred some controversy in recent years. See Lloyd E. Eastman, *The Abortive Revolution* (Cambridge, Mass.: Harvard University Press, 1974), pp. 283–313; Andrew J. Nathan, *Peking Politics, 1918–1923* (Berkeley: University of California Press, 1976), pp. 27–58; Richard H. Solomon, *Mao's Revolution and the Chinese Political Culture* (Berkeley: University of California Press, 1971).

[19] Liu Chien-ch'ün, *Fu-hsing Chung-kuo ko-ming chih lu* (The Way to Regenerate the Chinese Revolution) (n.p., 1934), p. 39, quoted in Eastman, *Abortive Revolution*, p. 305. Liu Chien-ch'ün was secretary to General Ho Ying-ch'in, a loyal follower of Chiang Kai-shek, and a leader of the fascistic Blue Shirts organization. He also trenchantly criticized the Kuomintang, hoping to convince the leadership to adopt reform measures for the good of the party. See *ibid.*, pp. 32–37.

where the *sheng-kuan fa-ts'ai* [to become an official and grow rich] mentality was deeply entrenched, the personal goals of the members usually—and especially after the faction had worked its way into power—began to overshadow their commitment to the impersonal goals. Chiang Kai-shek and his coterie provide, perhaps, the preeminent example of this strain between group principles and personal aggrandizement. Chiang himself seems to have been little concerned with personal enrichment and was probably firmly committed to broad national goals. Yet he also condoned flagrant corruption and notorious inefficiency on the part of his officials and military commanders as long as they remained loyal to him.[20]

Eastman and others have probably overstated Chinese indifference to abstract ideas; and disagreements between cliques often arose from divergent political orientations and, at times, notably dissimilar plans of action.[21] Nevertheless, it is probably true that disputes, whether stemming from conviction or interest, were generally perceived to involve status and position. A viewpoint at variance with Chiang's, for example, was interpreted as a direct challenge to his authority and could not be dealt with as merely an alternative solution for a complex problem.

The effects of these factional disputes within the Nationalist alliance were manifold. First, it proved impossible to have a strong, efficient, and determined government that could conduct a coordinated war or peace effort. Political decisions were tied up in an endless need to reconcile a variety of interests in each and every policy determination. When, in the early months of 1949, Li Tsung-jen decided to

[20] Eastman, *Abortive Revolution*, p. 304.

[21] "There has been much criticism of the Chinese government, both as to organization and as to personality. Such criticism, in China as elsewhere, is only partially justified. My own judgment is that while the moral level of officials should be raised, their intellectual level is even more in need of lifting and broadening. . . . Often I sat in cabinet meetings listening to discussions, indulging in the pastime of trying to fix the era to which the mentality of those present belonged. It was easy to detect German, Japanese, French, British or American educational backgrounds. But most common was the mentality of the old literatus, the one who mistook phrases for facts and decisions. If you told such a mind that it was out of date, the accusation would be resented." Tsiang Ting-fu Oral History Collection, p. 236, Chinese Oral History Project, Butler Library, Columbia University.

engage in negotiations with the CCP, Executive Yuan President Sun Fo moved the major part of the government to Canton. Sun was opposed to the idea of a compromise peace that fell short of Chiang Kai-shek's New Year's terms and simply refused to submit to Li's authority. He was able, at least initially, to divide the government, because he possessed a personal following within the Kuomintang and had the support of the CC Clique. The acting president of a nation at war had to journey to Canton and cajole Sun to return to the capital and participate in national affairs.[22]

Even when a decision was reached and a policy or military maneuver initiated, the government could never be certain that that policy or order would be carried out or in what form. The chief of staff of the Chinese armies found that his directives to field commanders were often countermanded by Chiang Kai-shek, who was in the habit of flying to various battlefronts or telephoning instructions to mere captains and lieutenants.[23] Chiang, as Generalissimo, had appointed members of his trusted Whampoa Clique to senior military positions, and their loyalty to him took precedence over their military ability and their integrity. Thus, even after his "retirement," he was able to overrule the directives of both civilian and military authorities. It was Chiang who rendered defense of the Yangtze River unmanageable, just as it was Chiang who forced General Pai Ch'ung-hsi to retreat into

[22] On March 7, 1949, Sun Fo finally resigned and was replaced by Ho Ying-ch'in, but by then Li had been to Canton (February 22) and Sun had returned the Executive Yuan to Nanking (February 28). Koo Oral History, vol. I, sec. 1, pp. 7–9; New York Times, February 19, 1949, p. 4, February 21, p. 1, February 22, p. 12, and February 25, p. 7; Li Oral History, vol. 5, pt. 7, ch. 48, pp. 10–11.

[23] Li Tsung-jen maintained that upon his return to Ch'ik'ou in Fenghua, Chiang had seven radio broadcasting stations erected from which he could direct military operations. Moreover, the chief of the General Staff, Ku Chu-t'ung, took orders only from Chiang. Li Oral History, vol. 4, pt. 7, ch. 49, p. 6. In a March 4, 1970, interview, Chang Fa-k'uei told V. K. Wellington Koo that there were occasions during the civil war when the minister of national defense was not informed of the whereabouts of troops taking orders directly from the Generalissimo. Koo Oral History, vol. J, sec. 4, p. 282. See also Wu Kuo-cheng (K. C. Wu) Oral History Collection, ch. 2, p. 70, Chinese Oral History Project, Butler Library, Columbia University (hereafter cited as Wu Oral History).

Kwangsi by ordering a withdrawal that left Pai's flank exposed.[24] Top army and navy officials told American observers that "if this situation continues, bloodshed may occur within the Nationalist army and navy because of divergent loyalties and directives." Almost constant disagreement over tactics and strategy was as disastrous to Nationalist forces as was actual combat with People's Liberation Army units. Li grew so desperate that he proposed American command of his forces to eliminate the Generalissimo's interferences.[25]

Li Tsung-jen's control of civil affairs was equally tenuous. He complained that members of his government would

[24] It was understood, Ambassador Koo notes, that the Generalissimo's order to General Liu An-ch'i, one of his favorite pupils from the Whampoa Military Academy, to withdraw south from the Kukong sector had, in large part, precipitated Pai's withdrawal from Hunan to Kwangsi. Koo continues: ". . . it was quite evident to the Generalissimo, to General Liu, as well as to the outside world, that this order to withdraw would cause General Pai's line of defense against the Communists to crumble. It may be that the Generalissimo felt this last attempt would be useless anyway, that it would be mere sacrifice to no purpose, and therefore he wanted to save his troops as much as possible." Koo Oral History, vol. J, sec. 1, pp. 39–40; 893.00/9-1749, no. 709, Karl L. Rankin to Secretary, RG 59. Chiang's biographer Brian Crozier blames this military debacle on the "provincial egotism" of Kwangtung Governor Yü Han-mou, who was trying to save his 50,000 regulars and keep Pai out of his province. (Crozier, The Man, pp. 341–42.) However, Yü was known to be a loyal follower of Chiang.

[25] According to Li and Pai in a September 12, 1949, interview with an American official, Chiang Kai-shek's interference was exemplified by withdrawal of air support over the battleground at Hengyang and removal of ammunition from Canton to Taiwan. Proof of the latter, they asserted, was the explosion of the transport ship Kaohsiung enroute. Office memo Butterworth (FE) to Humelsine (S/S), September 14, 1949, Records of the Office of Chinese Affairs, "Military Developments in China" folder, RG 59. General David Barr reported to the U.S. Department of the Army: "In an interview on 25th Jan with General Tang En-po, Defense Commander of the Nanking-Shanghai area, he stated that he was not going to obey the orders of Li Tsung-jen to discontinue work on defense installations in the Shanghai area, nor was he going to lift martial law as directed. He said he would also refuse to obey the instructions of any Communist influenced government. . . . He is strong Generalissimo man obviously not in sympathy with the policy being pursued by the present Peace Party in Nanking but he cannot hope to hold Shanghai under the circumstances." CYF771 GAGA, January 26, 1949, JUSMAGCHINA, Shanghai, Barr to Dept. of Army for Maddocks, ibid., "Military Developments" folder. Quote in text from Message COMNAVWESPAC, April 19, 1949, ibid., "Political Trends in China" folder. Also see Yin Shih (pseud.), Li-Chiang kuan-hsi yü Chung-kuo (The Li-Chiang Relationship and China) (Hong Kong: Freedom Press, 1954), pp. 103–28; and Liang Sheng-chun, Chiang-Li tou-cheng nei-mu (The Inside Story of the Struggle between Chiang and Li) (Hong Kong: Union Asia Press, 1954), pp. 29–169; and Clark, Canton, to Secretary of State, FR, 1949, 8:501–2.

clear orders with the Generalissimo before implementing them.[26] The leader of a small clique based almost entirely in his backward and underpopulated province of Kwangsi, Li was forced to recruit members of other groups to fill pivotal posts in his administration.[27] He could not replace entrenched representatives of factions that looked to Chiang Kai-shek for guidance, as did the Whampoa cadets. Thus when Chiang asserted his will, there was little that officials opposed to his actions could do. Chiang's July 1949 conference with President Elpidio Quirino at Baguio in the Philippines, at which he discussed the possibilities of a Pacific security pact, was reportedly not authorized by the government.[28] Similarly, the Generalissimo appointed Gen-

[26] U.S. Minister-Counselor Lewis Clark told Li Wei-kuo in a September 12, 1949, conversation that, prior to his departure from Canton, he had met with a depressed Li Tsung-jen. No important decision was possible without consulting Chiang and securing his approval first. Koo Oral History, vol. I, sec. 8, pp. 478–79; and Notes of Conversations, 1949, no. 77, September 15, 1949, Koo Papers. A reporter in the New Hope Weekly of April 4, 1949 (Shao Sheng, "Sidelights on Chikow," quoted in Chinese Press Survey, vol. 3, no. 5, April 7, 1949) wrote that the Lohsia airfield in eastern Chekiang was handling at least three flights per day as opposed to its normal one per month, and that all were high civilian and military missions. Similarly, Associated Press in Nanking reported that the Generalissimo was in daily telephone contact with key economic, military, and political people "who remain personally loyal to him even while supposedly under the direction of Acting President Li." "Chiang Activity Reported," New York Times, February 20, 1949, p. 19.

[27] The leadership of Kwangsi Clique was essentially oligarchic. Li Tsung-jen and Pai Ch'ung-hsi remained at the forefront throughout its history. Li Chi-shen was something of a mentor in the early years but later moved away into other affiliations such as the Kuomintang Revolutionary Committee. In the 1920s Huang Shao-hung shared power, maintaining the sanctity of Kwangsi while Li and Pai "crusaded" in the north. Although disagreements led him to sever intimate associations with the clique (he was replaced by Huang Hsu-ch'u), he often cooperated with Li in subsequent years. Below this level of leadership, however, there were few men of any particular talent. Shih Fen-wu, "Li Tsung-jen and His Following," Sinwen tienti (Newsland) (Shanghai), May 10, 1949, quoted in Chinese Press Survey, vol. 4, no. 3, May 21, 1949; The Far Eastern Bulletin (Hong Kong), ibid., no. 2, May 11, 1949; Huai Hsiang (pseud.), Lun Li Tsung-jen yü Chung-Mei fan-tung p'ai (A Discussion of Li Tsung-jen and the Sino-American Reactionary Clique) (Hong Kong, 1948), passim; Lary, Region and Nation, pp. 34–42, 157–58.

[28] Liang, Chiang-Li, pp. 156–63; Stuart Diary, July 16, 1949; "Prospects for Renewed Peace Negotiations between the Chinese Communists and the Kwangsi Clique," OIR 5017(PV), July 25, 1949, p. 5, reel 4, pt. 3, China and India, OSS/State Department Intelligence and Research Reports, University Publications of America, Washington, D.C. (hereafter cited as OSS/State Reports); Clark, Canton, to Secretary of State, FR, 1949, 8:423.

eral T'ang En-po governor of Fukien to replace General Chu Shao-liang without the approval of Li or his administration. Chu, angered, left his post before T'ang was ready to take over, and in the interim Fuchou fell to the Communists.[29] T'ang was also directed by the Generalissimo to arrest the governor of a neighboring province, Chekiang, for having implemented Li's reform measures, such as releasing political prisoners, and for talking peace.[30]

Prominent among the problems that Acting President Li was never able to solve was his dispute with the Generalissimo over control of China's finances. Chiang had directed the Bank of China to ship its assets to Taiwan in the autumn of 1948. The holdings at that time included gold bars, coins, U.S. and British banknotes, jewelry, and other items valued in all at U.S. $350 million. Although public outcry secured suspension of further shipments after the removal of the gold was discovered in early 1949, Li could never recover the already displaced bank assets, nor could he control their disbursement. Short of funds to meet administrative expenses or even to pay front-line troops, the acting president at best was able to arrange only limited transfers from Taiwan. Chiang retained authority over expenditures, and Canton bankers believed that he personally cleared all payments over $60,000 (Canton).[31]

[29] Koo Oral History, vol. I, sec. 8, p. 497, and vol. J, sec. 3, p. 181. K. C. Wu stated in his Oral History interview: ". . . I think future historians will be interested to know . . . how much influence Chiang still wielded after his official stepping-down from the Presidency. I can tell you that. Retirement or not, he was still the Government of China. . . . Take my own case. Chiang told me he wanted me to remain as Mayor of Shanghai. If Li had wanted to remove me, he simply could not have done it." Wu Oral History, p. 106.

[30] Li Oral History, vol. 4, pt. 7, ch. 49, pp. 8–9; and Joint Weeka no. 8, March 11, 1949, p. 3, and no. 9, March 18, 1949, p. 13.

[31] Estimates of the amount of gold transferred varied considerably, reaching a high of $300 million in the remarks of Senate Foreign Relations Committee Chairman Tom Connally on September 8, 1949. Press Conference, September 8, 1949, Senator Tom Connally Papers, "Speech File, 1949" folder, Library of Congress; Koo Oral History, vol. J, sec. 4, p. 281; Tillman Durdin, "Nationalist Funds Dwindle in China," New York Times, September 26, 1949, p. 12; and Li Oral History, vol. 4, pt. 7, ch. 51.

Conflict over financing continued throughout 1949, and late in the year the director of the Bank of China found himself under renewed pressure. The Generalissimo insisted that remaining assets be shipped to Taiwan while there was still time; Executive Yuan President Yen Hsi-shan wanted the stocks moved to Chungking to support the government when, as he expected, it shifted there; and Kan Chieh-hou served the bank with a written order from Li Tsung-jen demanding funds for his imminent trip to the United States. In a quandary as to whom to obey, the governor of the bank, Liu Kung-yun, consulted his predecessor O.K. Yui, a continuing power behind the scenes, who counseled him to ignore all others and carry out the Generalissimo's orders.[32]

Interference in the course of government affairs became easier for Chiang during the summer of 1949. On July 26 the Standing Committee of the Central Executive Committee of the Kuomintang, the party's most important organ, established a Supreme Policy Council to serve, on an emergency basis, as a coordinating agency for government and party policies. Because he was director-general of the Kuomintang, Chiang was named chairman of this new organization and Li Tsung-jen vice chairman, an arrangement that further circumscribed Li's already limited authority as president of the Republic.[33] Thereafter all government decisions had to be approved by the Policy Council before implementation, giving the Generalissimo final control of foreign and domestic, civil and military affairs. Further, on August 1, 1949, also in his capacity as director-general of the Kuomintang, Chiang set up his own "alternative government" in Taiwan. Although he claimed that this was a purely informal

---

[32] Liu Kung-yun described the situation as *i-kuo san-kung*, that is, three kings ruling one country. Koo Oral History, vol. I, sec. 4, pp. 117–18. With regard to Li's shortage of funds, Pai Ch'ung-hsi reportedly approached the U.S. consul-general in Hankow with a desperate appeal for financial aid. Joint Weeka no. 6, February 25, 1949.

[33] *China Handbook, 1950,* p. 239; Li Oral History, vol. 44, Part 7, ch. 51, p. 5; Clark, Canton, to Secretary of State, nos. 301, 303, 585, and 613, FR, 1949, 8:286–88, 383, 390.

structure, it closely paralleled the administrative divisions of the Canton government. Moreover, this director-general's office commanded the services of former Foreign Minister Wang Shih-chieh at a time when Li was unable to fill that post in his own cabinet. And Yui, the ex-governor of the Bank of China who told Liu Kung-yun to obey the Generalissimo's orders, coincidentally was the financial adviser.[34]

Kuomintang dissidents who had joined together to force Chiang out of the presidency recognized as early as February 1949 that this would not effectively eliminate his influence. Efforts to convince the Generalissimo to leave China following his retirement proved fruitless. Li sent emissaries to Fenghua district to convince Chiang to go. Ho Ying-ch'in and Pai Ch'ung-hsi both appealed to American Ambassador Stuart for assistance, hoping that an invitation from the United States might lure the Generalissimo abroad.[35] The Americans did not comply, but these were, in any case, unprofitable maneuverings, for Chiang was determined to stay on the scene. If his strength was inadequate to save the mainland, he must at least be sure that no one else could. He devoted his abilities, which were considerable, to thwarting his opposition. Li Tsung-jen never had a chance.

Factional rifts, debilitating in China, similarly impaired the country's representation abroad. The proliferation of Chinese observers and interveners in the United States, each making separate pleas for aid to various Chinese leaders, merely created confusion. Not only the major camps maintained such missions: Yen Hsi-shan sent a follower to protect

[34] China briefs from Chungking in Cantonese, July 20, 1949, *Foreign Broadcast Information Service* (hereafter *FBIS*), July 21, 1949, p. BBB-5, "Far East, China" section; "Tsungtsai Office Opened at Taoshan," from Chungking in Cantonese, August 3, 1949, *FBIS*, August 4, 1949, pp. BBB-2-3; "Prospects for Cooperation between Chiang Kai-shek and Other Non-Communist Leaders in China," OIR 5050(PV), September 19, 1949, p. 2, reel 4, pt. 3, OSS/State Reports.

[35] Joint Weeka no. 7, March 4, 1949, p. 2, and no. 8, March 11, 1949, p. 2; memorandum of conversation with General Ch'en Ming-shu, 893.00/3-1149, no. 36, Cabot, Shanghai, to Stuart, Nanking, Decimal File, RG 59; Stuart, Nanking, to Secretary of State, FR, 1949, 8:142; Stuart Diary, February 20 and 21, 1949; Seymour Topping, *Journey between Two Chinas* (New York: Harper & Row, 1972), p. 58.

the interests of the Shansi military clique; T. V. Soong and H. H. Kung ran personal networks from New York City; and beyond the frontier of Kuomintang membership, minor parties such as the Young China Party also had spokesmen on the scene.[36]

These factional politics placed severe strains on diplomatic relations, a fact that caused China's ambassador to Washington, V. K. Wellington Koo, who claimed to be nonpartisan but was identified by others variously as an adherent of Chiang or of Li, to complain bitterly.[37] Ignorant of the activities of other Nationalist Chinese, his efforts to organize publicity were hampered. Interviews with American leaders, which should have been arranged through the embassy, occurred haphazardly. Koo was never able to surmount such obstacles; and because his ambassadorial rank made him technically responsible, he was often berated for ineffective or inefficient work.[38]

[36] Koo Oral History, vol. I, sec. 4, p. 120, and vol. J, sec. 1, pp. 34–35. H. H. Kung (K'ung Hsiang-hsi), a banker and businessman, held posts in the Nationalist government as minister of industry and commerce and minister of finance. He was also the husband of Soong Ai-ling, Madame Chiang Kai-shek's eldest sister. T. V. Soong, a younger brother of Madame Chiang, also held the post of finance minister as well as other important government positions. Thus both men were "related" to the Generalissimo, and though they did not always agree with him or serve his interests, they remained prominent figures in Chinese Nationalist politics. See Boorman and Howard, *Biographical Dictionary*, 2:263–68, and 3:137–40, 149–53.

[37] "I was not taking sides between the Generalissimo and General Li, except that so long as the Generalissimo proposed to do something which would be in the interest of China, I would be on his side, as I had always been. . . . My position would also hold true if General Li was doing something for the good of China." Koo Oral History, vol. J, sec. 2, p. 165, and vol. I, sec. 3, p. 80. See also Chu Pao-chin, "V. K. Wellington Koo: The Diplomacy of Nationalism," in Richard D. Burns and Edward M. Bennett, eds., *Diplomats in Crisis* (Santa Barbara, Calif.: ABC-Clio, 1974), p. 131. Koo also noted that, whereas Li's representative in the U.S. Kan Chieh-hou and Yen Hsi-shan's representative P'an Ch'ao-ying were telling Congressional leaders that Koo spoke only for Chiang, the Generalissimo's followers, noting how much aid he had rendered Kan, believed Koo had joined Li's camp. Koo Oral History, vol. I, sec. 8, pp. 490–91.

[38] Koo Oral History, vols. I and J, *passim*; letter from Koo to George Yeh, July 20, 1949, Koo Papers, "George Kung-chao Yeh 1949–54" folder L21.a. Control of propaganda activities was uncoordinated not only in the United States; in China it was shaped by the Department of Information of the Foreign Ministry, the News Bureau of the Executive Council, the Defense Department, the Chinese News Bureau, and the Publicity Bureau of the President's Office. Koo Oral History, vol. I, sec. 4, p. 173.

Chiang Kai-shek operated on a variety of levels in America. Within the embassy itself he had a group of five officials, including the minister-counselor and the military attaché, who reported directly to him over the head of the ambassador.[39] Moreover, at least one important U.S. Congressional leader was told that Minister-Counselor Ch'en Chih-mai, not Koo, was the real power in the embassy.[40] Similarly, the Generalissimo designated H. H. Kung his special representative in the United States, an appointment that virtually established a second ambassadorship. However, Koo, whose diplomatic skills and command of English were considered irreplaceable, quashed this move by threatening to resign. In retrospect he realized

that Dr. Kung's appointment, the proposal for which was made prior to the Generalissimo's retirement, was desired . . . to keep in direct and confidential touch with the Administration in Washington, entirely separate from the government channels in China. The Generalissimo's retirement from the presidency . . . was not a step taken completely by preference, and there was certainly a general sentiment among the Generalissimo's entourage to have him return

[39] This coterie, revealed by Senator Wayne Morse's disclosure of a series of secret cables from the Chinese embassy in Washington to an unspecified, but obvious, destination in China, consisted of: Ch'en Chih-mai, the minister-counselor; Brigadier-General Peter T. K. Pee (Pi Tsung-kan), the military attaché; Lt. General P. T. Mow (Mao Pang-tsu), Chinese Air Force Procurement Mission; W. K. Lee (Li Wei-kuo), delegate to the Far East Commission; and K. H. Yu (Yü Kuo-hua), deputy director of the World Bank. Copies of the cables were published in the *Congressional Record*, vol. 98, pt. 3, 82nd Congress, 2nd session, April 10, 1952, pp. 3970–72, and pt. 5, June 6, 1952, pp. 6740–67. The subjects covered in these regular reports included information culled from the U.S. press and some received from friendly Congressional leaders. That the group was not delighted with Ambassador Koo was clear. January 17, 1950: "We think that Koo is not the ideal person. . . ." April 4, 1950: "Our diplomatic . . . officers are not at their posts and those who stay in America are not suitable persons to discharge their responsibilities." Styles Bridges Papers, "China Lobby, 1949 & 1952" folder, New England College Library, Henniker, N.H.; Paul P. Kennedy, "Senate Gets 'Files' on Secret Activity in U.S. to Aid Chiang," *New York Times*, April 11, 1952; Senator Wayne Morse writing in "Washington Merry-Go-Round," *Washington Post*, August 1952; Drew Pearson, "Cables Show Chiang's War Effort," *Washington Post*, June 4, 1952; and "Morse Seeks 'Lie' Probe of Chiang Envoys," *Washington Post*, June 10, 1952.

[40] Confidential memorandum from JAW to Senator Taft, March 1, 1948, Robert A. Taft Papers, Alphabetical File, "China 1948–49, Legislative Papers" folder, Library of Congress.

to power one day. In order to do that, during the interim period, it was very important and essential that an independent line of communication and information be kept up.[41]

Perhaps most embarrassing and difficult for the ambassador, however, was the sudden arrival in Washington of Madame Chiang Kai-shek on December 1, 1948.[42] Madame Chiang had set up headquarters in Riverdale, New York, and neither informed the embassy of her purposes nor used its services to conduct her business. Only rarely did she confer with Koo and then imparted as little information about her intentions as possible. Rather than tap his familiarity with the workings of American politics, she relied on her family— particularly H. H. Kung, Madame Kung, and their sons and associates. Koo found this personally galling and politically misguided. Madame Chiang, for instance, did not see the impropriety of appealing to Secretary of State George Marshall for aid when his retirement was imminent. She misinterpreted his friendship as encouragement and, worse yet, "[i]t was as if it were expected that an American Secretary of State would have the same ability to carry through a personal decision in the United States as the Generalissimo had in China."[43]

If the Generalissimo's followers regarded Koo with suspicion, so too did Li Tsung-jen and his prime supporter in the United States, Kan Chieh-hou. The Shanghai newspaper *Shih-shih hsin-pao* speculated that Kan's May 1949 trip to the United States had a special purpose, because Koo, an experi-

[41] Koo Oral History, quoted in vol. H, sec. 2, pp. 61–65; also see vol. I, sec. 4, pp. 151–52.

[42] Koo learned of Madame Chiang's imminent arrival from authorities in Taiwan on the day that the U.S. State Department press officer announced the visit. In the same telephone call of November 26, 1948, from Vice-Minister for Foreign Affairs George Yeh, Koo was reportedly told that Madame Chiang's visit was taking place despite the strong protests of Foreign Minister Wang Shih-chieh and efforts of the Generalissimo to dissuade her. She had been instructed by Chiang to stay in Washington a maximum of two weeks and make all arrangements through the embassy rather than the Kungs. Koo Oral History, vol. H, sec. 3, p. 81.

[43] *Ibid.*, p. 110, and vol. J, sec. 2, p. 96.

enced diplomat, needed no help. Koo himself, however, noted that "no correspondence from Acting President Li Tsung-jen to the United States government or President Truman ever went through the Embassy." [44] Kan also made it clear to everyone that he considered the ambassador to be working for Chiang's interests—interests that were now discredited and detrimental to China's welfare.

By confessing past errors of China's government and blaming its former leaders, Kan apparently hoped to convince Americans that Li, with creative new policies and a more liberal and honest staff, could be trusted to handle renewed aid.[45] His efforts, however, failed to have the desired effect on U.S. government officials. Kan's rhetoric and behavior merely deepened impressions of disunity and reinforced convictions in the White House and State Department that further aid to the Nationalists would be wasted.[46]

Factions competed in the United States with the same ardor with which they fought in China because the stakes were enormously high. Washington was seen not merely as the capital of a major world power but as the stage upon which China's vital struggle would be played out. A military victory over the Chinese Communists was clearly impossible after the

[44]*Ibid.*, vol. I, sec. 3, p. 81; Hu Nung-chih, "Will Kan Chieh-hou Become Foreign Minister?" *Shih-shih hsin pao* (Shanghai, a publication connected with H. H. Kung's son David), May 15, 1949, quoted in *Chinese Press Review*, no. 894, May 18, 1949. Li's view of Koo emerges clearly in the following: "My appointment of Dr. Kan as my personal representative to the United States in May, 1949, was due to Dr. Wellington Koo's neglect of his duties in Washington. Ambassador Koo took instructions only from Mr. Chiang. . . . Had I removed him from his position, he certainly would have rejected my order." Li Oral History, vol. 4, pt. 7, ch. 53, p. 5, and similar comments in ch. 48, p. 23 and ch. 50, p. 12.

[45]Kan described the tactic as *chang shuang huang*, that is, one person singing in two voices or playing a double role to one end. He told Koo on June 22, 1949, that though he was forced to condemn Chiang Kai-shek's performance as China's leader, he wasn't at all opposed to the Generalissimo. Koo Oral History, vol. I, sec. 4, pp. 185–87, and sec. 8, p. 491.

[46]Koo Oral History, vol. H, sec. 2, p. 65, and vol. J, sec. 3, pp. 241–42. "Our American friends both in the Administration and on Capitol Hill . . . feel confused. The State Department regards the situation here as a 'miniature China' reflecting the disunity in our country." Letter from Koo to George Yeh, January 6, 1950, Koo Papers, "Yeh 1949–54" folder.

Huai-hai debacle in January 1949. At most, the remnants of the Nationalist army might preserve a sanctuary south of the Yangtze River. To accomplish even this, however, American aid was believed to be essential. Though there were approaches to other Western powers and even efforts to come to terms with the Soviet Union, none of these attempts was more than a subsidiary, stopgap measure. All important plans, the energies of all, were dedicated to eliciting support from the United States.[47]

Chiang Kai-shek was certain that the United States would not finally abandon China. True, there might be painful defeats. The mainland might have to be sacrificed, temporarily. But in the end, arms and money would be forthcoming.[48] Meanwhile the Communists would smash his Kuomintang adversaries, who, bereft of the funds and weapons he still controlled, would not be able to fight on.[49] For the future, Chiang was convinced—and neither Koo in Washington nor American foreign service officers in China could disabuse him of the notion—that World War III would soon break out between the United States and the Soviet Union. During this confrontation he, Chiang, would reconquer China and thereby eliminate communism's eastern redoubt while the United States

[47] My interview with Philip Fugh, July 21, 1977. Koo advised T. L. Soong, Chinese representative on the Board of Governors of the International Bank for Reconstruction and Development (and also a brother of Madame Chiang), "as a general guide so often followed in our foreign policy, to lean on the side of the American view where the British insist upon an opposite stand. We have to depend more upon U.S. for financial and economic aid which U.K. is unable to give us at present." Koo Diary, February 4, 1949, Koo Papers.

[48] Fugh interview.

[49] Chiang "is reluctant . . . to provide [Li Tsung-jen and regional military leaders] . . . with sufficient material to permit them to offer an independent resistance to the Communists that is effective enough to threaten his own position of preeminence. . . . These objectives seem to have conditioned Chiang's strategic concepts—his refusal to defend the Yangtze line, his unwillingness to aid in the defense of the inland regions of south, southwest, and northwest China, and his preference for defending the coastal regions of Kwangtung and Fukien and Formosa—as well as his persistent interference in Li Tsung-jen's efforts to revitalize the resistance against Communism in China." OIR 5050(PV), reel 4, pt. 3, OSS/State Reports; see also Li Oral History, vol. 4, pt. 7, ch. 49, p. 18, and ch. 52, p. 12; Clark, Canton, to Secretary of State, FR, 1949, 8:453.

destroyed it in the west. Chiang was not alone in expecting a war, and similar views held by the Japanese, many Europeans, and several doomsayers in the United States reinforced Nationalist expectations. So, too, did the signing of the North Atlantic Treaty in April 1949, which was interpreted as a military alliance that would heighten world tensions and provoke a violent Soviet response. General Cheng Chieh-min, head of the Kuomintang military secret service and vice minister of national defense, told Wellington Koo in November 1949 that Chinese government policy was to conserve resources on Taiwan until World War III provided the Kuomintang with an opportunity to oust the Communists.[50]

Short of the hoped-for war, the Nationalists made other efforts to keep the United States involved and on their side. In September 1949 U.S. Consul-General Walter P. McConaughy in Shanghai reported to the secretary of state that the Chinese air force was dropping pamphlets over the city signed "Tiger Airforce Squadron." As McConaughy noted, this title bore a striking resemblance to Chennault's "Flying Tigers" and could only be interpreted as a flagrant attempt to involve the United States directly in China's struggle.[51] Similarly, the use of Japa-

[50] On the imminence of World War III: OIR 5050(PV), pp. iv, 6, reel 4, pt. 3, OSS/State Reports; Stuart, Nanking, to Secretary of State, FR, 1948, 7:625–27; memorandum of conversation by Ambassador-at-Large (Jessup) on talk with Chiang Kai-shek, January 16, 1950, FR, 1950, 6:280–83; Cantel no. 1281 to Secretary of State, November 25, 1949, file 350, Consul-General Hong Kong, RG 84; 893.00/5-949, no. 1565, Confidential Decimal File, RG 59; Andrew Roth, "Chiang under Fire," Nation (January 8, 1949), p. 35; Fugh interview; Koo Oral History, vol. I, sec. 3, pp. 65–66 and sec. 8, p. 479, vol. J, sec. 2, pp. 90–94, 131, 139. Li also based his policies on the imminence of World War III, according to Koo; see Koo Diary, February 24, 1949. On the role of the North Atlantic Treaty in the coming of World War III: the Kuomintang-connected newspaper Sinwen tienti maintained that World War III would be brought on by Soviet attempts, which the Atlantic pact made unavoidable, to consolidate its position in Eastern Europe, and that it would occur within the year. Kung Sun-wang, "Peace Talks in China before the World's Gathering Storm," Sinwen tienti, April 21, 1949, no. 67, quoted in Chinese Press Review, April 21, 1949, no. 877, pp. 12–15; Inside the Chinese Communists (Shanghai, a publication connected with the Kuomintang secret service), April 1, 1949, no. 2, ibid., April 1, 1949, no. 862, pp. 11–12; "Safeguarding World Peace," Ta-kung pao, April 5, 1949, ibid., April 5, 1949, no. 864, pp. 3–4.

[51] 893.00/9-649, No. 3659, McConaughy, Shanghai, to Secretary of State, Decimal File, RG 59; "Chinese 'Tiger Air Force' Not Related to American 'Flying Tigers,' " Department of State Bulletin (October 3, 1949), 21(535):515.

nese mercenaries to fight for the Nationalist armies and advise the government on economic matters, at a time when American troops occupied Japan and General Douglas MacArthur was responsible for Japanese policies and actions, could not but confirm suspicions that the United States was participating in the Kuomintang military effort.[52]

A still more imaginative plan called for indicting the USSR on grounds of disregarding its obligations under the 1945 Sino-Soviet Treaty of Friendship. The Russians had pledged themselves to give Chiang moral, military, and material aid and to abstain from aiding his enemies in return for substantive concessions by the Chinese government.[53] By accusing the Soviets of treaty violations in the United Nations, Chinese leaders hoped to arouse world sympathy for China. They also wanted to make clear that any government, coalition or communist, that emerged in China was a creation of the USSR and not an independent regime entitled to recognition.[54] But "[i]n reality," the State Department's Policy Planning Staff believed, "the end purpose of the Chinese

[52] T. V. Soong is credited with the decision to use Japanese technical personnel for economic development projects. Ch'en Yi, "T. V. Soong's New Mission," *Niu shih* (connected with the Kuomintang), May 19, 1949, no. 20, pp. 11–13, quoted in *Chinese Press Review*, May 24, 1949, no. 898. The CCP contended that General Douglas MacArthur recommended Horiuchi Kanjō and others to Soong; see "Henchmen of the Invading Americans" (Peiping, in Japanese), July 24, 1949, *FBIS*, July 26, 1949, pp. 1–17, "Far East Articles and Speeches" section. The CCP also claimed to have captured major Japanese war criminals fighting with Yen Hsi-shan's army. See "Japanese Generals Captured at T'aiyuan" (Shengyang, in Japanese), May 3, 1949, *FBIS*, p. CCC-3, "China—Communist Control" section. Further, the Chinese Communists noted a July 18, 1949, speech by Yen Hsi-shan calling for "international volunteers" including Japanese and using U.S. aid. Yen was the former governor of Shansi and was serving as president of the Executive Yuan in July. "Kuomintang Trying to Recruit 100,000 Japanese Mercenaries," NCNA, *Weekly Bulletin* August 19, 1949, no. 114, p. 3. An undated, unsigned memorandum claiming to represent the views of the people of Shansi province and calling for Japanese volunteers because of Japan's proximity to China appears in the Claire L. Chennault Papers, Freedom Cause—Correspondence, "Raising of 100,000 International or Japanese Volunteers to Prevent the Spread of Communism in China by Using American Military Aids," reel 12, Library of Congress. Also see Donald G. Gillin, *Warlord: Yen Hsi-shan in Shansi Province, 1911–1949* (Princeton, N.J.: Princeton University Press, 1967), pp. 286–88.

[53] Immanual C. Y. Hsu, *The Rise of Modern China* (New York: Oxford University Press, 1970), p. 707; and Tang Tsou, *America's Failure in China, 1941–50* (Chicago: University of Chicago Press, 1963), 1:284.

[54] Koo Oral History, vol. J, sec. 1, pp. 11–12, 28.

effort . . . is to involve us in an obligation of further support to the Chinese government."[55]

Foreign Minister Wang Shih-chieh broached the idea of bringing a case before the United Nations to Secretary of State George C. Marshall in November 1948. Marshall warned that the disadvantages of raising the matter before the UN would almost certainly outweigh the advantages. Although the United States strongly believed that the USSR had surreptitiously aided Chinese Communist advances in Manchuria, three years of surveillance had yielded no concrete evidence. If the UN were to act at all, it would merely send an observer group whose chances of seeing more than the Americans had seen were slight, especially since it would inevitably be hampered by a Soviet member.

In spite of Marshall's negativism and Ambassador Koo's opposition, enthusiasm for such a policy increased among the leaders of the Kuomintang. It was hoped that if the General Assembly would not vote sanctions against the Soviet Union—an admittedly unlikely prospect—it would at least censure Soviet behavior, thereby embarrassing the USSR and distracting international attention from repeated Kuomintang military defeats. In February 1949 Executive Yuan President Sun Fo was reported to have called for a UN appeal as the only solution to China's problems. Though rarely agreeing on anything, Chiang Kai-shek and Li Tsung-jen were both eager to make this case and Yen Hsi-shan added his approval. Finally, to overcome the Foreign Ministry's hesitancy, the Legislative Yuan passed a resolution calling on the government to act.[56]

The Chinese therefore presented their strategy to Department of State officers with the expectation, however illfounded, of eliciting a positive response.[57] Surprisingly, a

[55] Memorandum, Dean Rusk to Philip C. Jessup, September 8, 1949, Records of the Policy Planning Staff, Country and Area files, "China 1949" folder, RG 59 (hereafter cited as PPS Records).

[56] Koo Oral History, vol. H, sec. 1, pp. 38, 40–42, and vol. J, sec. 1, pp. 11–12.

[57] That this occurred only shortly after publication of the White Paper on China (discussed below) gave Ambassador Koo added reason to anticipate a poor reaction.

sympathetic Deputy Undersecretary of State Dean Rusk encouraged them. Subsequently T. F. Tsiang, China's permanent representative to the UN, was informed that the United States would support a complaint based on treaty and UN Charter violations, though not a call for nonrecognition of a Chinese Communist regime.[58] In September, when he presented the National Government's case, Tsiang was hopeful that a strong indictment would emerge. Beneath the surface of State Department good will, however, uneasiness began to spread during the autumn of 1949. Charles W. Yost (adviser to Ambassador-at-Large Philip C. Jessup), the Policy Planning Staff, and Minister-Counselor Lewis Clark all argued against American involvement in the issue. Nationalist Chinese unreliability made the potential for embarrassment too high, they said. Yost, moreover, thought that the damage such an entanglement would do to American relations with the Chinese Communists weighed strongly against it. By November Tsiang was aware that American support had slipped and would tolerate only a very weak resolution.[59] The subsequent measure, sponsored jointly by the United States, Australia, Mexico, Pakistan, and the Philippines, merely reiterated traditional formulas regarding China's independence and integrity without touching on Soviet actions or the matter of recognition.[60]

Meanwhile, events in China had significantly altered Nationalist assessments of their prospects at the UN. On October 1, 1949, a new Communist Chinese government had been created at Peking. The People's Republic promptly demanded membership in the General Assembly and China's permanent seat in the Security Council. Frightened by this

---

[58] Koo Oral History, vol. J, sec. 1, pp. 16, 29; conversation with Assistant Secretary of State Dean Rusk, no. 80, September 21, 1949, Koo Papers, box 130, "Notes of Conversation 1949."

[59] 761.93/9-749 memorandum Fosdick to Jessup, Rusk, Hickerson, Butterworth, Bancroft, Freeman, 761.93/10-349 memorandum Clark to Jessup, 761.93/11-1149 memorandum Noyes to Jessup, and 761.93/11-1149 memorandum Yost to Jessup, Decimal File, RG 59; Koo Oral History, vol. J, sec. 1, p. 61; memorandum Rusk to Jessup, September 8, 1949, PPS Records.

[60] Tsou, *America's Failure*, 1:521–22.

challenge, the Nationalists desired simply to avoid controversy. Thus, on December 5 they allowed their complaint
to be sent to the General Assembly's Interim Committee for
further study. This retreat, however wise, seemed to State
Department critics of the Kuomintang regime proof that their
skepticism had been justified. Lewis Clark remarked to Jessup that "in this as in so many other heartbreaking experiences I have had with the Chinese in the past two years, the
Chinese just seem unable to do anything positive themselves.
They always want the United States to do it first and for
them."[61]

Chiang Kai-shek's inauguration of a Pacific security pact
similarly sought to maneuver Washington into rendering the
Nationalists more aid and support. Although the concept of
an eastern association to parallel the fledgling North Atlantic
Treaty Organization had been discussed, no concrete plans
existed in the spring of 1949. Chiang's enthusiasm for a military and political alliance, offering heightened stature in domestic affairs and enhanced legitimacy and forcefulness in
dealing with the United States, struck responsive chords
with Philippine President Quirino and South Korea's Syngman Rhee, both of whom likewise occupied vulnerable political positions. Chiang and Quirino thereupon met in Manila
in July to launch the pact, and Rhee indicated that South
Korea would adhere shortly. According to former Shanghai
mayor K. C. Wu and the Generalissimo's son, Chiang intended to utilize his new allies to secure "indirect assistance" from the United States by asserting his more pressing
need for whatever they might acquire.[62]

[61] 761.93/11-749 memorandum Clark to Jessup, Decimal File, RG 59. Stuart expressed similar views; see the Ambassador in China (Stuart) to Secretary Marshall,
September 20, 1947, in Van Slyke, White Paper, pp. 830–31; also Koo Oral History,
vol. J, sec. 1, pp. 74–75.

[62] "Chiang and Quirino in Philippine Talk," New York Times, July 10, 1949, pp.
1 and 20; "Anti-Red Bloc Plan of Chiang, Quirino," ibid., July 11, 1949, p. 8; Ku Jen,
"The Influence of American Aid and the Pacific Pact on the Peace Talks," Ho-p'ing
jih-pao (Shanghai, a publication with ties to the Nationalist army), April 13, 1949,
quoted in Chinese Press Review, April 15, 1949, no. 872, p. 9; "Developments in the

However, the United States, whose leadership a Quirino spokesman claimed was indispensable to the project, had already demonstrated its opposition. Secretary of State Acheson announced in May that the United States would not join a Pacific defense union, maintaining that internal disruption in Asia made such a plan premature. Nevertheless, State Department officials recognized that considerable interest existed in Asia for establishing cooperative relations. Secretly, therefore, they suggested that a non-Communist rather than anti-Communist, economic rather than military, association might be welcomed by Washington. Such a venture must also exclude Nationalist China, the Americans cautioned, lest the burden of an impossible crusade doom it to failure.[63]

Other Kuomintang efforts to win American cooperation could not be so easily avoided by the United States. One tactic, political as well as military, was the imposition of a seacoast blockade, coupled with selective bombing of American and Chinese Communist targets. Although the damage inflicted upon the Communists did handicap industry in Shanghai, the major urban center of China, the Nationalists knew they were not able to severely threaten Communist power.[64] Their aim was rather to overwhelm a group that lacked personnel equipped to operate a huge city, thus embarrassing an enemy that could not adequately protect the people under their control, demoralizing the Westerners who remained in Communist territory, and ensuring that Western aid and trade would not establish a bridge between the Communists and the Nationalists' own wavering allies. As

---

Pacific Pact Plan," *Shih-shih hsin-pao*, May 18, 1949, *ibid.*, May 19, 1949, no. 895, p. 1.

[63] Memorandum by Policy Information Officer of the Office of Far Eastern Affairs (Fisher) to Butterworth, *FR, 1949*, 7:1160–64; Acheson to Embassy in Korea, *ibid.*, pp. 1177–78; McDonald, Taipei, to Secretary of State, *ibid.*, p. 185. See also *ibid.*, pt. 2, *passim*.

[64] By late October 1949 Shanghai industry was operating at only 30 to 40 percent of normal capacity in spite of shipments made by blockade runners. Despatch No. 88, November 8, 1949, file 510, "Trade Relations," Consul-General Hong Kong, RG 84.

intensely as the Soviets, Chiang desired to keep the Chinese Communists isolated and dependent upon Russian aid.

Legally, the National Government could not proclaim a blockade. Belligerency status, a prerequisite, had never been granted to the Communist "bandits." To do so at that time, as Ambassador Stuart pointed out, would imply that Shanghai was in Communist hands by right of conquest, in which case it was doubtful that a Kuomintang declaration would have any effect. Moreover, under a blockade foreign shipping would automatically be entitled to the rights of neutrals in the conflict, thereby handicapping Nationalist naval patrols. Thus, on June 20, 1949, the Chinese government announced that, in its capacity as the only recognized ruling authority on the mainland, it was closing ports from Fuchou to Manchuria to international traffic.[65] Western powers, however, could not honor what was so transparently a naval blockade unless it effectively stopped all trade, and this the Chinese navy was not equipped to do. Great Britain promptly made clear its determination to resist, threatening to convoy its merchant craft if necessary.[66]

The United States' position was less consistent. Although publicly declaring the blockade illegal, the Truman administration made it clear to private shippers that entering closed ports was dangerous business and no escort service would be provided by the United States Navy. With presi-

---

[65] 893.801/6-2449, no. 1373, Stuart, Nanking, to Secretary of State, Decimal File, RG 59; and "Blockade of Reds in China Ordered," New York Times, June 21, 1949, p. 1.

[66] Great Britain maintained that the Chinese Nationalist decree, closing ports occupied by insurgents without the maintenance of an effective blockade, was simply an attempt to secure the rights of war without assuming the accompanying responsibilities dictated by international law. Memorandum by the Director of the Office of Far Eastern Affairs (Butterworth) to the Secretary of State, FR, 1949, 9:1110–12. On British convoying of merchant craft, see memorandum by Secretary of State to the President of the United States, ibid., pp. 1150–52; Andrew Roth, "How the Communists Rule," Nation (November 19, 1949), 169:488; and memorandum by R. H. Hillenkoetter, Director of Central Intelligence, to the President of the United States, January 12, 1950, in Harry S. Truman Papers, President's Secretary's Files, Intelligence, "Central Intelligence Memorandum 1950–52" folder, Harry S. Truman Library, Independence, Mo.

dential direction and encouragement, the State Department maintained a hands-off policy, despite provocation (American commercial ships were shelled) and pleas from the Isbrandtsen Shipping Lines.[67]

A similar position was taken by the United States in the matter of raids conducted by the Chinese air force over heavily populated Chinese cities, particularly Shanghai. Although it was clear that the Chinese were not restricting their strikes to military targets, and American foreign service officers reported "indiscriminate destruction" and "butchery of unknown numbers," the American government seems to have limited itself to ineffectual protests.[68] For the United States the situation was especially difficult. Despite Chinese assurances that American property would not be deliberately bombed, Department of State reports left no doubt that easily identifiable installations such as the Shanghai Power Company, which provided all the electric power for the city of Shanghai, were being hit repeatedly.[69] Robert C. Strong, the

[67] Secretary of State to Consul-General Rankin at Hong Kong, September 16, 1949, FR, 1949, 9:1133–34; memoranda of conversations with the president by Acting Secretary of State James E. Webb, October 1 and 3, 1949, Memoranda of Conversations with the President 1949–52, Records of the Executive Secretariat, Lot Files, RG 59; Dean Acheson, "Attacks on United States Shipping by the Chinese," *Department of State Bulletin* (December 12, 1949), 21:908.

[68] 893.00/10-1549, no. 4351, McConaughy, Shanghai, to Secretary of State, Decimal File, RG 59.

[69] Acheson, Secretary of State, to Embassy in China, FR, 1950, 6:306–7. The February 6, 1950, attack on the Riverside plant of the Shanghai Power Company caused severe damage estimated at U.S. $4.15 million. It put approximately 40 percent of the company's generating capacity out of commission for an estimated twelve-month period during which it expected to lose an additional U.S. $970,000. "Synopsis of Telephone Conversation between Mr. Gehrels in Shanghai and Messrs. Robertson and Kopelman in New York," January 24, 1950, and letter from Troy L. Perkins, Officer in Charge, Political Affairs, Office of Chinese Affairs, Department of State, to W. S. Robertson, American and Foreign Power, N.Y., March 18, 1950, communicating confidential information from Gehrels in Shanghai, in Shanghai Power Company Papers, box 271–26, Boise Cascade Archives (hereafter cited as SPC Papers). On the day prior to the attack, Kuomintang leaflets warned Shanghai residents to keep away from all utilities. Cablegram from Gehrels in Shanghai to Ebasint, N.Y., February 6, 1950, *ibid.*, box 226–34. Yet, in May 1949 John M. Cabot, the American consul-general in Shanghai, had secured a Nationalist promise, which he verbally communicated to Paul S. Hopkins of the Shanghai Power Company, that the company would not be attacked. Paul S. Hopkins, "Memorandum Regarding Shanghai

chargé d'affaires in Taipei, observed, "In my opinion Chinese navy and CAF both have idea U.S. will not retaliate in any serious way almost regardless of what they do."[70] And Foreign Minister George Yeh's half-hearted attempts to justify the attacks on the grounds that Shanghai Power's output was being used for military purposes merely reinforced Strong's view.[71]

At the same time the United States was being blamed for these raids in Shanghai, for whose people the erratic destruction was "like someone pounding on [a] festering boil."[72] The Communists loudly decried what they called imperialist murder: American-made planes dropping American-made bombs, purposelessly incinerating the congested wooden neighborhoods of the city.[73]

Yet the United States was in a difficult position. Director of the State Department's Office of Chinese Affairs Philip Sprouse argued that:

It should not be overlooked that the Chinese Government, in effect, exists and maintains its representation in the UN solely because of American support and that it would probably collapse overnight if that support were withdrawn. It seems incredible, therefore, that

---

Power Company's Position in Shanghai, China," March 21, 1950, *ibid.*, box 268–14. On similar problems faced by Stanvac, see 893.00/12-3049, no. 5456, McConaughy, Shanghai, to Secretary of State, Decimal File, RG 59; "Pootung Terminal Damage Protested by State Department," *Stanvac Meridian*, March 1950, p. 1, Mobil Oil Corporation Archives, New York City.

[70] Strong to Secretary of State, FR, 1950, 6:307n.4.

[71] Strong to Secretary of State, *ibid.*, pp. 307–8. The State Department had had indications that the Nationalists were firing upon highly visible American property as early as May 1949. A cable from Consul-General John M. Cabot in Shanghai reported: "Consulate offices have been repeatedly hit during afternoon by rifle and machine gun fire. All but two possible cases are clearly Nationalist side. Majority of cases appear accidental if utterly irresponsible but [in] several instances it can only be deliberate despite American flags on pole and both entrances. . . . If Department wishes it can quote me to press as saying, Nationalists have wantonly fired on American flag, that is the simple fact." Koo Papers, "U.S. Diplomats in China" folder B75.1.

[72] McConaughy, Consul-General at Shanghai, to Secretary of State, FR, 1950, 6:302–3.

[73] Paul S. Hopkins, Shanghai, to K. R. MacKinnon, July 8, 1949, SPC Papers, box A: 271–27; and *Ta-kung pao* editorial, February 13, 1950, *ibid.*, box 268–14.

we permit the Chinese government brazenly to do the damage to our position in China that it is doing. It is all the more incredible that we do not take stronger steps than we have already taken to make clear to that Government that, if it continues bombing attacks of this nature, we will stop all aid or at least all shipments of military supplies from this country. We cannot afford to let the Chinese Government take us further down the primrose path than it has already led us.[74]

What his analysis did not mention, what the Nationalists obviously were counting on, was the political threat the Truman administration was thought to be facing should it abandon "the cause." In fact, power over China's future immobilized the United States government. The Chinese Nationalists therefore were gambling. If their supporters in the United States were adept, the stakes would continue to be too high for the Democrats. As time passed, the United States became more and more closely identified with the brutality of the bombings, more and more tied into the Kuomintang fight.

The use of pressure politics in the United States on behalf of the Nationalists was intense and purposeful, if poorly planned and coordinated. Approaching varied segments of American society to recruit friends and engender sympathy, the Chinese employed paid lobbyists as well as the energies of Nationalist officials and interested allies. The Chinese believed that, with their understanding of American political institutions and American ways of thinking, they could shape public opinion into a powerful pro-Kuomintang instrument as they had during World War II.

China's Ambassador V. K. Wellington Koo vigorously pursued this objective. American-educated, with an illustrious diplomatic career going back to 1912, Koo was an astute, if idealistic, observer of the American scene.[75] He was con-

---

[74] Memorandum by Sprouse to Deputy Assistant Secretary of State for Far Eastern Affairs Livingston Merchant, FR, 1950, 6:312.

[75] At the age of twelve Koo began his Western-oriented education at the Anglo-Chinese Junior College (Chung-hsi Shu-yuan) in Shanghai. Later he attended the Talent Fostering School (Yu-ts'ai) and St. John's University in China and the Cook

vinced, perhaps to an exaggerated degree, of the efficacy of "enlightening the public," which "in a democracy like the United States," he believed, "was as important as informing the administration of the major issues and the significance of particular problems arising in one's country or between one's country and the United States." [76] Utilizing his post as senior representative and spokesman for his government, Koo lectured widely and wrote often on Chinese affairs and the need for foreign, that is, American, aid. Impressed by the political influence American interest groups seemed to wield, he worked at winning the support of labor unions, veterans' organizations, and women's clubs.[77] He met frequently with members of Congress and repeatedly with State Department officials, even though he found many of them unsympathetic and unpleasant.[78] He was sensitive to the effect on prominent figures of ill-timed or poorly executed appeals and worked assiduously, although ultimately to little effect, to coordinate China's publicity work.

Academy and Columbia University in the United States. At Columbia he earned his B.A., and both an M.A. and Ph.D. in political science. His diplomatic career began soon after with an appointment as English secretary to then-Foreign Minister W. W. Yen (August 1912). In 1915, when only twenty-seven years old, he became minister to the United States. Subsequently he represented China at the Versailles Conference in 1919, at the League of Nations, as minister to Great Britain and France, and at a host of international conferences. Boorman and Howard, *Biographical Dictionary,* 2:255–59; and Chu, "Koo," pp. 125–29.

[76] Koo Oral History, vol. H, sec. 2, p. 70.

[77] On Koo's efforts to influence the AFL-CIO, the Federation of National Women's Clubs, and the Veterans of Foreign Wars through prominent persons such as Perle Mesta, the American minister to Luxembourg, Mrs. Hamilton Wright, crusader for narcotics control, and Fanny Holtzmann, a New York lawyer, see *ibid.,* vol. I, secs. 4 and 8.

[78] Koo was especially distressed by the attitude of W. Walton Butterworth, assistant secretary of state for Far Eastern affairs, who seemed to take "glee" in making him uncomfortable. "I felt Butterworth looked upon me as if I were the Soviet Ambassador, judging from the caution and reserve he assumed, so unusual for an American diplomat in his attitude and action toward an accredited Chinese representative. I have not experienced quite the same situation in my 35 years of dealing with Americans." Koo Oral History, vol. H, sec. 4, pp. 148–49 (taken from Koo Diary, January 13, 1949), and sec. 1, p. 36; vol. J, sec. 2, p. 132. On the attitudes of Acheson and Webb, see Koo Diary, February 15, 1949, and March 3, 1949, respectively.

Most lobbying for the Nationalists was, in fact, carried on outside the control of the ambassador. Koo did not disburse the funds or have a say over the selection of agents to carry out propaganda efforts. In the case of William Goodwin, a paid lobbyist, his "letter of employment, of which the Embassy knew nothing, was drafted, revised and approved by 'Riverdale,' even against the objection of the Director of the Chinese News Service, whose official business was to look after publicity, and who, in this case, was the hiring agent." "Riverdale" was, of course, Madame Chiang Kai-shek.[79]

The struggle for a "Free China" attracted a wide range of Americans. Anti-Communist religious leaders, industrialists, and congressmen publicized the crusade through organizations such as Alfred Kohlberg's American China Policy Association and Frederick McKee's Committee to Defend America by Aiding Anti-Communist China.[80] The Chinese embassy kept in touch with many prominent participants in this so-called China lobby. Koo entertained them, met with them at

[79] Koo Oral History, vol. I, sec. 8, pp. 466–68, and sec. 4, pp. 144–46.

[80] Alfred Kohlberg, a "mild mannered, unassuming little man who rarely raised his voice," was among the bitterest critics of United States China policy. Having made his not-unappreciable fortune importing Chinese laces, silks, and embroidery, he maintained a lifelong interest in Chinese affairs. His unhappy associations with the American Bureau for Medical Aid to China, United China Relief, and the Institute of Pacific Relations launched his second and more prominent career as the guiding light of the American China Policy Association and the "man behind McCarthy." Joseph Keeley, *The China Lobby Man* (New Rochelle, N.Y.: Arlington House, 1969), pp. 4, 11, 21–25, 55–70, 75–103. See also Alfred Friendly, "Man Behind the Man Who Is Accusing Lattimore," *Washington Post*, April 23, 1950; Edward A. Harris, "The Men behind McCarthy," *New Republic* (April 24, 1950), 122:10–11; Malcolm Hobbs, "Chiang's Washington Front," *Nation* (December 24, 1949), 169:619–20; and Ross Koen, *The China Lobby in American Politics* (New York: Harper & Row, 1974), pp. 50–52. Frederick McKee's activities spanned the foreign policy field rather than concentrating on China as Kohlberg's did. A Pittsburgh industrialist and philanthropist, he was active in the American Committee for Non-Participation in Japanese Aggression and the American Association for the United Nations and Free World Inc., among other such groups. Koen, *China Lobby*, p. 53. Other studies of the China lobby include a contemporary exposé printed by the *Reporter* magazine in April 1952, and Stanley D. Bachrack's *The Committee of One Million: China Lobby Politics, 1953–71* (New York: Columbia University Press, 1976). On the Congressional China bloc, see James Fetzer, "Congress and China, 1941–1950" (Ph.D. diss., Michigan State University, 1969).

dinners arranged by Goodwin, Kohlberg, or McKee, and appeared at functions throughout the United States at the invitation of *Time-Life* publisher Henry Luce and others.[81] Members of Congress, whether cold warriors, anti-New Dealers, partisan Republicans, or sincere friends of China, were constant targets for Kuomintang appeals. Some, such as New Jersey Senator H. Alexander Smith, traveled to China and corresponded regularly with government officials. These few supported their arguments for aid to Nationalist China with firsthand knowledge. But up-to-date "evidence" provided by the Nationalists also appeared in the Congressional speeches of many who personally knew little about Chinese affairs.[82] On occasion, the embassy even drafted such speeches.[83]

From their American sympathizers the Nationalists solicited and received confidential information about the inner workings of government agencies. They ascertained who might be well disposed to their cause, where bureaucratic squabbles might operate in their favor, and how best to rephrase an appeal that had already been modified or denied several times. Most helpful in providing such intelligence

[81] Koo Diary and Oral History, *passim*. Other Chinese officials who dealt with politicians and the press included H. C. Kiang of the Chinese delegation to the United Nations, who wrote Joseph Alsop on November 25, 1949: "I think I do not have to say how much we shall appreciate it if you and your brother will write about our [UN] case for the better information of the people in this country." Joseph and Stewart Alsop Papers, General Correspondence, "China lobby" folder, Library of Congress.

[82] Senator Smith's papers are filled with correspondence he exchanged with various Kuomintang notables. He also circulated among his Congressional colleagues a report on his autumn 1949 trip to the Far East and sent copies to State Department personnel, the White House, newspaper publishers, and reporters, among others. See especially H. Alexander Smith Papers, box 98, Mudd Library, Princeton University. Representative Walter Judd of Minnesota was generally credited with being the China expert in Congress, a distinction he accepted proudly. See Floyd R. Goodno, "Walter H. Judd: Spokesman for China in the United States House of Representatives" (Ph.D. diss., Oklahoma State University, 1970). Others associated with the China bloc in Congress were less directly motivated by China's plight. Senator Pat McCarran, for example, could not, in Wellington Koo's view, help but represent the interests of his silver-producing state (Nevada), which would benefit if China's silver needs were met. Koo Oral History, vol. I, sec. 3, pp. 84–85, sec. 4, pp. 132–35, and sec. 6, p. 263.

[83] Koo Oral History, vol. J., sec. 5, p. 395.

were congressmen like Walter Judd, State Department representatives like John Foster Dulles, and the military. Koo
found both American military officers and the Department of
Defense willing, even anxious, to cooperate with him. Admiral Oscar C. Badger, special adviser on Far Eastern affairs at
the Navy Department, virtually authored China's December
1949 aid request and then directed the timing and manner of
its submission. The assistant secretary of defense and his
deputy provided Koo with regular reports on top-level policy
discussions in the Department of Defense. They recounted
secret debates in the National Security Council and disclosed
the details of State Department and Pentagon planning.[84]

When emotional and political inducements failed to secure help, the Chinese Nationalists used less subtle means.
Chiang Kai-shek maintained a secret fund in the United
States under the control of Yü Kuo-hua, deputy executive
director of the International Monetary Fund. These monies
were intended for special purposes, such as a payment to
Colonel M. Preston Goodfellow to organize a foreign legion
for China.[85] In September 1949 General Albert C. Wedemeyer
was offered a large amount of money to serve as an adviser
to the Chinese government, the aim being, the State Department speculated, to ensure "U.S. involvement, together

[84] On Admiral Badger's role, see *ibid.*, vol. I, sec. 5, pp. 159–73; Koo Diary,
December 9, 20, 22, 27, and 30, 1949; and Notes of Conversation, no. 86, Admiral
Oscar C. Badger, December 20, 1949, Koo Papers, box 130. On the Defense Department and the assistance Koo obtained from Secretary Louis Johnson, Undersecretary
and later Assistant Secretary of Defense Paul Griffith, and Colonel Victor O'Kelliher,
liaison between the department and the Chinese embassy, see Koo Oral History,
vol. I, sec. 4, p. 172, sec. 5, pp. 244–45 and 249–50, vol. J, sec. 2, pp. 94 and 112–13,
sec. 3, pp. 160, 184–86, 223–24, 234–35; and Koo Diary, June 8, 1949.

[85] Koo Oral History, vol. J, sec. 5, p. 396; Koo Diary, January 4, 1950; Clark, Canton, to Secretary of State, FR, 1949, 8:455. During World War II M. Preston Goodfellow, a deputy director of the Office of Strategic Services, served in Axis-occupied
Europe and Asia as a guerrilla movement organizer. In 1946 he was attached to the
commanding general's headquarters in Korea as a political adviser. Although he returned to his prewar profession of newspaper publishing later that year, his interest
in anti-Communist activism remained strong. According to Koo, he continued assist-
ing the Rhee government in training undercover operatives for work in North Korea.
Times Biographical Edition (New York, September 1973), 4(9):1476; Koo Diary, January 4 and 12, 1950.

with U.S. military and economic aid."[86] And in March 1949, when the European desk in the Department of State opposed his efforts to secure U.S. tanks, Colonel David Li of the Chinese procurement mission in Washington asked Ambassador Koo "whether he should promise rewards to Am. officials." Koo noted in his diary:

I warned him to be very careful lest it should cause scandals hurting the good name of the Ch. Gov't and damaging the prospects of further aid legislation by Congress. I told him I would rather not know the people he had in mind and the amounts they asked, and I particularly asked if he had the funds already remitted to them from China. He said none yet, but he had already reported to Col. Chiang Wei-kuo [Chiang Kai-shek's son] who had entrusted the purchasing mission to him.[87]

Whether money was in this instance actually paid to anyone is unclear, but there can be no doubt that such a tactic was considered.

The importance that the Chinese placed upon these efforts at persuasion, whether overt or covert, sheds light on their conduct in other areas as well. If impressing American opinion, especially such opinion leaders as Congressional representatives, were the way to secure aid, then American sensibilities must be catered to. Thus Hu Shih was invited to become foreign minister because of his standing in American eyes. Similarly, there was talk of establishing a liberal party to pose as a front for the Kuomintang government in hopes of impressing the United States. A liberal cabinet enlisting the services of virtually every Chinese who had a vigorous and honest reputation in Washington, would, it was hoped, serve as a convincing example of Chinese unity and purpose.[88] Na-

[86] Analysis of Pawley memorandum by W. W. Stuart and Philip D. Sprouse, Records of the Office of Chinese Affairs, "Civilian Advisors to China" folder, RG 59. In an interview with the author on November 30, 1977, General Wedemeyer confirmed that the Chinese government had solicited his services but that he never actually filled the position.

[87] Koo Diary, March 2, 1949.

[88] The individuals most often mentioned, in addition to Hu Shih, were James Y. C. Yen, famous for his rural reform and educational projects, and K. C. Wu, the

tionalist requests for American guidance in reforming their political system also were meant to serve this end. Perhaps the most striking example of such accommodation, however, was the Nationalist response to the publication popularly known as the China White Paper.

To explain and defend its China policy, the State Department published this abundantly documented, 1,054-page study on August 5, 1949. Even before its release, rumors of its contents sparked virulent criticism and acrimonious debate throughout the United States. Pro-Chiang elements accused the Truman administration of stabbing their hero in the back. Not only had aid to China been inadequate and the Yalta talks with Stalin a betrayal of China's interests, they said, but now "Communist sympathizers" and "fools" in the State Department had written Chiang's obituary and condemned his still-valiant armies. Even Democrats loyal to Truman, while pointing out the paper's compelling arguments, were hardpressed to justify publication of confidential reports.[89]

Ironically, the reaction of China's government lacked the bitterness so evident in America. Officials and their spokesmen in the news media denounced the document, decrying its effects on China's future. But the mood of the CC Clique newspaper *T'ien-feng jih-pao* was one of dismay rather than resentment, as it cautioned:

[O]ne must not put too much faith in one-sided words of diplomats. [The] Chinese government has undeniably inevitably made mistakes but not so serious as [the] White Paper would have us believe. Countries are not alike, thus Marshall and Wedemeyer proposals may have been fine for America but not for China. . . . Republicans

---

widely admired mayor of Shanghai. Koo Oral History, vol. J, sec. 2, p. 101. On reform plans, see Edgar, Taipei, to Secretary of State, FR, 1949, 8:422–43; 893.00/8-1349, no. 38, Clark, Canton, to Secretary of State, Decimal File, RG 59, in which General Ho Ying-ch'in suggests that "U.S. advice and supervision" would convince "the Old Man" to stop interfering in government affairs.

[89] See Lyman P. Van Slyke's introduction, in White Paper, for a concise discussion of the background of and reception given to State Department publication 3573, *United States Relations with China, with Special Reference to the Period 1944–1949.*

and rest of American people still love China. We must so arrange our affairs that no White Paper can harm China's brilliant future.[90]

This calm on the part of the most antiforeign elements in Chiang's Kuomintang coalition testified to both the Generalissimo's control and the pervasive agreement among all segments that American aid was the ultimate and only barrier to total annihilation. Thus, a lengthy refutation of the White Paper was postponed until U.S. Congressional opinion regarding China aid crystallized. Chiang reviewed the brief statement prepared by the Supreme Policy Council of the Kuomintang and eliminated its querulous and anxious tone.[91] Venting fury at this American betrayal might bring momentary satisfaction, but the necessity of securing further support from these same Americans compelled restraint.

It is evident, therefore, that the leadership of Nationalist China looked to the United States for deliverance and that, as the painful months wore on, no other options were seriously entertained. Whether the Nationalists had a viable alternative is arguable, but if they did not, it only makes their behavior harder to understand.

Having demonstrated military ineffectiveness and political vulnerability, the Nationalists proceeded during 1949 and early 1950 to display their diplomatic ineptitude as well. In the face of disaster, Kuomintang leaders refused to work together, distrusting their colleagues and seeking to preserve what personal power they could. This disunity hampered innovative thinking, much as it convinced observers abroad that the Chinese government could not be energetic, honest, or efficient. Similarly, efforts to embarrass the United States into providing support, although somewhat successful in the

[90] 026CHINA/8-1049, no. 906, Clark, Canton, to Secretary of State, and 026CHINA/8-1549, no. 387, MacDonald, Taipei, to Secretary of State, Decimal File, RG 59.

[91] 026CHINA/8-1849, no. 981, Clark, Canton, to Secretary of State, and 026CHINA/8-2549, no. A-84, Edgar, Taipei, to Secretary of State, *ibid.*; and "Draft of Reply to White Paper Finished," August 14, 1949, Chungking, in Mandarin, *FBIS*, August 15, 1949, p. BBB-1, "China" section.

Congressional realm, aggravated pivotal American officials and produced but meager results.

Nevertheless, dependence on American aid, absolute during World War II, had become addictive. In the subsequent years of civil strife, China's Nationalist leaders could not see around or beyond that precedent. They listened to the rhetoric of their supporters in the United States and seemed convinced by propaganda that they, in part, generated themselves. Even after Nationalist hopes of a Republican presidency were dashed in 1948, they—and particularly Chiang Kai-shek—persisted in the belief that the tide would turn and the United States would come to the rescue. When the entire Chinese mainland fell under the control of the Communists, reliance on ultimate United States assistance continued on the small island of Taiwan. And it is a fine irony of history that, after the major battles were lost and only a fortress remained to be defended, the outbreak of a new war in Korea did after all bring the Americans back into the fight.

SUMMARY OF DISCUSSION
Dorothy Borg

IN OPENING the discussion of her paper Nancy Tucker explained that she had focused on the deterioration of the Chinese Nationalists because she felt it was a major factor in Sino-American relations in 1949 and early 1950 that American scholars had for the most part neglected. While they had been intensely interested in the effect of the so-called China lobby and the China bloc in Congress on America's China policy, they had paid little attention to the disorder within the Kuomintang and its negative impact on the attitude of the United States government toward the almost obsessive appeals for aid from the Chinese Nationalists.

Walter LaFeber, who served as the main commentator for the Tucker paper, emphasized the need to view the relations between the United States and the Chinese Nationalists during the 1949-early 1950 period in a larger context. This was a period, he said, in which the Cold War became so different in degree that it became different in kind. The United States no longer limited itself to ideological and economic commitments but entered into fundamental military commitments. While there were many possible causes for the hardening of American policy, such as the triumph of the Communists in China and the beginning of McCarthyism in the United States, in his view the most compelling explanation was the explosion of the Soviet atom bomb.

Granted the Cold War current of United States policy, LaFeber continued, historians had questioned why in the late 1940s the United States had done so little to keep Chiang

172

Kai-shek on the mainland and, even more remarkably, had done still less to protect him on Formosa until the middle of 1950. Among the various reasons commonly given were the United States' military limitations and the administration's "Europe First" approach.

Nancy Tucker had now advanced another major consideration: the pluralism, verging at times on total disarray, within the Kuomintang leadership which had frustrated the Nationalists' efforts to draw the United States more deeply into the Chinese civil war. By showing the extent of the dissension among the Nationalists, she had explained why the China lobby, which subsequently was to assume almost mythic proportions, had been so ineffective at the precise moment that Nationalist China's life was at stake in 1949 and 1950. LaFeber felt that, devoid of any concerted backing, the China lobby was unable to activate the China bloc in Congress, which meant that the Nationalists could not obtain the aid they so desperately wanted.

As a measure of the inactivity of the China bloc LaFeber cited a March 29, 1950, executive session of the Senate Foreign Relations Committee which Dean Acheson addressed and Senator H. Alexander Smith, a prominent member of the bloc, attended. The secretary declared flatly that the Generalissimo was "not the person . . . to liberate China," that by bombing the mainland he was "going to solidify everybody against him," and that the Chinese Communists were "criminally crazy" if they did not put an end to the Nationalists' attacks as soon as possible. Despite the bluntness of the secretary's comments, Senator Smith limited himself to saying that he was not in accord with Acheson's opinions but neither would he argue with him. Aside from Senator Smith no one on the committee gave any indication of disagreeing with the secretary.

LaFeber stated that he, personally, welcomed the Tucker paper. United States policy, in his judgment, had been formed in large part by the "world views and personal assessments" of top administration officials and not by the members of a Congressional bloc whose attitudes had been shaped by a supposedly monolithic and all-powerful China lobby. Nor, for that matter, were these officials heavily influenced by any other segment of public opinion.

James Fetzer, who was also a formal commentator, agreed with LaFeber that Tucker had added an important dimension by demonstrating that the dissension among the Nationalists had frustrated their efforts to secure large-scale American assistance. As for the China lobby, he asserted that the Tucker paper should dispel any lingering notion that in 1949 the Nationalist component of the lobby formed a "centrally controlled machine which efficiently pumped money, charm, and propaganda into the American political system."

Fetzer did not agree, however, with the implication that the actions of the China bloc were conditioned by the China lobby. Admittedly, he said, the China bloc included members, like Walter Judd, who supported the Nationalists with a missionary fervor. By 1949, however, the bloc consisted largely of Republicans for whom the China question was primarily a matter of party politics. Before the 1948 presidential election, confident of victory, the Republicans had treated the China problem with caution, assuming it would soon be their responsibility. But with Truman's return to office they adopted a gloves-off approach and promoted the Nationalist cause for their own political purposes. The China lobby and the China bloc were therefore motivated by quite different considerations, and the China bloc, headed by some of the most powerful Republicans in Congress, proceeded largely on its own momentum.

In the subsequent discussion some participants took issue with LaFeber's basic thesis that, in the making of China policy, top American officials had enjoyed a wide latitude, free from any significant outside constraints. Robert Blum and Michael Baron not only maintained that the administration had been subjected to a variety of pressures, but asserted that it had made important concessions. Outstanding among the cases they cited was the administration's endorsement in

October 1949 of a $75 million grant for use in the "general area of China," an endorsement admittedly made in response to the China bloc and perhaps indirectly to the China lobby.

The significance of this example, though largely overlooked by historians, is that it has long served to distinguish the scholars who attach great importance to the influence of the China bloc and the China lobby in the late 1940s from those who do not. The former have relied heavily on the argument that while the $75 million grant admittedly involved only a negligible sum, it kept alive the tie between the United States and the Chinese Nationalists, thereby preventing the administration from carrying out its policy of disengagement. Some have gone even further to claim that the grant amounted to a moral commitment to the Nationalists on the part of the United States government. In contrast, the scholars who share LaFeber's view that neither the China bloc nor the China lobby had an important impact in the late 1940s have regarded the grant as no more than a token gesture designed to appease a few prominent Republicans in Congress at minimum cost. While the conference did not resolve this difference of opinion, it at least brought the controversy into sharper relief.

Complementing the discussion of the China bloc and the China lobby, Michael Baron opened up a new area for consideration concerning the Nationalists' efforts to influence American policy. Whether or not the China lobby had been useful, he said, the Nationalists had attempted to influence the United States government through less obvious but more powerful channels. Nationalist officials maintained close contacts with the American military on many different levels. There was a constant interchange between members of the Nationalist government and United States army and navy officers stationed in East Asia. On various occasions when the China issue was debated within the administration in Washington, the Nationalists were alerted in advance, to all appearances by the United States military, and were therefore able to put pressure on the State Department, at times with telling effect. Moreover, on December 23, 1949, the Joint Chiefs of Staff, reversing their earlier position, recommended sending a mission, including military advisers, to Taiwan. The recommendation, as one State Department official remarked, paralleled with such "extraordinary fidelity" an appeal for aid, received the same day from the Nationalist government, that it suggested a striking readiness on the part of the Joint Chiefs to meet the Nationalists' wishes despite the likely opposition of the State Department.

Warren Cohen strongly supported the general tenor of Baron's comments. He added that, although complete documentation is still lacking, he felt that the contacts between the leaders of the Nationalist government and high-ranking United States Defense Department officials, including not only members of the Joint Chiefs but also Secretary Johnson, may have been particularly significant.

The conference then turned to a consideration of conditions within the Kuomintang, a subject that formed much of the heart of the Tucker paper. It soon became evident that any discussion of the Kuomintang was equivalent to a discussion of Chiang Kai-shek, as his influence had been all-pervasive. Some of the China specialists present criticized American China specialists in general for dealing with the Generalissimo too harshly. They asserted that, partly because of the lack of interest among American scholars in Nationalist China of the 1930s and 1940s, little thought had been given to the variety and magnitude of the problems the Generalissimo faced. Moreover, even though Chiang had failed disastrously in many areas, including his relations with Washington, he should be credited with having been in office for an exceptionally long time, during which he provided the Nationalists with leadership, a sense of continuity, and a competence that enabled them ultimately to establish an effective government on Taiwan.

Other China specialists at the conference, however, differed profoundly with this assessment. They contended that Chiang Kai-shek lost China because he was incapable of meeting any of the basic military, political, and social problems with which he was confronted. They maintained further that the Nationalist successes on Taiwan were not due to Chiang's efforts but to a variety of other factors, primarily the assistance procured from the United States. In their judgment it was the Generalissimo's obsessive desire to retain exclusive power and control every aspect of the Nationalists' activities which led to the complete disorientation of his government in the 1949-early 1950 period.

Akira Iriye stated that it was precisely the disorientation of the Kuomintang that explained the inability of the Nationalists to involve the United States more extensively on their behalf. In the context of Sino-American relations in the years before the Korean War, the attempts of the China lobby and even of the China bloc to obtain American assistance were of secondary importance. He agreed with Tucker's point that dependence on the United States had become addictive for the Chinese Nationalists by the close of World War II and added that the same could be said of other regimes in Europe and the Middle East as well as Asia. This, he asserted, opened up a whole set of questions about the receiving end of American aid. Dependency in the abstract was one thing, but its concrete application was quite another. The effectiveness of American aid was determined not by decisions made in Washington but by the capacity of the recipient nations to realize the desired results. In the late 1940s and early 1950 it was the lack of any viable political structure in Nationalist China able to use help constructively that doomed the Nationalists' efforts to secure extensive American support by whatever means. One of the most challenging questions Tucker had raised was whether the Nationalists would have obtained the kind of American involvement in the Chinese civil war they wanted if they had possessed a government that commanded the confidence of the United States.

PART III
Chinese Communist Policy

In the very lively conference discussion provoked by Michael Hunt's paper, Steven Goldstein offered a contrasting (and in some ways complementary) view of the issues. Believing that a fuller exposition of Goldstein's ideas would be valuable, the conference organizers commissioned him to write the paper that here follows Hunt's presentation. Since Goldstein's contribution could not be considered at the conference, in order to avoid imbalance the editors have dispensed with a report of the discussion of Hunt's paper though a number of ideas presented at the discussion have been incorporated in Goldstein's essay. The purpose of these introductory comments is to delineate in broad outline the major approaches taken by scholars to the study of Chinese Communist Party (CCP) foreign policy in the late 1940s so that the presentations by Hunt and Goldstein may be viewed in context.

INTRODUCTION
Steven I. Levine

FOR MANY years the actions of China's new leaders in forming an alliance with the USSR in February 1950 and intervening in the Korean War against the United States eight months later were seen as the results of a pell-mell rush toward an ideologically determined destiny. More recently, the counterargument has been propounded that as late as May 1949 Mao Tse-tung and the CCP were vigorously signaling their desire to avoid a dependent relationship with the USSR and to establish ties with the United States. According to this thesis, inattentive, ill-formed, or ideologically biased American leaders were responsible for missing an historic chance to avert twenty years of Chinese-American enmity. A key question, then, is just how committed the CCP was on the eve of victory to the pro-Soviet, anti-American foreign policy which it espoused during the first decade or so of its rule. What degree of flexibility, if any, was there in the CCP's world view and its foreign policy tactics at the time? The great merit of the essays by Hunt and Goldstein is that, by critically examining the years preceding the Chinese-American confrontation in Korea, they analyze the motive forces of Chinese Communist foreign policy in this period.

Unlike his Americanist colleagues who are liberally supplied with documents of every description, the student of Chinese Communist foreign policy in the 1940s is confronted by the locked doors of the CCP archives and an unusually opaque political process. Scholars negotiating this difficult terrain have taken divergent approaches with different results. The papers by Hunt and Goldstein in many respects represent the two principal tendencies in the literature. Hunt's approach may be described as situational, Goldstein's as ideological.

Proponents of the situational interpretation believe that the most striking characteristic of Mao and his colleagues in the late 1940s was their pragmatic approach to politics in spite of their adherence to Marxism-Leninism. Although there was a genuine pro-Soviet tendency within the CCP, the dominant attitude toward the USSR, which Mao shared, was profoundly nationalistic and strongly averse to an exclusive dependency upon the Soviet Union. The experience of strained relations with Stalin's Russia dating from the 1920s made Chinese leaders even more wary of the USSR.

Thus the Party leadership wanted to maintain a certain distance from the Soviet Union lest China's independence be compromised. It saw the establishment of a relationship with the United States primarily as a means of accomplishing this end. In addition the CCP believed that, as the dominant economic power in the postwar world, the United States could provide China with much of the financial, technological, and economic assistance necessary to modernize China's backward society. If only Washington could be made to understand that the Party was not Stalin's stalking horse in Asia, mutually advantageous Chinese-American relations could develop without threatening the integrity of China's revolutionary values. In 1944–46 and again in 1949, the CCP leadership made serious attempts to convey to the United States its desire for good relations, but the attempts were ignored or misinterpreted except by junior diplomats who lacked policy-making authority.

Supporters of the ideological approach take the position that Mao and his colleagues perceived world politics through a Leninist prism as a zero-sum game in which China would naturally join the revolutionary forces doing battle with the imperialists. Despite Mao's rejection of Stalin's counsel concerning Chinese revolutionary strategy, he and his colleagues believed that the Soviet Union would shelter China during its period of greatest vulnerability to attack from the imperialists and provide it with the economic and technical assistance and political support necessary to emulate the Soviet developmental model. Such intraparty differences as existed were not sufficient to make consideration of an alternate course likely or feasible. However, within the context of its primary relationship with the Soviet Union the new China might seek relationships with other countries that accepted the fact of China's Revolution and treated the People's Republic of China on terms of equality. According to the ideological interpretation, although practical circumstances mattered, ideology was the key to CCP leadership thinking. Even though Chinese-American conflict in Korea may not have been preordained, a period of tension, misunderstanding, and mutual revilement was almost inevitable.

Mao Tse-tung
and the Issue of Accommodation
with the United States, 1948–1950
Michael H. Hunt

BY LATE 1948 the leaders of the Chinese Communist Party
(CCP) knew that the triumph of their revolution against "feu-
dalism" and "imperialism" was at hand. Already the CCP
controlled 900,000 square miles of territory and a population
of 168 million, and major successes lay ahead. Victories by
Lin Piao's army in Manchuria, the main arena of military
conflict, and Ch'en I's forces in Shantung led in turn to the
capture of the Peking-Tientsin area, Nanking, and (by May
1949) Shanghai. But these successes by the People's Liberation Army (PLA) created difficulties as well as opportunities
for the CCP. There were massive and interrelated problems of
consolidation of power, political integration, and economic
reconstruction. At the same time, the Nationalist collapse,
coming as it did a year or more earlier than anticipated and
with remarkable suddenness, forced the CCP to cope with
these major new responsibilities with relatively little preparation.

The most urgent of these problems was on the home
front. Foremost on the new agenda was the complete elimination of Nationalist forces on the mainland. Already demor-
alized by defeat and hyperinflation and then thrown into
disarray by Chiang Kai-shek's resignation as president in January, the Nationalist armies offered little resistance to the

185

PLA's rapid advance, thus enabling the CCP to move quickly ahead to its next goal, the establishment of firm control over Chinese territory.

Securing physical control was only the first step; beyond were enormous organizational and administrative tasks.[1] With a membership somewhat in excess of 3 million at the end of 1948, the CCP would have to govern a population of roughly half a billion. Party leaders had to meld together newly liberated areas with the old, take control in the cities where their experience was by-and-large limited, secure the cooperation of experienced bureaucrats and technicians until the party faithful grew in numbers and expertise sufficient to displace those of questionable loyalty, and demobilize and integrate into the economy a 4-million-man army. Within the general population the party had the task of isolating those elements deemed reactionary, whether by virtue of their overt hostility to the new regime, of their support of the old order within China, or of their collaboration with imperialism. At the same time the party had to cultivate, as it had throughout the civil war, the political liberals and neutral elements, including the small but influential intelligentsia of bourgeois origins and those entrepreneurs not tainted by reactionary associations.[2]

Finally, China's disrupted economy required attention after more than a decade of deterioration and destruction.[3]

[1] Ezra Vogel, Canton under Communism (Cambridge, Mass.: Harvard University Press, 1969), captures in microcosm the problems facing the new regime. The military background is concisely recounted in Lionel Max Chassin, The Communist Conquest of China: A History of the Civil War, 1945–49, translated by Timothy Osato and Louis Gelas (Cambridge, Mass.: Harvard University Press, 1965).

[2] Suzanne Pepper, "The Student Movement and the Chinese Civil War, 1945–49," China Quarterly (October–December 1971), no. 48, pp. 726–35; and Suzanne Pepper, "Socialism, Democracy and Chinese Communism: A Problem of Choice for the Intelligentsia, 1945–49," in Chalmers Johnson, ed., Ideology and Politics in Contemporary China (Seattle: University of Washington Press, 1973), pp. 208–13.

[3] On economic conditions, see Shun-hsin Chou, The Chinese Inflation, 1937–1949 (New York: Columbia University Press, 1963); Chiang Chia-ngia (Chang Chia-ao), The Inflationary Spiral: The Experience in China, 1939–1950 (Cambridge, Mass.: MIT Press, 1958); Alexander Eckstein, Communist China's Economic Growth

Industrial production had fallen to roughly half of its prewar peak; agricultural output was down by a quarter; and foreign trade had fallen by about 30 percent between 1947 and 1949. China's transport system, never well developed, was either in disarray, damaged beyond repair, or devoted to military tasks. Hyperinflation ravaged the urban economy. To master these problems party leaders foresaw "three years of recovery" to be followed by "ten years of development."

The agenda on the foreign policy side was neither so full nor so pressing, yet it was important. China's primary international relationship would be with the USSR, though the precise nature of that tie had yet to be defined. Even less clear was China's stance toward those Western powers which retained a stake in China through their resident nationals and the enterprises they operated and which in some cases also had control or influence in colonies, concessions, and autonomous territories along China's periphery. Of those powers, one, the United States, could to a significant degree impede the CCP's consolidation of power. Its navy and air force dominated the western Pacific from island bases acquired at the end of World War II. Its economy had grown enormously during the war, and prosperity and growth continued into the postwar period. By 1949 the United States headed an impressive coalition of Western European states. The colonial possessions of its European allies together with its Asian clients in South Korea, Japan, and the Philippines made the United States a formidable political force at both ends of the Eurasian land mass.

The United States further commanded the attention of the leaders of the CCP because by the late 1940s it had become deeply involved in China, perhaps more deeply than any other country. The United States had lent military sup-

and Foreign Trade (New York: McGraw-Hill, 1966), p. 186; Jacques Guillermaz, The Chinese Communist Party in Power, 1946–1976, translated by Anne Destenay (Boulder, Colo.: Westview Press, 1976), pp. 6–7; and Helen Yin and Yi-chang Yin, Economic Statistics of Mainland China (1949–1957) (Cambridge, Mass.: Harvard Center for East Asian Studies, 1960), pp. 3, 24, 42.

port to the Nationalists throughout the civil war. Continuation of that support could prolong the internal conflict, raise its costs, and impede the CCP's efforts at consolidation and recovery. Another more subtle threat lay in the notable influence which, for over a century, American missionary, cultural, philanthropic, and economic enterprises had had on Chinese intellectuals, educators, and businessmen. Although it would not be immediately apparent to the Communists how deep an impress the United States had made, they were wary of its potential power to use its influence to create and exploit disaffection. Finally, on the positive side, the United States and American-occupied Japan figured as important trading partners, and some in the Party appear even to have regarded the United States as a potential source of technical and material aid. Whether or not the United States would provide such assistance and maintain its trade, especially in essential manufactured goods, until China's own industry recovered would have a crucial bearing on economic planning for the years immediately following liberation.

What were American intentions vis-à-vis China? For the leaders of the CCP the answer would be important not only in formulating domestic policy but also in setting a course in foreign affairs. That the CCP would at least initially align itself closely with the USSR was beyond doubt. What was still at issue was how close that alignment would be and to what extent it would carry over into economic and national security affairs. If American policy were to accord China a position of equality and respect, then China would be spared primary dependence on the Soviet Union. If, on the contrary, the United States proved hostile to a people's democracy in China, then the CCP would have but one place to turn for military security and economic assistance.

Mao's Policy Framework
Available evidence points to Mao Tse-tung as the leading figure within the CCP. By the late 1940s Mao had occupied a

preeminent position within the party for over a decade. Aside from guiding the party toward its approaching seizure of power, he had set the tone and direction of its position in foreign affairs. His published writings and comments, which in sum offer a fuller long-term view on the CCP's foreign policy than do those of all its other leaders combined, highlight Mao's key role in shaping relations with the United States between the triumph of the revolution and the outbreak of the Korean War.

Faced with the task of defining foreign policy in a dangerous and uncertain Cold War context, Mao did what perhaps most policy makers do—rely for policy orientation on deep-seated assumptions validated by experience. The foreign policy views that were to guide Mao in his dealings with the United States were cast in a Marxist-Leninist ideological framework given special form by China's long experience of foreign intrusion. These views even now are difficult to reduce to a single, simple formula, and hence it is easy to understand that they were not easily grasped by most American observers, whose discovery of Mao dated back no more than a decade and who knew nothing of his ideas and their historical context. In retrospect, however, it is possible to follow Mao's ideas through a lengthy and complex process of intellectual evolution and exploration in a distinctly Chinese context. The outcome of that process was an amalgam of nationalism, anti-imperialism, and cultural conservatism.

Mao was, first of all, a nationalist. He was deeply committed to realizing the time-honored goal of the late 19th century self-strengtheners—"wealth and power" to save China from foreign peril—even if it meant going down the previously untried path of Communist revolution. Mao's nationalism in turn carried him almost at once to anti-imperialism and a determination to overturn foreign privileges and concessions and to secure China a position of equality and respect in the world.

Mao had come early to his nationalism and his anti-imperialism. His studies—not to mention events within his own

lifetime, such as the loss of Korea and Taiwan, the occupation of Peking, the repeated payment of indemnities to
foreign powers, and the informal partition of Manchuria—left
Mao with an imposing picture of foreign power and an
alarming vision of Chinese vulnerability in an international
order governed by amoral struggle. Sometime, probably in
the early 1910s, Mao picked up an 1896 pamphlet on China's
imminent dismemberment that so impressed him that years
later he could still recall its opening line—"Alas, China will
be subjugated"—and his own feeling of depression "about
the future of my country" and the dawning realization "that
it was the duty of all people to help save it."[4] After an intellectually exciting period in Peking in the winter of 1918–19
Mao's views had become (as he himself later described them)
"definitely anti-militarist and anti-imperialist."[5] Soon Mao,
like many of his contemporaries, was caught up in the May
Fourth Movement, initiated by anti-Japanese demonstrations
in Peking that quickly spread to the provinces.

Henceforth, Mao would be under the sway of what might
be called the May Fourth approach to foreign policy. Its goal
was the recovery of lost territory and abrogation of the unequal treaties that gave foreigners their privileged standing
in China and were a source of humiliation and resentment. In
place of those treaties China was to claim a relationship of

[4] Edgar Snow, Red Star over China (New York: Grove Press, 1961; originally
published in 1938), p. 131; Stuart Schram, ed., The Political Thought of Mao Tse-
tung (New York: Praeger, 1963), p. 95 (April 1917); and Mao Tse-tung, "The Great
Union of the Popular Masses" (July 1919) translated by Stuart Schram, China Quarterly (January–March 1972), no. 49, p. 76.

The most important source for Mao's youth is his own account related to Snow
in 1936; see particularly Red Star, pp. 127–29, 132–34, 141–42. But neither Li Jui,
The Early Revolutionary Activities of Comrade Mao Tse-tung, translated by An-
thony Sariti and James Hsiung (White Plains: M. E. Sharpe, N.Y., 1977), nor Hsiao
Yü (Siao-yu), Mao Tse-tung and I Were Beggars (Syracuse, N.Y.: Syracuse University
Press, 1959), should be neglected. Stuart Schram, Mao Tse-tung (New York:
Penguin, 1967), sets the material from these and other lesser accounts in historical
context. See also Jerome Chen, Mao and the Chinese Revolution (London and New
York: Oxford University Press, 1965), which has a helpful chronology on pp.
375–79.

[5] Snow, Red Star, pp. 147–48.

full juridical equality that would at last bring the foreign presence under control. With the new relationship would have to go a new Chinese style—of self-reliance and national pride. "Be independent, not submissive; progressive, not conservative; outspoken, not reserved; cosmopolitan, not parochial; practical, not formalist; and scientific, not imaginative."[6] These were the cardinal virtues which Ch'en Tu-hsiu, one of the intellectual leaders of the period, emphasized China would need to secure strength and respect in the world. Mao himself had struck the same theme when he had insisted in 1917 that the Chinese had to cultivate "courage, dauntlessness, audacity, and perseverance" in order "to overcome national weakness." By 1919 Mao could optimistically predict that the May Fourth virtues of independence and courage, developed in a unified Chinese people, guaranteed China "a great future." "Our golden age, our age of glory and splendor lies before us!"[7]

In the 1920s Mao turned his attention to Marxism and in 1921 participated in the formal founding of the CCP. To Mao the nationalist and anti-imperialist, the new ideology offered an appealing explanation of the wellsprings of imperialism, a convincing description of its impact on China, and a promising revolutionary method to win power and turn back imperialist inroads. "We knew that we ought to fight against imperialism and its lackeys," he observed much later, "but we did not know how to do it."[8]

As a Marxist Mao was never interested in the driving force behind imperialism. The theme that engrossed him and to which he returned almost obsessively time and again throughout the rest of his life was the impact of imperialism

[6] Quoted in Lucien Bianco, *Origins of the Chinese Revolution, 1915–1949*, translated by Muriel Bell (Stanford: Stanford University Press, 1971), pp. 37–38.

[7] Schram, *Political Thought*, p. 99 (April 1917); Mao, "Great Union," p. 87 (July 1919).

[8] A comment made in 1964 to a group of Nepalese educators, in Jerome Chen, *Mao Papers: Anthology and Bibliography* (London and New York: Oxford University Press, 1970), p. 22.

on China. He was deeply troubled by the ability of the imperialists to seduce and subvert sections of the Chinese population. The government in Peking had become "the counting house of our foreign masters," foreign-backed warlords kept China divided and in disorder, and the native bourgeoisie contributed to the impoverishment of the worker and peasant masses by facilitating the invasion of foreign goods.[9] With the assistance of these collaborators, imperialist powers destroyed the national unity necessary to resist foreign aggression. The collaborators who so preoccupied Mao would once have been called "Chinese traitors" (Han-chien). But Mao, preferring other labels, called them "lackeys" and the "reactionary class."

With Mao's turn to Marxism naturally went a rapid rise in his estimate of his Russian neighbor. The success of the Russian revolution endowed the Communist Party of the Soviet Union with a prestige and authority which not even the blunderings in China of Stalin and the Comintern could extinguish and which by all evidence persisted until the conquest of power in 1949. Conversely, Mao's conversion to Marxism (and to a degree his disillusionment with Wilson's betrayal of China at Versailles[10]) undermined what had been a favorable if somewhat hazy conception of the United States.[11] Through the 1920s and well into the 1930s, he fit the United States to its new stereotype as an imperialist, one of the "foreign masters" alternately contending against and cooperating with Japanese, British, and French imperialism

[9] See, for example, Schram, Political Thought, pp. 142 (August 29, 1923) and 144–46 (February 1926); Mao Tse-tung, Selected Works of Mao Tse-tung (Peking, 1965–77) (hereafter Mao, SW), 1:65 (October 5, 1928) and 121 (January 5, 1930).

[10] Li, Revolutionary Activities, p. 109.

[11] By Mao's own admission, he had not even known of the existence of the United States until he was seventeen. But soon he learned of the American Revolution and the Civil War, events that struck a sympathetic chord in the Chinese experience. He enshrined Washington and Lincoln in his pantheon of foreign heroes, and he became familiar with some of the rudiments of the American political system. By the late 1910s Mao also counted himself "a strong supporter of America's Monroe Doctrine and the Open Door." Snow, Red Star, p. 154.

for the chance to control and exploit China. Mao worried that many Chinese retained their illusions about the United States, what he called "a superstitious faith in America [as] a good friend who helped China." Americans, he warned twice in 1923, were a two-faced people who used "a pretense of 'amity' in order that they may squeeze out more of the fat and blood of the Chinese people."[12]

Beginning in the late 1930s Mao's view of the United States began to warm, primarily because of his growing recognition of the American potential for resisting Japan. Granted that in contrast to the Soviet Union—the country "most reliable, most powerful and most capable of helping China to resist Japan"—the United States was politically opportunistic, wavering uncertainly between appeasing Japan and resisting its encroachments on American trade and investment. Still, Mao ranked the United States along with France and Britain as prospective adherents to the "international peace front" that had taken shape under Soviet leadership in opposition to fascist aggression.[13] And in 1941 Mao became convinced that "popular" forces in the United States led by Roosevelt had gained ascendence over reactionary "isolationists" and that as a consequence American resistance to Japan was assured. By early 1943 he seemed certain

[12] Schram, Political Thought, p. 142 (August 29, 1923). See also ibid., p. 266 (July 11, 1923); and Mao, SW, 1:120 (January 5, 1930). Materials recently become available (the wan-sui collections) offer evidence that Mao continued at least up until the late 1950s to believe that economic needs fundamentally shaped American foreign policy and that "the U.S. devotes its energies to making money." See John Gittings, "New Light on Mao: His View of the World," China Quarterly (December 1974), no. 60, pp. 755, 757, 759.

[13] It is possible to follow the course of Mao's views down to Pearl Harbor in Mao, SW, 1:256 (December 28, 1936); Chang Kuo-t'ao, The Rise of the Chinese Communist Party, 1928–1938 (Lawrence, Kan., University of Kansas Press, 1972), p. 478; Mao, SW, 1:286 (May 7, 1937), and 2:17 (July 23, 1937); Edgar Snow, "Chinese Communists and World Affairs: An Interview with Mao Tse-tung," Amerasia, (August 1937), 1:264–66; Mao, SW, 2:129, 130, 136 (May 1938), and 276 (September 28, 1939); Schram, Political Thought, pp. 269–70 (January 1939) and 275 (September 1939); Edgar Snow, Random Notes on Red China (1936–1945) (Cambridge, Mass.: Harvard University Press, 1957), p. 69 (September 1939); Mao, SW, 2:385 (January 28, 1940) and 443 (December 25, 1940), and 3:27 (May 25, 1941); and Schram, Mao, p. 224 (November–December 1941).

that the power the United States had marshaled in the Pacific guaranteed victory over Japan.[14]

With the end of the war in sight, Mao grew interested in securing the support of the United States. "Its growing power in China and in the Far East" had already become "decisive." American support might strengthen the CCP's postwar domestic position while restraining the Nationalists' claims to a monopoly of political and military power within China. Mao's hope was that a program of military, cultural, and even economic collaboration—always on a basis of mutual advantage and respect—would strengthen ties with progressives in the United States, neutralize the doubts that American reactionaries and "hardheads" harbored about Chinese communism, and ultimately align American policy more closely with Yenan's interests. From August 1944 to January 1945 Mao took steps to realize this hope. The Communists invested scarce military resources in cooperation with American forces in China. Yenan opened its doors to American reporters and officials and lavished attention on them, while Mao made a considerable effort to take seriously Roosevelt's emissary, Patrick J. Hurley, whom the Chinese soon took to calling Ta-feng ("the big wind"). The effort came to a proper climax in January with a request from Mao and Chou to visit Washington "as leaders of a primary Chinese party."[15]

[14] Schram, Mao, pp. 224–27; and manifesto of the Central Committee of the CCP, July 7, 1943, in Stuart Gelder, The Chinese Communists (London: Gollancz, 1946), p. 141.

[15] "CCP Central Committee Directive on Diplomatic Work," August 18, 1944, in Problemy Dal'nego Vostoka (Problems of the Far East), no. 1, March 24, 1972, translated in U.S. Joint Publications Research Services (hereafter JPRS), no. 57230, October 12, 1972; Mao interview with John Service, August 23, 1944, in U.S. Congress, Committee on the Judiciary, Senate Internal Security Subcommittee, 91st Congress, 1st Session, The Amerasia Papers: A Clue to the Catastrophe of China (2 vols.; Washington, D.C., 1970), pp. 786–97; Mao interview with Col. David Barrett, December 10, 1944, in U.S., Department of State, Foreign Relations of the United States (hereafter FR), 1944, 6:727–32; and Mao's telegraphic request of January 9, 1945, in Barbara Tuchman, "If Mao Had Come to Washington: An Essay in Alternatives," Foreign Affairs (October 1972), 51:44. For the reference to the August 1944 directive I am indebted to James Reardon-Anderson, whose recently completed Yenan and

But the plan did not work. By July 1945, if not somewhat earlier in the year, it had become clear to Mao that American policy was not going to become more favorable. Indeed, following Roosevelt's death in April he had detected an upsurge in reactionary sentiment in Washington that boded ill for the Chinese Communists. Washington had turned aside his requests for talks. Hurley had struck Mao a blow by publicly announcing exclusive American political, economic, and military support for the Nationalist government. And somewhat earlier, Hurley had begun what was in time to become a full-scale purge of the government's China experts, whom Mao and his colleagues had carefully cultivated. Their disappearance from the China scene cost Mao sympathetic contacts through whom he had hoped to make his views known. John Service's arrest in June was taken by Mao as strong evidence of the unfavorable direction in which American China policy was moving. At first Mao directed his fire at Hurley and his reactionary supporters in the U.S. government. By August he had broadened his indictment, blaming American imperialism for wanting "to help Chiang Kai-shek wage civil war and turn China into a U.S. dependency." Through mid-1946 Mao set aside all restraint. He described General George Marshall's efforts at mediation as "a fraud" and "a smoke-screen for strengthening Chiang Kai-shek in every way and suppressing the democratic forces in China." Behind Marshall was the Truman administration, "a reactionary capitalist clique" that had set its face against the Chinese revolution. Thus Mao defined the propaganda line that was to persist more or less unchanged for the following two years.[16] A period that had begun with doubts about

---

the Great Powers: The Origins of Chinese Communist Foreign Policy (New York: Columbia University Press: 1980) does much to illuminate Communist policy toward the United States. See also Robert G. Sutter, China-Watch: Toward Sino-American Reconciliation (Baltimore, Md.: Johns Hopkins University Press, 1978), ch. 2.

[16] For key expressions of Mao's views in this period, see "On Coalition Government," April 23, 1945, translation of the original text in Gelder, Chinese Communists, pp. 21, 49–51; two editorials, July 12 and 19, 1945, in Schram, Political

American policy and given way to high hopes ended with mistrust deeper than ever before.

The Mao who was coming to power in 1948 was neither an ideologue nor a blank slate. His long-established general views on China's foreign relations and his perceptions of the United States gave his policy coherence and consistency. But at the same time his essential principles were broad enough and his sense of China's and the CCP's immediate needs was strong enough that he retained a degree of flexibility and adaptability to changing circumstances. In his earlier dealings with the United States Mao had already demonstrated his capacity for making adjustments in his views and striking bargains in his policy. Between 1937 and 1941 he had twice redefined the threat of American imperialism out of existence to suit changing Chinese and Soviet interests in the struggle against Japan. Later, in the closing year of the Pacific War, he had sought American political support in recognition of the Communist military contribution. Then and later he had dangled the bait of trade and investment opportunities in China in hopes of weakening the American infatuation with the Nationalists while simultaneously securing needed assistance in reconstruction. Now, in 1948, Mao needed to know how the United States would react to his new regime.

Formulating a Policy toward the United States, November 1948–April 1949

In late 1948 the most immediate foreign policy question that the leaders of the CCP had to consider concerned the handling of foreigners and foreign interests in China. The occupation of Mukden in November placed under Communist control a substantial foreign community, including diplomats. Still larger communities lay ahead in Peking, Nanking, and Shanghai. The CCP's second task, less pressing at the

Thought, pp. 276–79; manifesto of July 7, 1946, in FR, 1946, 9:1310–16; and items in Mao, SW, 4:20 (August 13, 1945), 97–107 (August 1946), 109 (September 29, 1946), 117 (October 1, 1946), 120 (February 1, 1947), and 170–73 (December 25, 1947).

turn of the year but of considerable long-term import, was to formulate terms for diplomatic relations with the powers.

The fashion in which Mao grappled with these foreign policy issues and the extent to which he consulted with his associates are frustratingly obscure to the historian. There was certainly no time for leisurely deliberation. In March 1947 Mao had fled Yenan just before its capture by Nationalist troops. The Politburo—whose core consisted of Mao, Chu Te, Liu Shao-ch'i, Jen Pi-shih, and Chou En-lai—had had to divide and travel as two separate groups. Not until May 1948 was the Politburo reunited. In all probability, by the time of its first official gathering in September 1948 foreign policy had become an important item on its agenda. The fall of Mukden and Tientsin was in sight; moreover, the party had to interpret and respond to the Cominform denunciation of Tito, made in June. The P'ingshan conference of the party's Central Committee, held between March 16 and 23, 1949, rounded out whatever formal discussions the party had on foreign policy. But there is no clear evidence on the substance of any of those discussions, nor do we know how Mao approached them, whether as forums for serious debate or as opportunities to rubber-stamp his own ideas or perhaps to give pro forma approval to a consensus reached informally beforehand with his close colleagues.

Mao did at least have his own "barbarian experts" available for consultation. To them fell much of the daily burden of dealing with Western imperialists in 1949 and early 1950. The group was headed by Chou En-lai—suave, well born, widely traveled, and since the late 1930s the party's leading diplomat, dealing alternately with the Soviets, the Nationalists, and the Americans.[17] The aides that Chou gathered around himself—principally Chang Han-fu, Ch'iao Kuan-hua, the K'ung sisters (P'u-sheng and P'eng, married to Chang and

---

[17] Kai-yu Hsu, *Chou En-lai: China's Gray Eminence* (Garden City, N.Y.: Doubleday, 1968), chs. 1-4; and Donald W. Klein and Anne B. Clark, *Biographic Dictionary of Chinese Communism, 1921–1965* (2 vols.; Cambridge, Mass.: Harvard University Press, 1971), 1:204–19.

Ch'iao respectively), Huang Hua, and K'o Pai-nien—had backgrounds that were in essential respects carbon copies of Chou's. With the possible exception of K'o and Huang, all came from Kiangsu. All had attended modern schools in China (Tsinghua, Yenching, or Shanghai missionary institutions) or abroad. All had a command of at least one foreign language (in most cases English). All had engaged in diplomatic and propaganda work during World War II and the immediate postwar years. In early 1949 they had staffed the alien affairs offices organized to deal with foreign interests in Peking, Nanking, and Shanghai; later in the year they were brought into the new Foreign Ministry.[18]

Whatever the process, Chinese terms for dealing with the United States had been formulated by April 1949. There was no simple comprehensive statement to spell out the policy; rather it took shape by degrees. In general terms the policy that emerged had a positive and a negative side. On the positive side, it was accommodating at least in principle toward private American interests. Foreign residents could be allowed to remain, it was argued, because under the regulations of a people's government they would no longer serve as instruments of imperialist penetration. The CCP may have been moved by the practical desire to restore production and foreign trade (in which case the presence of American business may have seemed a real asset worth preserving through the period of reconstruction). At any rate, this tolerant policy toward American businessmen and missionaries became evident even before the first large cities fell into Communist hands and was subsequently maintained as the Communists extended their control southward to the major cities of east China.[19] Following the liberation of major cities, the alien af-

[18] Biographical information from entries in Klein and Clark, *Biographic Dictionary*; and Union Research Institute (hereafter URI), *Who's Who in Communist China* (rev. ed., Hong Kong, 1969).

[19] FR, *1948*, 7:456–57 (September 1948 report on missionaries in Shansi), 102–3 (PLA proclamation of December 24, 1948), 816 (radio broadcast monitored in Mukden, May 8, 1948); and *China Digest* (Hong Kong) (November 30, 1948), 5:10 (CCP Central Committee announcement of November 21, 1948). For two recent assess-

fairs offices began to tackle the problems affecting foreigners and handled them with fair success. The major exceptions were the labor disputes involving foreign employers where overlapping jurisdictions and intense worker unrest hampered settlement.[20]

CCP policy was by contrast negative in its approach to official relations with the United States. It was adamant and inflexible in its demand that official intervention be brought to an end. American military forces were to leave Chinese soil and American bases were to be liquidated. All American agreements concluded with the Nationalists were subject to repudiation. And above all else American military and political support for the Nationalists, particularly on Taiwan, had to end.[21] The fulfillment of these demands was the precondition for diplomatic relations with the United States, and until then the Communists would not recognize the official status of American diplomatic personnel in China and would instead treat them like any other foreign residents. This point was repeatedly made clear to American diplomats in China both in private conversations and in published regulations governing foreign residents, though in practice diplomats often received special privileges and considerations.[22]

---

ments of the response of private American interests in China to this CCP policy, see Nancy Bernkopf Tucker, "An Unlikely Peace: American Missionaries and the Chinese Communists, 1948–1950," *Pacific Historical Review* (February 1976), 45:97–116; and Warren Tozer, "Last Bridge to China: The Shanghai Power Company, the Truman Administration and the Chinese Communists," *Diplomatic History* (Winter 1977), 1:64–78.

[20] See, for example, the labor disputes in Shanghai in which both the consulate-general and private Americans became embroiled, detailed in *Department of State Bulletin* (September 19, 1949), 21:440–41; and FR, *1949*, 9:1350–51. The ill-starred Mukden consulate also had labor problems, described in *China Digest* (December 14, 1949), 7:6–8; and *Department of State Bulletin* (July 11, 1949), 21:956–57.

[21] Statement by Central Committee of the CCP, February 1, 1947, repudiating any future agreement concluded by the Nationalist government, in U.S., Department of State, *United States Relations with China, with Special Reference to the Period 1944–1949* (Washington, D.C., 1949), p. 720 (hereafter cited as *China White Paper*); PLA manifesto of December 1947, in FR, *1948*, 7:19; and Central Committee statement of November 21, 1948, in *China Digest* (November 30, 1948), 5:10.

[22] FR, *1950*, 7:353, and John Leighton Stuart, *Fifty Years in China* (New York: Random House, 1954), p. 256, provide examples of special treatment.

The conclusion of diplomatic relations was not, however, to be automatic once the United States ended its intervention. It was contingent upon American willingness to accept "equal and friendly relations." The Central Committee of the CCP used those terms in a statement (made public on November 21, 1948) that gave the formula for diplomatic relations preliminary expression. In late April 1949 that formula assumed its definitive form when Mao took the unlikely occasion of an incident with a British gunboat to make public—though not under his own name—a call for diplomatic relations based on "equality, mutual benefit, mutual respect for sovereignty and territorial integrity and, first of all, on no help being given to the Kuomintang reactionaries."[23] So that foreign observers would make no mistake about the importance of this second public statement, the CCP's English language propaganda outlet in Hong Kong, the *China Digest*, headlined it on May 17, 1949, as "The Way to Establish Diplomatic Relations with China," while an editorial in the nonparty daily *Ta-kung pao* on June 1 not only underlined the importance of the April statement but linked Mao's name to it. In amplifying its meaning the editorial referred to sections of Mao's "On Coalition Government," published four years earlier.[24]

Mao was actively involved in formulating the terms for dealing with the United States, but it is doubtful that he was in full agreement with the policy line that resulted from the collective decisions of his colleagues. To begin with, he seems to have been noticeably less tolerant than they toward the continued presence of private American interest groups in China. In March and April 1949, when he first dealt with this issue, he appears to have agreed on the need to protect "ordinary foreign nationals" who had "legitimate interests" or were "engaged in legitimate pursuits." But while the Cen-

[23] Central Committee statement of November 21, 1948, cited in n.21; and Mao, *SW*, 4:402 (April 30, 1949).

[24] *China Digest* (May 17, 1949), 5:5; and *Ta-kung pao* (The Impartial) editorial of June 1, 1949, in U.S. Consulate-General, Shanghai, *Chinese Press Review*.

tral Committee the previous November had gone out of its way to reassure "American nationals" in China, Mao seemed less obliging. Rather than referring specifically to Americans, he used only the blanket term "ordinary foreign nationals." Moreover, he made a special effort to insist that "imperialist economic and cultural establishments," a phrase nowhere evident in the earlier Central Committee document, be subject to restrictions. Diplomatic and press offices were to be closed, while all other institutions that fell into this category would have to sacrifice some of their autonomy and accept Chinese "supervision and control." In any case, their existence was guaranteed only "for the time being"; they were ultimately "to be dealt with by us after countrywide victory." [25]

In similar fashion Mao's views on official relations with the United States perceptibly diverged from those of his colleagues. His March comment on diplomatic relations is notable for its careful avoidance of any specific reference to the United States (in marked contrast to the November 1948 statement of the Central Committee) and for its pessimistic judgment that the imperialists "will definitely not be in a hurry to treat us as equals." To judge from the more inviting call to conclude diplomatic relations that he issued (though not in his own name) in late April, he had at least formally softened his position, probably as a result of the discussions held at the March meeting of the Central Committee. But that he did not openly link his name to the invitation suggests that he may have had reservations about it. In any case, Mao was careful to make no specific reference to the United States except in calling for an end to outside support for the Nationalists. Mao's private doubts about dealing with imperialists thus persisted, to reemerge dramatically within only a few months.

The terms for dealing with the United States that developed between November 1948 and April 1949 bear the un-

[25] Mao, SW, 4:370 (March 5, 1949) and 402 (April 30, 1949).

mistakable mark of May Fourth nationalism. Mao and his colleagues shared a general commitment to setting foreign relations on a basis of equality and mutual advantage and ending imperialist interference in China. What separated them may have been a difference of opinion over what constituted "imperialist interference" and how soon it had to be brought to an end. Mao's seeming impatience to sweep China clean flowed from that preoccupation with national self-reliance and pride that had its origins in his student days. Even in the midst of his attempt to cultivate the United States in 1944–45, Mao repeatedly referred in public and private to the need for self-respect (though he was not always above telling visiting journalists and American officials what he thought they wanted to hear about the nature and goals of the CCP in order to disarm their suspicions). "We are not like Chiang Kai-shek. No nation needs to prop us up. We can stand erect and walk on our own feet like free men." And again: "We stand for self-reliance. We hope for foreign aid but cannot be dependent on it."[26]

With the triumph of the revolution in 1949 Mao exulted that the Chinese people had "stood up," as he put it in March and once again in exactly the same words in September.[27] His sense of national pride inclined him to put diplomatic recognition on a "take it or leave it" basis. He wished recognition, but to obtain it he would not have the new China seem overeager or humble itself, particularly before an imperialist power such as the United States and particularly not with the suspicion (springing from recent experience) that Washington was unlikely to reciprocate any Chinese advances. Mao's abiding concern with self-reliance may also have prejudiced his attitude toward foreign educators, doctors, and businessmen. However much such foreigners might contribute to the realization of Mao's vision of "a prosperous and

---

[26] Ibid., 3:191 (January 10, 1945); "CCP Central Committee Directive on Diplomatic Work" of August 18, 1944, cited in n. 15; and Mao quoted in FR, 1944, 6:729.

[27] Ibid., 4:370 (March 5, 1949) and 16–18 (September 21, 1949).

flourishing country," Chinese rather than outsiders were more likely to serve Chinese interests and eliminate vestigial imperialist influence. Mao's impulse toward self-reliance seems generally not to have intruded into the area of international economic relations nor to have gotten in the way of his sharing his colleagues' desire to promote foreign trade.[28] But even here Mao betrayed an occasional doubt. At least once in 1949 he made the extraordinary and revealing statement that independence from foreign trade was one of China's ultimate goals.[29] Together these considerations of self-reliance and restored national pride served as a brake on a diplomatic initiative that may have appeared to Mao a precipitate, unseemly, perhaps even dangerous effort to come to terms with a confirmed enemy of China's independence and integrity.

Measuring American Intentions,
November 1948–June 1949

At the same time Mao and other leaders of the CCP were deciding on the principles to guide their policy toward the United States, they were also estimating the likelihood of an American acceptance. By late 1948, with the Nationalist cause in clear decline, there was good reason to scan for signs that the United States was willing to accept its loss and at last to make that long-deferred peace with Chinese communism.

The Mukden consular affair provided the inauspicious beginning to this period of testing. Mukden was the scene of the first contacts between American officials and the now-victorious Communists. It was no doubt regarded on the Chinese side (as it certainly was on the American) as a test of intentions and good will. Initial contacts in early November went smoothly, even cordially, with Angus Ward, the Ameri-

---

[28] Mao, SW, 4:371 (March 5, 1949) and 408 (June 15, 1949).

[29] Takeuchi Minori, comp., Mao Tse-tung chi (Collected Works of Mao Tse-tung) (Tokyo, 1970–73) (hereafter Mao chi), 10:304 (June 30, 1949).

can consul-general, making clear his interest in cooperating with the new administration and promoting closer contacts, while the new Communist mayor, Chu Ch'i-wen, left Ward from the time of their first meeting with the "definite impression of desiring [to] be friendly and helpful."[30] But before the month was out, relations changed drastically for the worse. The critical element appears to have been the discovery by Communist security forces of an American spy network. As early as 1946 the External Survey Detachment No. 44, based in Shanghai and attached to the commander of U.S. Naval Forces in the Western Pacific, had begun gathering intelligence through Chinese agents in Manchuria. In October 1948, anticipating complete Communist victory in the region, the unit's main office in the Mukden consulate (another had operated out of the Ch'angch'un consulate until its close) set up a network of Chinese agents equipped with small transmitters, code books, and money. By November 20 the city authorities had learned of the network, arrested eight agents, seized Ward's radio equipment, and put the consulate and its personnel under close confinement.[31]

Other impressions of American intentions in China were no less discouraging. American troops had not intervened to save the Nationalists from defeat (as some CCP commentators seem to have feared), but neither had the United States abandoned its counterrevolutionary role. By early 1949, with the

[30] Chu was a 39-year-old political scientist from Kiangsu. He had joined the party in the early 1930s and had served in Manchuria since 1946. He remained as mayor until August 1950. Thereafter he was active first in law and political science associations and later (well into the 1960s) in foreign relations. URI, Who's Who, pp. 180–81.

[31] This account of the Mukden case is drawn from FR, 1948, 7:809–10, 813–15, 828–31, 833–35, 837, 840, 849; Shen-yang Mei-kuo chien-tieh an (The American Spy Case in Mukden) (Canton, 1950); China Digest (December 14, 1949), 7:9 and 24; Department of State Bulletin (July 11, 1949), 21:955–57; and Angus Ward, "The Mukden Affair," The American Foreign Service Journal (February 1950), 27:14–17ff.

The recently released FR, 1949 volume 8 contains nothing to give direct support to the Chinese charges of espionage. There is, however, in a telegram from Clubb (who had earlier served in Mukden) a censored reference to the Mukden consulate's "previous . . . connections" (p. 936). There are also Huang Hua's private hints to Philip Fugh in early June 1949 (before charges were made public) that spying was the issue (p. 959).

Nationalist cause on the mainland doomed, the Communists saw an awakening American interest in Taiwan. For example, the Chinese press reported in March that the National Security Council had urged President Truman to provide assistance for the Nationalists' defense of Taiwan as well as Hainan,[32] while at the same time American officials appeared to be establishing contacts with the Taiwan independence movement. One way or the other, the United States would obtain indirect control of this important forward base in its Western Pacific defense system.[33] As for dealing directly with the Communists, Washington gave no hint of interest. It is true that diplomatic and consular personnel had stayed at their posts on the mainland, but on the other hand they had studiously avoided treating the CCP as the de facto authority in China. In May the Chinese press somehow uncovered and promptly publicized the recently initiated American effort to organize its allies into a united front opposed to switching diplomatic recognition from the Nationalists to the CCP.[34] Finally, as if to banish any lingering doubts, a sharp reminder of continuing support for the Nationalists came in late June as American bombs began falling on Shanghai from American planes flown by Nationalist pilots. At the same time the Nationalists tightened the squeeze on Shanghai by initiating a blockade that some in the CCP regarded as American-instigated. There is no question that the United States acquiesced. Although the State Department declared the blockade illegal, Acheson limited his response to ineffectual notes of protest.[35]

[32] In fact, it was the Joint Chiefs of Staff, not the National Security Council, that favored "some form of military support" for Taiwan. FR, 1949, 9:291. The opposition of the State Department forced the military to back down in April, but the issue of aid was to reemerge later in the year.

[33] See, for example, New China News Agency (hereafter NCNA) comments on Taiwan, March 15, 1949, in Chuang Chia-nung, Fen-nu ti T'aiwan (Taiwan in Fury) (Hong Kong, 1949), pp. 199–201; and Chuang's commentary in ibid., pp. 152–83.

[34] China Digest (May 31, 1949), 5:5.

[35] Department of State Bulletin, vol. 21, July 11, 1949, p. 34, and December 12, 1949, p. 908; FR, 1949, 9:1126 (recording Ch'en I's conviction that Admiral Badger was behind the blockade).

A second broad source of concern was the buildup of American influence along China's periphery—in French Indochina, in the Philippines, in South Korea, and, above all, in Japan. For several years American occupation policy toward Japan had aroused widespread and emotional opposition in China. Only four years had passed since the end of the Pacific War, which had brought a halt to a half century of Japanese aggression against China. But in those four years the American occupation, rather than eradicating Japanese militarism as promised, had instead restored it, thereby (in Mao's words) fostering "'the forces of aggression in Japan." MacArthur's headquarters in Tokyo had rehabilitated political and military personalities implicated in the criminal policy of aggression against China, revived the armed forces in the guise of a "police force," reversed the policy of breaking up Japanese industry, canceled reparations due China and other injured countries, and suppressed domestic "progressive" forces fighting for democracy and demilitarization. The Chinese called for the early conclusion of a peace treaty that would bring the American occupation to an end and make Japan a less threatening neighbor.[36] Washington, which had previously excluded China from a real role in the occupation, paid no attention.

Perhaps the decisive test of American intentions came in April and May, with the launching of confidential overtures to Washington. The decision to approach the American government probably came out of the March Central Committee meeting, where some more confident than Mao of American flexibility successfully argued for at least a try at opening private lines of communication. Evidence on the make-up of the prevailing coalition can be only circumstantial in part

[36] See, for example, Mao, SW, 4:316 (January 14, 1949); and NCNA, Daily News Release, April 26, 1949, p. 3, May 19, 1949, p. 21, June 21, 1949, p. 2, June 22, 1949, pp. 2–3, and June 27, 1949, p. 1. The breadth and intensity of postwar Chinese concern over U.S. policy toward Japan is documented in David Griggs, Americans in China: Some Chinese Views (Washington, D.C., 1948), pp. 42–43; and Dorothy Borg, "America Loses Chinese Good Will," Far Eastern Survey (February 23, 1949), 18:43–44.

and pure speculation for the rest. It seems a fair assumption that the foreign affairs experts (including Chou En-lai himself) placed more faith in the efficacy of their special diplomatic skills than did Mao. Those same experts also had ties of education, language, and even friendships with the imperialist United States, in contrast to the more insular figures such as Mao and those with more experience with the Soviet Union such as Liu Shao-ch'i. There is also fragmentary evidence that some military figures in early 1949 either regarded the United States kindly or believed it could be maneuvered out of the final stages of the civil war, thus making the People's Liberation Army's task easier. Finally, those closely involved with economic planning, such as Minister of Industry and Commerce Yao I-lin, may also have recognized the likely limits of Soviet aid, the attractive possibility of American credits, and the importance of unimpeded trade with Japan and the United States.[37]

Bowing to this dominant view of his colleagues, Mao authorized Chou En-lai to make confidential contacts with the American embassy. The teacher-student relationship between Huang Hua (one of Chou's Kiangsu associates) and Ambassador John Leighton Stuart (once president of Yenching University) ensured the desired conditions of informality and confidentiality. In early May, soon after reaching Nanking to take over the alien affairs office there, Huang got in touch with Stuart. On June 28 Huang went as far as to indicate that both Mao and Chou wanted to talk.[38] While Huang pursued

[37] See, for example, the messages from Generals Nieh Jung-chen and Yeh Chien-ying received by Clubb in Peking on December 15, 1948 (FR, 1948, 7:648–49), Yeh's endorsement of trade relations with capitalist countries in February 1949 (FR, 1949, 8:1058), and the not entirely persuasive and perhaps somewhat dated report in January 1950 (FR, 1950, 6:289–93, 296–302) that General Ch'en I had aligned with a party faction seeking ties with the United States to balance off the USSR. For some contemporary journalistic speculation that largely coincides with my generalizations in the text, see Tillman Durdin's reports from Hong Kong in the New York Times, September 17, 1949, p. 5.

[38] FR, 1949, 8:741–42, 745–48, 752–54, 766–67. See also Seymour Topping, Journey between Two Chinas (New York: Harper & Row, 1972), pp. 82–88, which draws on Stuart's personal diary and conversations with Huang Hua and Stuart's private

his contacts in Nanking—with the hope of making way for a discussion of outstanding political issues—officials in Peking had already set in motion a parallel effort to restore Sino-American trade, or at least to determine the American attitude on economic relations. This less well known, but equally important, secret initiative was directed by Yao I-lin, a Christian and party member fluent in English and educated in missionary schools and Tsinghua University. In late April he had subordinates approach the American consul-general in Peking, O. Edmund Clubb, to propose a bargain on trade between China and American-occupied Japan. Concurrently Huang Hua, Ch'iao Kuan-hua, Ch'en I, and local authorities in Shanghai lent Yao their public support by making statements that underlined the importance of economic relations with the United States, including financial and technical aid as well as trade. In private it appears (on the basis of evidence both fragmentary and indirect) that even Mao and Liu Shao-ch'i stood behind this effort, at least with respect to securing American trade.[39]

By June neither Huang nor Yao could report any sign of a favorable American response. Huang's proposals were met

secretary Philip Fugh. It goes far beyond the expurgated version Stanley Hornbeck worked into Stuart, *Fifty Years*, pp. 247–48.

[39]See *FR, 1949*, 9:976–77; Yao entry in Klein and Clark, *Biographic Dictionary*, pp. 998–1001; and *FR, 1949*, 8:350, 370, 373, 377–78, 379–80, 763.

A curious incident in late May suggests that Chou may even have injected himself into this effort. Clubb in Peking received word secondhand from Australian newspaperman Michael Keon that Chou wished to communicate with "highest American authorities on top secret level without his name being mentioned." Aside from laying bare a split within the CCP between Liu Shao-ch'i's radical wing and Chou's moderates, the message expressed an interest in U.S. aid (which the USSR would not be able to supply in quantity) and in the establishment of de facto working relations (which would allow China to play a mediatory role between the United States and the USSR). The State Department, in a response endorsed by President Truman, asked the Chinese to demonstrate their interest in better relations with deeds not words. When Clubb tried to send this response directly back to Chou's office in late June, contact was abruptly cut, presumably because, as the original message indicated, Chou expected no specific reply and did not want his name linked to the message. The denouement of this strange episode came in August when Keon was scared out of the country by intimations that he was about to be charged with spying. *FR, 1949*, 8:357–60, 373, 384–85, 388, 389, 397–99, 496–98, 780.

with a silence imposed by President Truman and Yao's with a variety of obstacles thrown in the way by MacArthur's headquarters with the backing of the State Department. By July, if not sooner, Yao had concluded that "American authorities would not permit such trade" as he had proposed.[40] Mao's initial pessimism about American policy toward China now found confirmation and in his view justified a formal shift in policy.

Formalizing the "Lean-to-One-Side" Policy, June 1949

In late 1948 and early 1949 Mao had been faced with the acute problem of not alienating the Soviet Union (as he tested American intentions) while avoiding Stalin's smothering embrace (which experience warned him against). Mao's efforts to strike a balance between autonomy and dependency in relations with the USSR are reflected in his policy decisions. On the one hand he ignored Stalin's cautious advice in the closing phase of the civil war and instead ordered the PLA to cross the Yangtze and deal a final blow to the Nationalists. But in his brief flirtation with the United States in the spring of 1949 Mao was cautious and discreet. He put out the April recognition formula under a name other than his own to avoid close identification with an initiative that might not find favor in Moscow. He also tried to make the announcement of the Chinese position seem routine, leaving it to the Chinese English-language press to draw its importance to the attention of American observers. Finally, Mao kept the Huang-Stuart liaison and the trade proposals confidential to spare Stalin any alarm. (It is also possible that Mao wanted to keep these dealings with the Americans out of the eyes of the Chinese public so as not to encourage false expectations of a rapprochement or to seem to go out of his way to encourage contacts with the major imperialist power.)

In the realm of ideology the need to keep a line open to

[40] *Ibid.*, p. 769, and 9:987–88, 992–94.

Moscow also forced a balancing act on Mao. Forceful endorsement of the two-bloc view and an attempt at downplaying the originality of Maoist theory would have helped to put Mao in Stalin's good graces. But Mao instead moved relatively slowly and half-heartedly toward meeting Soviet desires. Early in November 1948, following the Cominform's condemnation of Tito, the Central Committee of the CCP endorsed the decision as a necessary contribution "to the cause of preserving world peace and democracy, and of defending the peoples of Yugoslavia from the deception and aggression of American imperialism." Both Mao and Liu Shao-ch'i in turn (one as head of the party and the other as the most vocal exponent of Mao's way) openly acknowledged the leading role of the Soviet Union in the socialist camp. Liu's was the sharpest statement, a long and partisan piece that elaborated the two-camp view of the world and developed in detail the dangers the United States posed as the head of the imperialist camp. He warned those inside and outside the party against the "illusions that American imperialism would in good faith help the Chinese people to achieve real independence, peace and democracy." Mao's statement by contrast was far briefer and milder. It refrained from any open attack on Tito and instead stressed the need for unity among the revolutionary forces of the world.[41]

By mid-June 1949 the failure of the Huang and Yao feelers coming on the heels of the Mukden affair must have prompted Mao to reassess China's relations with the two powers, for at that time the CCP's public attitude toward the United States began to harden. In mid-June attacks on the United States in the official press resumed after the period of relative silence that predated the Huang-Stuart conversations. The Mukden consular case, long kept under wraps, was made public on June 19 and the charge of espionage taken to court with much fanfare. It would appear in retro-

---

[41] URI, *Collected Works of Liu Shao-ch'i* (Hong Kong, 1969), 2:123–51 (November 1, 1948); and *Mao chi*, 10:185–89 (November 4, 1948).

spect that Ward and his staff had been held hostage to be forgiven and released if relations with the United States improved. But with no improvement in sight, the case was brought into the open—some six months after the fact.[42]

Mao himself played the dominant role in publicly defining the new foreign policy. In a speech to a national political assembly on June 15, he warned that "the imperialists and their running dogs, the Chinese reactionaries, will not resign themselves to defeat in this land of China." They would, Mao charged on the basis of information not yet made public, "smuggle their agents into China" and "blockade China's ports." It was a time not for rapprochement but for "vigilance against the frenzied plots for revenge by the imperialists and their running dogs." Mao not only added to the April formula for diplomatic relations a new precondition—"an attitude of genuine, and not hypocritical, friendship towards People's China"—but now also gave play to an intense anti-imperialism hitherto held in check by the preferences of his more moderate colleagues.

China must be independent, China must be liberated, China's affairs must be decided and run by the Chinese people themselves, and no further interference, not even the slightest, will be tolerated from any imperialist country.[43]

Having identified the threat from American imperialism, Mao dealt with its implications on June 30 in a second address, "On the People's Democratic Dictatorship," a comprehensive statement of the national policy the CCP intended to follow in the years immediately ahead. The sections on foreign policy received the closest attention both within China and abroad as the first authoritative statement of the course Mao had charted for China. It is best known and most important for Mao's announcement that China would lean to

[42] These generalizations are based on a reading of NCNA, *Daily News Release* for April–June 1949; and FR, *1949*, 8:933.

[43] Mao, SW, 4:407–8.

one side. "Not only in China but also in the world, without exception, one either leans to the side of imperialism or to the side of socialism. Neutrality is a camouflage, and a third road does not exist." Mao blamed the "reactionaries" for blocking recognition on the basis of the April formula and preventing the resumption of foreign trade, and he stressed as he had earlier in June the danger of flirtation with the United States. "Imperialism is still standing near us, and this enemy is very fierce." Mao argued that consequently China had only one way to go—toward the USSR, a true ally bound to China by a common revolutionary experience and ideology and also the only dependable source of assistance in China's reconstruction.[44]

Mao's decision to announce his choice publicly and emphatically may seem like a costly personal indulgence (in that it further alienated the United States), unless one considers that the speech addressed three audiences and served three purposes largely unrecognized at the time. In one sense the speech was aimed at a small domestic audience, primarily party comrades who—even after Huang's failure to elicit some encouraging sign from Washington—still wished to establish China in a position more equidistant between the United States and the USSR than Mao had in mind. Despite Huang and Yao's lack of success, these and perhaps other party leaders may have still favored delaying any dramatic commitment to the side of the USSR and instead maintaining room for diplomatic maneuver in the months ahead. They may have been sufficiently uncertain about the Soviet Union as a source of economic and military support to want to extend the period of probing. They may have felt that the American government needed more time to consider and respond or that perhaps the probes had not been forceful enough to capture the attention of high level American policy makers. Perhaps they hoped that if formal diplomatic relations could not be reached, they might at least preserve infor-

[44] Ibid., pp. 415–17. Both quotes come from Mao chi, 10:297 and 304.

mal lines of communication by developing economic and cultural ties with Americans in China and with groups in the United States sympathetic to the CCP. Mao's speech, couched in language that his colleagues would have to take as a definitive rejoinder to their views, was intended, if not to change their minds, at least to put an end to the inner party debate.

Mao may also have been speaking to another small but influential group within China—intellectuals, liberals, and patriotic bourgeoisie in the cities recently occupied by the PLA. Mao's address could in this light be viewed as a step in political consolidation intended to draw to the side of the CCP those, particularly among students and older intellectuals, who had earlier protested American support for the Nationalists and the resulting prolongation of the civil war. Mao may also have wanted to reach those in the treaty ports who had absorbed political illusions from their contacts with imperialism. His concern with this group was to grow in importance in the months ahead.

Mao's speech had another important audience—Stalin—and another purpose—to assuage his doubts about the orthodoxy of the Chinese party and convince him that it was an ally worthy of support. As Mao recalled in 1956, "Stalin suspected that ours was a victory of the Tito type, and in 1949 and 1950 the pressure on us was very strong indeed."[45] With his speech Mao made an ostentatious attempt to reassure Stalin that the CCP was solidly planted in the socialist camp and looked to the USSR for leadership, assistance, and instruction. He assured Stalin (while warning his comrades and countrymen) that in a two-bloc world there could be no "sitting on the fence" and no "third road." The identity of Chinese and Soviet interests and ideology, so Mao now argued in public, permitted China to go in only one direction.

The decision to lean to the side of the USSR must have given Mao some uncomfortable moments. While dependency

[45] Mao, SW, 5:304 (April 25, 1956).

on the USSR might benefit China in economic and military affairs, it was also nearly impossible in June 1949 to calculate even in gross terms the degree of benefit Stalin would be willing to bestow on his Chinese ally and to weigh against it the cost in terms of worsened relations with the United States. Behind the uncertain calculus of advantage there must have existed on Mao's part a deep ambivalence about the Soviet Union, rooted in personal experience. On the one hand the USSR occupied a unique place in Mao's public rhetoric as the "fatherland of socialism." "The interests of the Soviet Union," Mao had proclaimed in September 1939, "will always conform and never conflict with the interests of China's national liberation."[46] On the other hand the tangled skein of Sino-Soviet relations offers considerable evidence for a good deal of tension between the fraternal Communist parties of China and the Soviet Union and between their respective leaders. Those tensions dated back, as far as the Chinese were concerned, to the poor advice the Comintern and Stalin had given the party from the mid-1920s down to the mid-1930s, when Mao gained control. But more to the point were the repeated collisions of interest that had marked the post-1945 relationship. Stalin had pursued a course more czarist than fraternal. The sack of Manchurian industry in 1945, the pact with the Nationalists restoring Soviet privileges in southern Manchuria the same year, the support for independent Mongolia, and the privileges obtained in Sinkiang from the Nationalists in their last moments of power on the mainland all caused consternation and no doubt much irritation inside the party.[47]

[46] Ibid., 2:277–78, 281 (quote, September 28, 1939). See also Schram, Political Thought, pp. 293–94 (December 30, 1939). For some acute remarks on Mao's ambivalent attitude toward the USSR, see Benjamin Schwartz, Communism in China: Ideology in Flux (Cambridge, Mass.: Harvard University Press, 1968), p. 37; and his essay in Dick Wilson, ed., Mao Tse-tung in the Scales of History (New York: Cambridge University Press, 1977), p. 27.

[47] Warren Cohen, "American Observers and the Sino-Soviet Friendship Treaty of August, 1945," Pacific Historical Review (1966), 35:347–49; James P. Harrison, The Long March to Power: A History of the Chinese Communist Party in Power, 1921–1972 (New York: Praeger, 1972), pp. 383–85; and FR, 1949, 8:391.

Throughout the civil war Stalin did more to obstruct than to facilitate Communist victory. He seems to have feared that a Communist victory might cause the United States to intervene militarily in China, thus opening a second Cold War front that the Soviet Union was ill prepared to deal with. In the summer of 1945 he had urged Mao to avert civil war by entering a coalition with the Nationalists and dissolving his army. When to Stalin's dismay Mao resorted to force, the Soviets indicated their neutrality by keeping the Soviet ambassador with the Nationalist government until it abandoned the mainland, longer than any other country. Even at the eleventh hour, with a Communist victory in sight, Stalin is supposed to have suggested to Mao an armistice and partition along the Yangtze River. Mao, who in 1939 had confidently asserted that the USSR "actively supports just and non-predatory wars of liberation" as a fundamental principle of its policy, must have felt chagrin looking back over the postwar Soviet record.[48]

Tensions over the ideological relationship between the two Communist parties created further difficulties for Mao. While Stalin called Mao a "margarine Marxist" afflicted by "chauvinism" and a "petty bourgeois ideology,"[49] the Chinese for their part put forward with increasing frequency the claim that Mao was an original Marxist thinker whose way in China provided a model for other Asian Communist parties. As early as 1936 Mao himself had cited the "international revolutionary significance" not to mention the uniqueness of

[48] Harrison, March to Power, pp. 383–85; Mao, SW, 2:277, 281 (September 28, 1939), 5:304 (April 25, 1956); Stuart Schram, ed., Chairman Mao Talks to the People: Talks and Letters, 1956–1971, translated by John Chennery and Tieyun (New York: Pantheon, 1974), pp. 103, 191; Adam B. Ulam, Expansion and Coexistence: The History of Soviet Foreign Policy, 1916–67 (New York: Praeger, 1968), pp. 470–95, 514–18; O. B. Borisov and B. T. Koloskov, Soviet-Chinese Relations, 1945–1970, edited with an introduction by Vladimir Petrov (Bloomington, Ind.: Indiana University Press, 1975), pp. 21–24, 60–62, 116–25.

[49] Harrison, March to Power, p. 384; Nikita Khrushchev, Khrushchev Remembers, translated by Strobe Talbott (Boston: Little, Brown, 1970), p. 462; and Wolfgang Leonhard, Three Faces of Marxism, translated by Ewald Osers (New York: Holt, Rinehart and Winston, 1974), pp. 227–30.

the Chinese revolution. His comrades, especially Liu Shao-ch'i, later elaborated on the Chinese contributions to the theory and practice of revolution, making what must have seemed to the Soviets extravagant claims for a party still struggling for power.[50]

Thus while it may be tempting to explain Mao's June enunciation of policy essentially in terms of an inherited proclivity for the socialist camp, a review of Sino-Soviet relations indicates that Mao was prompted by something more than an unthinking faith in a special relationship with Stalin and the USSR. Mao was above all concerned with the position of the United States. The apparent hostility of the world's greatest power and the close proximity of its western Pacific system of bases and allies left Mao only two alternatives—to alter the course of the revolution to accommodate American preferences or to seek an ally who might provide a modicum of insurance against possible attack either direct or by proxy. The former course would have meant in large measure a repudiation of the May Fourth foreign policy, and there is no evidence that even hints that Mao or other party leaders considered this course. Thus Mao had in effect only one remaining alternative to embrace.

Neutralizing the United States, July 1949–June 1950

A propaganda campaign against the United States had begun in June, apparently as a prelude to Mao's "lean-to-one-side" pronouncement. Thereafter, rather than trailing off, the campaign continued with new intensity. The main purpose it now served was a broader one—to secure popular understanding and support for Mao's new policy of offsetting American power in East Asia and neutralizing American influence in China.[51] The first sure sign that the campaign was

[50] Mao, SW, 1:194 (December 1936); and Schram, Political Thought, pp. 113–14 (October 1938). See, for example, Liu Shao-ch'i's address of May 1945 in Stuart Schram and Hélène Carrère d'Encausse, Marxism and Asia: An Introduction with Readings (London: Allen Lane, 1969), pp. 259–61.

[51] See the coverage in NCNA, Daily News Release, July–September 1949.

assuming serious dimensions came on July 7, when Mao put out a statement signed by the leaders of twenty-two different "popular" parties and organizations endorsing China's adherence to the "anti-imperialist camp" and attacking U.S. policy toward Japan.[52] The launching of the Sino-Soviet Friendship Association in Peking on July 16 underlined the importance now attached to popular support for the leaning toward the USSR. A month later Mao stepped in again, this time with his commentary on the China White Paper and Secretary of State Dean Acheson's covering letter, which were released together by the Truman administration on August 5, 1949 as a defense against charges it had lost China to communism.

Mao's response took the form of a series of five articles (published pseudonymously between August 14 and September 16) pointing out the illusions some Chinese still harbored about the United States, recounting the history and ultimate failure of American aggression against China, and dissecting the misperceptions, failures, and confusions plaguing American policy in the wake of the Communist victory.[53] The appearance of these commentaries by Mao became in turn the occasion for public discussion of American imperialist activities in Taiwan and Japan and for comment by non-Communist political figures in support of the new policy.[54]

Mao's commentary on the White Paper seemed on the surface little more than a tirade directed at the United States. The embassy in Nanking, which was unaware Mao was the author, described the first installment as "vehement" in its hostility and "violent," while the second—directed at the departing Ambassador Stuart—was reported as "sinking to [a] new low in lampooning, personal defamation [of a] great

[52] Mao chi, 10:309–13.

[53] Mao, SW, 4:425–31 (August 14, 1949), 433–39 (August 18, 1949), 441–45 (August 28, 1949), 447–49 (August 30, 1949), and 451–58 (September 16, 1949).

[54] See the reports from Shanghai, Nanking, and Peking in FR, 1949, 9:1403, 1407–9.

friend of China."[55] There was, indeed, a remarkable emotional intensity to these writings, but it reflected less hostility to the United States per se than Mao's old preoccupation with the wound imperialism had inflicted on Chinese society. From the 1920s onward Mao had turned time and again to the general question of China's classes and their relation to imperialism.[56] With the civil war Mao as well as party propagandists had begun to express specific concern about the ties between American imperialism and the Chinese bourgeoisie and intellectuals. American imperialism, a mid-1946 party manifesto warned, "breeds traitors." By early 1948 Mao was directing the attention of "certain democratic personages" to the danger of falling victim to illusions about American friendship and a "third road" in either foreign or domestic policy. By December 1948 he was accusing those same elements of serving as tools of American imperialism in its effort to organize "an opposition faction within the revolutionary camp . . . [and] to halt the revolution where it is or, if it must advance, to moderate it and prevent it from encroaching too far on the interests of the imperialists and their running dogs." In March 1949, now in a more temperate mood, Mao warned his comrades to guard against the "sugar-coated bullets" of the bourgeoisie while correcting the mistaken views of "non-Party democrats" through "serious and appropriate criticism or struggle."[57]

Mao was not a victim of a fevered imagination. "Certain democratic personages" who had rallied to the Communist side in 1948 and early 1949 did indeed have illusions about

[55] Ibid., pp. 1399, 1400.

[56] For evidence of the persistence of Mao's early concern with the bourgeoisie and its links to imperialism, see Mao, SW, 1:157–58 (December 27, 1935), 264, 272–73 (May 3, 1937), 290–91 (May 7, 1937), 331–32 (August 1937); 2:288–91, 294 (October 4, 1939), 320–22 (December 1939); 4:19 (August 13, 1945), 207–10 (March 1, 1948), 220–21 (March 20, 1948), 374 (March 5, 1949), 418–19 (June 30, 1949).

[57] Manifesto of the Central Committee of the CCP, July 7, 1946, reproduced in FR, 1946, 9:1314; Mao, SW, 4:220 (March 20, 1948); NCNA editorial, May 24 and 30, 1948, in China White Paper, pp. 859–64; Mao, SW, 4:301, 304–5 (December 30, 1948), 374 (March 5, 1949).

taking a third road. They fancied playing an intermediary role between Peking and Washington, and for that reason they maintained contacts with remaining American diplomats in China. They wanted to strike a modus vivendi with the United States, particularly to facilitate economic reconstruction. And they told Mao as much.[58] Dean Acheson's open appeal in early August to these embodiments of Chinese "democratic individualism" to take their stand against a Soviet-controlled CCP confirmed Mao's fears and provoked him to action.

Mao thus wrote his commentary with the intention of popularizing the policy line he had defined in June. Though he may still have had in mind those within the CCP not yet fully won over to the new foreign policy, he seems to have been more concerned with a broader segment of the population—those Chinese who had "foreign characteristics" (as Mao had phrased it in 1926) and the same illusions about the United States that he himself had once entertained. Mao wanted to unite, not split, with the patriotic bourgeoisie. His "people's democracy" envisioned a period of three to five years during which the bourgeoisie would have an important role to play in political organization and economic reconstruction. With his commentary on the White Paper, Mao began in earnest the task of reintegrating the bourgeoisie back into the body politic. For the moment education prevailed over coercion as the instrument for national unification, and so it would remain until the Chinese-American collision in Korea slightly over a year later further diminished Mao's tolerance of national division and produced a dramatic reversal of methods.

After completing his commentary in mid-September Mao fell silent on the subject of United States-China relations. For example, when Acheson sallied forth in January and again in

---

[58] Chow Ching-wen, *Ten Years of Storm: The True Story of the Communist Regime in China*, translated and edited by Lai Ming (New York: Holt, Rinehart and Winston, 1960), p. 282; Carson Chang, *The Third Force in China* (New York: Bookman, 1952), p. 279; FR, *1949*, 8:496, 750–51, 756, and 9:382–83.

March to take what a State Department aide called "the first step . . . in gaining support in the United States for our Asiatic policies," Mao this time did not respond; instead he left the principal rebuttal to others—first to Hu Ch'iao-mu, a party propagandist, and later to Chou En-lai.[59] Even so, the Chinese press continued to cover American transgressions—the persecution of the American Communist Party, the American role in the bombing of Shanghai, persisting support for the Nationalist forces on Taiwan, and, above all else, MacArthur's continued remilitarization of Japan. This unfavorable comment continued to appear right down to the outbreak of the Korean War, though compared with earlier the coverage was sporadic and contended for space with the inauguration of the People's Republic on October 1, the promotion of friendship with the USSR, and the formation of a world peace bloc against American imperialism.[60]

On the level of practical policy the turn to the USSR formally and publicly signaled by Mao in June took concrete form through the second half of 1949 and the first half of 1950. A series of economic agreements concluded between July 1949 and April 1950 assured China not only needed industrial products but also technical assistance and a $300 million credit[61] in the wake of American economic restrictions first imposed in early 1949 and later expanded.[62] Politi-

[59] Shih-chieh Chih-shih Ch'u-pan She, comp., Chung Hua Jen-min Kung-ho Kuo tui-wai kuan-hsi wen-chien chi (Collected Documents on the Foreign Relations of the People's Republic of China), vol. 1, 1949–50 (Peking, 1957), pp. 92–94, 109–11 (hereafter cited as CHJM). Hu, like many of the Chinese who dealt with American affairs, came from the lower Yangtze delta (Kiangsu), studied at Tsinghua University, and knew English. His ties appear to have been closer to Mao than to Chou. See Klein and Clark, Biographic Dictionary, pp. 374–77; and URI, Who's Who, pp. 285–86. The quote is from Undersecretary of State James E. Webb in FR, 1950, 6:35.

[60] My reading of NCNA, Daily News Release, September 1949–June 1950.

[61] M. I. Sladkovskii, History of Economic Relations between Russia and China, translated by M. Roublev (Jerusalem: Israel Program for Scientific Translation, 1966), pp. 226–28, 240–43, 244–47, 249. Sino-Soviet trade still constituted only 23 percent of China's foreign trade in 1950.

[62] For an overview of U.S. restrictions and an evaluation of their effectiveness, see Gunnar Adler-Karlsson, Western Economic Warfare, 1947–1967: A Case Study in Foreign Economic Policy (Stockholm: Almquist & Wiksell, 1968), pp. 201–8; FR,

cal relations were established immediately after the founding of the new government. And after much general celebration of Sino-Soviet friendship (with a special emphasis on China's need for aid), Mao departed for Moscow in December. His extended stay provided him opportunity to pay elaborate public tribute to his host, discuss the cooperative measures the two might take together, and finally conclude a series of economic, cultural, and political agreements. Easily the most important from the Chinese point of view was the February treaty guaranteeing China against attack by Japan or "any state allied with her," a scarcely veiled reference to the United States.[63]

But the implementation of Mao's "lean-to-one-side" policy did not eliminate older tensions in the Sino-Soviet relationship; if anything it created new sources of friction. The Moscow talks had proven long and difficult. Mao later remembered that trying to get help from Stalin was like getting "meat out of the tiger's mouth."[64] To solve the questions concerning Chinese interests, it took Mao ten weeks, much longer than he had expected and an extraordinary length of time for the head of a new state to stay abroad.[65] Although Mao got his alliance, the economic aid was meager compared to Chinese needs or (to judge from the frequent references in the press in the fall of 1949) CCP expectations. Moreover, the Moscow agreements carried with them some marked disadvantages. Joint stock companies allowed the Soviets to main-

---

1949, 9:895, 950, 955–57, 976–77, 987–88, 992–95, 1003–4, 1016–19, 1028–29; and FR, 1950, 6:619–20, 622–25, 638–39.

[63] URI, Liu Shao-ch'i, 2:161–66 (speech of October 5, 1949) and 171–72 (speech of November 7, 1949); Ting Wang, "Mao Tse-tung hsuan-chi" pu-i (Supplement to The Selected Works of Mao Tse-tung), vol. 3, 1949–59 (Hong Kong, 1971), p. 5 (Mao's tribute to Stalin of December 21, 1949); Chung-kuo Jen-min Wai-chiao Hsueh-hui, comp., Oppose the Revival of Japanese Militarism (Peking, 1960), pp. 1–4 (for the text of the February 14, 1950, treaty).

[64] Quoted in Gittings, "New Light on Mao," p. 761.

[65] Hsin Hua yüeh-pao (New China Monthly) (January 15, 1950), 1:579. For an extended report on Chinese resentment of Soviet policy on the eve of the Moscow meeting, see FR, 1949, 8:632–36.

tain their influence in Sinkiang. Elsewhere on the border, in Manchuria, the Soviets retained special rights in Dairen and Port Arthur and over the Ch'angch'un railroad, though they did promise eventual relinquishment.[66] Not surprisingly, Chinese press treatment of the new accords was restrained and at times even defensive in attempting to meet the objections that greeted them.

On the ideological front the CCP made no concessions. It still claimed a special role in the world revolutionary movement. For example, in November 1949 Liu Shao-ch'i immodestly described the Chinese way as "the way that should be taken by the peoples of many colonial and semi-colonial countries in their fight for national independence and people's democracy." And just after he reached Moscow, Mao's original theoretical insights received special attention from one of the CCP's foremost ideologues, Ch'en Po-ta. Ch'en managed to square the circle by explaining that Mao had developed his ideas on the Chinese revolution independently of Stalin yet reached conclusions compatible with Stalin's own observations.[67]

Although Mao's "lean-to-one-side" formulation carried China toward the USSR, Mao seems not to have regarded it as inconsistent with diplomatic initiatives directed toward states outside the socialist camp. Chou En-lai, whose de facto position as the CCP's foreign minister was regularized under the new government,[68] turned his hand to this new project in the fall, certainly with the intention of undermining the American policy of diplomatic isolation but also, perhaps,

[66] Allen S. Whiting and Sheng Shih-ts'ai, Sinkiang: Pawn or Pivot? (East Lansing, Mich.: Michigan State University Press, 1958), pp. 98–123; and Sladkovskii, Economic Relations, pp. 240–42.

[67] Liu text in Schram and Carrère, Marxism and Asia, p. 271; and Ch'en on "Stalin and the Chinese Revolution," in NCNA, Daily News Release, December 20, 1949, pp. 149–52, and December 21, 1949, pp. 160–64.

[68] Chou was concurrently foreign minister and premier in the central government. On the creation of the Ministry of Foreign Affairs in 1949, its antecedents, and staffing, see Donald W. Klein, "The Management of Foreign Affairs in Communist China," in John M. H. Lindbeck, ed., China: Management of a Revolutionary Society (Seattle: University of Washington Press, 1971), pp. 305–13.

with hopes of avoiding an exclusive diplomatic relationship with the USSR. Mao gave the effort his blessing in his October 1 proclamation of the new central government of the People's Republic. Invoking the April formula, he expressed his government's wish to establish relations with "whatever foreign governments sincerely observe the principles of equality, mutual advantage, and reciprocal respect for territorial sovereignty." The next day Chou issued an identically worded invitation to all governments. Two weeks later K'o Pai-nien, one of Chou's subordinates in the Foreign Ministry, provided an authoritative outline of policy that conceded the possibility of coexistence with imperialism (while affirming the two-bloc view), emphasized interest in diplomatic and trade relations with all countries, and reaffirmed the commitment to protect resident foreign nationals, including Americans. The immediate—and probably from the Chinese point of view the single most important—result of Chou's effort was to divide Britain from the United States on the issue of recognition and to accentuate tensions between (as the Chinese saw it) ostensible allies with conflicting imperialist aspirations in Asia. By April 1950 Chou had secured recognition not only from Britain but also from leading Asian states (including India, Burma, Indonesia, and Pakistan), the Scandinavian countries, Switzerland, and the Netherlands, not to mention virtually all of the socialist camp.[69] The other facets of Chou's campaign—establishing a claim to the Nationalist seat in the United Nations and a signatory role in the Japanese peace treaty—fared less well, for these were areas where American will prevailed.[70]

Official lines of communication between China and the United States had one by one disappeared. The Chinese had ordered the U.S. Information Service closed in July and called a halt to the operations of American news agencies in

[69]Mao chi, 10:362; CHJM, pp. 5–32; and FR, 1949, 9:93, 117, 120–22, 138–39. K'o's overview of policy appears in Hsueh-hsi (Study) (October 15, 1949), 1:13–15.

[70]FR, 1949, 9:195; and CHJM, pp. 85–87, 90, 91–92, 96, 114–15, 118–19, 127, 128.

October. Ambassador Stuart had left in August. In Mukden Ward had been tried on assault charges in November, convicted, and at once deported, thus bringing to an end the year of confinement suffered by the consular staff. In January 1950 the final split was precipitated by the Chinese seizure of land acquired by the "unequal treaty" of 1901 to house troops in Peking and still held by the United States as well as by France and the Netherlands. Although Washington had warned that it would retaliate by recalling all remaining diplomatic personnel in China, the Peking Military Control Commission went ahead with its announced intention of taking back the land and requisitioning the buildings on it (with property rights to be worked out subsequently).[71] By April the remaining American consulates in Peking and Shanghai were officially closed, and by early May all officials had departed, leaving behind businessmen and missionaries either hopeful of a place in the new China or unable to leave for legal reasons.

By June domestic issues had come to overshadow the question of American imperialism. In a series of meetings held through that month Peking gave priority to land reform and economic reconstruction, both particularly important after a winter in which food had been in short supply.[72] The military struggle was all but over. Although Tibet was still unredeemed, it posed none of the problems of Taiwan, one hundred miles from the mainland and with an American interest in its fate. But even Taiwan now seemed a less imposing problem to tackle than it once had. High-level American policy statements had given the Chinese some grounds to expect no active opposition to an invasion. Truman's January statement on Taiwan disclaimed any intention of military interference (though he did add the qualifier "in the present situation") and any interest in military bases there (though here too he hedged with the phrase "at the present time"). As

[71]FR, 1950, 6:270–71, 276–78, 286–87, 327, 329; Department of State Bulletin (January 23, 1950), 22:119–23; and Hsin Hua yueh-pao (February 15, 1950), 1:854.

[72]Mao, SW, 4:26–31, 33–35 (June 6, 1950), and 38–40 (June 23, 1950); URI, Liu Shao-ch'i, 2:193–95, 199–200, 203 (April 29, 1950), and 224–25 (June 14, 1950).

late as June 24 Acheson reaffirmed Truman's position, which he interpreted publicly as a policy of no direct aid to the Nationalists on Taiwan. The capture of Hainan in April had proven the People's Liberation Army could master amphibious operations. An attempt to take Taiwan would come next, once the army was adequately prepared and political agitation on the island among students and others and propaganda appeals to the military had rendered the Nationalists' position uncertain.[73]

The CCP was thus well on its way to mastering the problems of political and territorial consolidation. But the calculations on which this domestic policy rested were rudely and unexpectedly deranged by international developments. The conflict in Korea began on June 25. At first the official press gave it only perfunctory attention (although the leaders of the CCP may have been privately far more concerned than their public silence and the press treatment might indicate). But Truman's decision on June 27 to interpose the Seventh Fleet between Taiwan and Communist forces on the mainland unmistakably shocked Peking and elicited from both leaders and press a rapid response. On June 28 Mao indicted Truman for going back on his January pledge, a point underscored by a *People's Daily* editorial the next day. Mao characteristically demanded that the United States leave Asian affairs to Asians, a theme he had developed earlier in private conversation with the Indian ambassador. The West had "unbalanced the life of Asia, and the work of this generation of liberators was to recover the balance." On the same day Chou En-lai charged the United States with armed aggression against China as well as provocation in Korea. And Chou too appealed for Asian solidarity against "American imperialist war-makers."[74] On several occasions much later he was to

[73] Allen S. Whiting, *China Crosses the Yalu: The Decision to Enter the Korean War* (Stanford: Stanford University Press, 1960), pp. 20–22; and Acheson in the *New York Times*, June 25, 1950, p. 18.

[74] *Important Documents Concerning the Question of Taiwan* (Peking, 1955), pp. 11–15; *Jen-min jih-pao* (People's Daily) editorial, June 29, 1950, in *T'ai-wan wen-t'i chung-yao wen-hsien tzu-liao chi* (A Collection of Important Materials on the Tai-

argue that Truman's sudden shift in policy on Taiwan constituted a "new aggression" against China (though it is possible Chou was engaging in a post facto effort to put the United States in the worst possible light).[75]

Despite its concern, Peking seemed reluctant to divert energy or attention from urgent domestic problems. Yet within days the new Asian crisis had begun reshaping foreign and domestic policy. A People's Daily editorial of July 1 still defined the two chief tasks ahead as achieving a "radical improvement in the economic and financial conditions of the state" and carrying through agrarian reform in newly liberated areas. But to these goals had now been added in third place the defeat of American intervention and the liberation of "Taiwan and all other territory of China." Within the month Chinese troops, some previously scheduled for the Taiwan operation, had moved north to Manchuria and Shantung, closer to the war zone. Meanwhile at home the regime took the first steps toward mobilizing popular support against this new American aggression.[76] The prospect of war between the United States and China, unimaginable a month before, had already taken shape like a growing cloud on Peking's horizon.

Mao and Misperception

It might be tempting to see Mao as an ideologue whose distorted vision of the world in general and the United States in particular translated into a flawed foreign policy. That Mao

---

wan Question) (Tokyo, 1971), 1:121–23; and K. M. Panikkar, In Two Chinas: Memoirs of a Diplomat (London: Allen & Unwin, 1955), pp. 80, 81.

[75]Edgar Snow, The Other Side of the River: Red China Today (New York: Random House, 1961), p. 116 (for a 1960 interview); and Topping, Journey, p. 398 (for a 1971 interview).

[76]Jen-min jih-pao editorial, July 1, 1950, in Boyd Compton, Mao's China: Party Reform Documents, 1942–44 (Seattle: University of Washington Press, 1952), pp. 277–78; Wei-ta ti k'ang-Mei yuan-Ch'ao yun-tung (The Great Resist-America Aid-Korea Campaign) (Peking, 1954), pp. 641–49; and Whiting, China Crosses the Yalu, pp. 64–67.

knew and perhaps even cared little about the United States as an abstraction is evident from his collected works. For example, of the historical parallels and illustrations in Mao's writings, most came from the Chinese experience, a few from Europe, more from the USSR and its revolution, and virtually none from the United States. Mao's incidental comments on the contemporary United States were more numerous, but they were never written with the verve or conviction of which he was capable when addressing issues closer to home and his heart. What emerges from those comments is a predictable picture, consistently maintained, and from all evidence reflecting his real views. For Mao, the United States was a country divided between oppressive reactionary capitalists and progressive popular forces, a country always on the verge of economic crisis with its ruling elite feverishly struggling to avert a collapse through the control of foreign markets, a country whose imperialist thrust abroad was generating the forces of opposition necessary to encompass its defeat. A 1947 analysis of American strength drew together these strands:

The economic power of U.S. imperialism . . . is confronted with unstable and daily shrinking domestic and foreign markets. The further shrinking of these markets will cause economic crises to break out. . . . Irreconcilable domestic and international contradictions, like a volcano, menace U.S. imperialism every day [and have] driven the U.S. imperialists to draw up a plan for enslaving the world, to run amuck like wild beasts in Europe, Asia and other parts of the world.[77]

It is easy to fault these superficial and often erroneous views. American imperialism, supposedly in irreversible decline, proved far stronger and more persistent a force in Asia than Mao had imagined. The American ruling elite maintained its power, easily containing those popular revolutionary groundswells that Mao hopefully glimpsed just below the surface. The economic crisis never came.

[77] Mao, SW, 4:172 (December 25, 1947).

Americans in the late 1940s—and perhaps some of those Chinese liberals that worried Mao—saw the shortcomings of his views. Ambassador Stuart's characterization, made on the eve of his talks with Huang Hua, offers as good an illustration as any: "CCP leaders, while extremely intelligent, probably see [the] world—especially [the] U.S.—largely through a murky haze of [their] own self-indoctrination."[78] Even Mao would have conceded that he had gathered his information in a slapdash way. Though he called on his comrades to do "systematic, thorough social research," he admitted in 1941 that neither he nor the party had done so in regard to world affairs generally, not to mention the American scene in particular. And he was aware of the consequences: "For a person who shuts his eyes, stops his ears and totally cuts himself off from the objective world there can be no such thing as knowledge." The kindliest verdict would thus have been that Mao was guilty of "looking at flowers on horseback," a phrase he frequently flung at superficial observers in the early 1950s.[79]

Mao's lack of insight is accounted for only in part by the limitations, in terms of both quantity and variety, of his sources of information. Until his trip to Moscow in December 1949 he had never traveled abroad. The visit to Washington that Mao had proposed first in early 1945 and then again (at best only half seriously) in early 1946 might possibly have introduced more nuance into his stereotyped view of the United States. But, as things stood, Mao was thrown back on an exclusive reliance on secondhand information about the United States. One source was foreign news services and foreign radio broadcasts, though these had not always been available (as for example during the years in the wilderness from 1927 to 1935 or in the months following the flight from Yenan in 1947). Another source available to Mao, at least as

[78] FR, 1949, 9:14.

[79] Mao, SW, 1:303 (July 1937), 3:13 (March 17, 1941) and 18 (May 1941); and Compton, Mao's China, pp. 67–68, 70.

early as December 1948, was the "News for Reference" (Ts'an-k'ao hsiao-hsi), a limited-circulation compilation that included a substantial amount of foreign news presented in a straightforward fashion and with a minimum of editorial comment.[80] (The Chinese daily press, once it fell under CCP supervision, had less utility as a full source of information. With few exceptions, international news carried the credits of the official Soviet news agency TASS or the official Chinese news agency Hsin-Hua. Only occasionally did the latter base its reports on information drawn from such foreign sources as USIS news releases or despatches from the Associated Press or Reuters.) An alternative source of second-hand information came in the form of a steady stream of curious Americans who passed through Yenan in the late 1930s (beginning with Edgar Snow's visit in 1936) and again in the mid-1940s. And, finally, Mao could turn to aides such as Chang Wen-t'ien (Lo Fu), who had lived in San Francisco in the early 1920s and acquired a good command of English,[81] and Huang Hua, with his extensive contacts with Americans in China.

However, the major problem for Mao was not the availability of information but the way his settled assumptions distorted it. By the mid-1930s he had worked out the essentials of his view of the United States, and nothing in his experience from that time down to the late 1940s had given him cause to reconsider. Thus those assumptions served as a filter through which "objective" reports such as foreign press accounts had to pass. And those same assumptions shaped Mao's line of inquiry in ways both predictable and banal when he actively sought information. For example, Mao

[80] Henry Schwarz ("The Ts'an-k'ao Hsiao-hsi: How Well Informed Are Chinese Officials about the Outside World?" China Quarterly [July–September 1966] no. 27, p. 57) dates "News for Reference" back to the mid-1950s. For evidence of its earlier existence, see Ch'en Chen et al., Chung-kuo chin-tai kung-yeh shih tzu-liao, ti-erh chi (Historical Materials on Modern Chinese Industry, Second Collection) (Peking, 1958), p. 298; as well as Derk Bodde, Peking Diary, 1948–1949: A Year of Revolution (New York: Henry Schuman, 1950), pp. 206–7.

[81] Klein and Clark, Biographic Dictionary, pp. 61–67.

asked Snow in the late 1930s when he expected revolution in the United States. Would Snow join in? Why were the Republicans, who represented "big finance capital," loathe to have the United States enter the war? "Was there a strong religious conflict in America?" And even: "How did most people get married?"[82]

Mao's biases not only shaped the information he gleaned but also narrowed the range of sources he turned to in the first place. From among visiting Americans Mao for the most part sought out those such as Snow or Anna Louise Strong who were (as Mao would have put it) "progressive" in their outlook. Mao's reliance on experts on the United States from within the CCP still further insulated him from points of view at odds with his own. For example, Huang Hua (according to Seymour Topping's recollection of a 1946 encounter) was curious about the United States but "carried out discussion in terms of communist dialectics." Three years later Ambassador Stuart recorded Huang's view of the United States: "people were oppressed and knew it—would some day revolt—intellectuals aroused."[83]

Mao's parochial perspective did on occasion lead to mistakes in policy, but it is not clear that a better understanding would have induced Mao to change the essential policy line that he had pursued. Take the case of Mao's misplaced belief that a crisis-prone American economy needed the China market, and that opening it or closing it might be a card he could play in his dealings with Washington.[84] In 1944–45, when Mao had tried to tempt Americans with the prospect of postwar trade with China, he had found Washington unmoved. In 1949, when Mao again attempted to use the China market as bait, he was treated to the spectacle of the United States itself

[82] Edgar Snow, Journey to the Beginning (New York: Random House, 1968), p. 168; and Snow, Random Notes, pp. 69–70, 72.

[83] Topping, Journey, pp. 88, 275.

[84] See Mao's interview with Service on August 23, 1944, cited in n. 15, p. 796; Mao's "On Coalition Government," April 23, 1945, in Gelder, Chinese Communists, p. 46; and also his interview with Snow, Amerasia (August 1937), 1:265, 266.

cutting off trade with China. Indeed, the efforts of CCP spokesmen at that time to emphasize China's interest in trade may have had a result exactly the reverse of that intended by helping to convince Washington that trade was for Peking a necessity American policy could exploit rather than an avenue of mutual advantage and political accommodation. Undeniably, Mao's initiatives turned out contrary to expectations, yet even a better informed Mao probably could not have found in 1949 an alternative means to neutralize apparent American hostility to Chinese communism, to hasten reconstruction, and to avoid exclusive reliance on the USSR. In the final analysis, the gamble had cost him nothing.

Some observers might further fault Mao for his public attacks on the United States between June and September 1949, which confirmed official American assumptions of Chinese dependence on the USSR and of the irrational and virulently antiforeign character of Chinese policy. It is unlikely Mao intended or for that matter even anticipated that the end result would be to deepen American hostility to Chinese communism (and hence in a measure to limit China's future range of diplomatic maneuver). But an examination of the context of Mao's public pronouncements shows him guided not by some abstract notion of American imperialism but rather by specific and pressing policy concerns. American intentions had been tested and found wanting. The United States had failed to respond to CCP overtures in the spring, and it refused to disengage from the civil war. Having thus been forced to rule out the possibility of accommodation with the United States, Mao had already by the summer of 1949 given up on trying to manipulate American policy. He turned his attention instead to mobilizing support within the CCP, within China, and within the Kremlin for a policy that took into account an unmistakably hostile American policy.

A broader, more sophisticated knowledge of the United States might have become important to Mao had Washington agreed to his demands for a relationship of equality and respect. Mao then would have been launched on treacherous waters where he would have needed a clear understanding of American policy, including both its domestic and its global ramifications. However, by refusing to meet Mao's preconditions for an accommodation, American policy makers spared him the complications and pitfalls of developing a Chinese-American relationship in a difficult Cold War context. As it turned out, Mao needed little sophisticated information to determine the American position. He had only to judge United States policy by its concrete impact on China. American policy makers would not stand back and let the revolution run its course. They would not end support for the Nationalists or cease trying to turn to their advantage lingering American influence over the treaty port elite. They would not, in sum, accept a new relationship with China. In the final analysis it was American actions themselves that confirmed old deeply embedded assumptions Mao held about the role of imperialism in China. And those assumptions in turn served as the foundation for policy at least after June 1949.

What is striking in retrospect is that Mao and his associates seem at least down to June 1949 to have in a measure suspended their ideological assumptions, carefully sized up China's position, and rationally sought some way out of a difficult international situation. The question that arises and that this study does not answer is this: What personal qualities, what traditions of Chinese statecraft, what elements in Chinese Communist thought, and what developments in Sino-Soviet relations provided these Chinese Marxists the flexibility to seek a highly pragmatic solution to China's problems rather than the rigidly ideological one that contemporary observers and subsequent critics have seen in Peking's performance? Perhaps this is a question that students of China should put high on their agenda, for a clear sense of the historical dynamics of Chinese foreign policy is now more than ever essential for the light it can shed on contemporary East Asian international relations.

ENDNOTE
This paper relies heavily on a reading of Mao's works. For both speed and convenience I have used the official English-language compilation of the *Selected Works of Mao Tse-tung* (5 vols.; Peking, 1965–77). For the period December 1947 through June 1950 I have also consulted the new authoritative Chinese-language edition, *Mao Tse-tung chi*, compiled by Takeuchi Minoru (10 vols.; Tokyo, 1970–73), and other collections containing writings by Mao, for omissions and revisions in the official edition. Stuart Schram, whose major works are cited below, has no peer as a guide through this corpus of writings by Mao.

Reading in the official and semiofficial press is important for setting Mao's views in context, in the sense of establishing the background to his pronouncements and measuring the direction and tone of general Chinese foreign policy. For this purpose I have made most intensive use of the New China News Agency's *Daily News Release* for April 1949 through June 1950. I have also surveyed portions of *China Digest* (published in Hong Kong) for November 1948 through February 1950; *Hsin Hua yueh-pao* (New China Monthly) for November 1949 through July 1950; *Hsueh-hsi* (Study) for September 1949 through June 1950; and the *Chinese Press Review* (a regular translation service provided by the U.S. consulate-general in Shanghai) for spring and summer 1949. Shih-chieh Chih-shih Ch'u-pan She (World Knowledge Publishing House) put together a convenient compilation of official statements on the establishment of diplomatic relations and other important foreign policy issues that arose during the first year of the People's Republic. It appears under the title *Chung Hua Jen-min Kung-ho Kuo tui-wai kuan-hsi wen-chien chi* (Collected Documents on the Foreign Relations of the People's Republic of China), vol. 1, 1949–50 (Peking, 1957).

Chinese Communist Policy Toward the United States: Opportunities and Constraints, 1944–1950*

Steven M. Goldstein

OFTEN REVISIONIST historians meet the McCarthyite charge that the State Department "lost" China because of a strong sympathy for the Chinese Communists with the equally simplistic assertion that the State Department "lost" China because of its blind hostility to them. Both theories suffer from an overestimation of the influence of American officials on the actions of the Chinese Communist Party (CCP). This paper seeks to analyze Chinese Communist foreign policy from the late 1930s to the late 1940s in order to show the possibilities it offered and those it foreclosed for better Sino-American relations.

Perspectives on International Affairs: The Early Years [1]
Mao's statement of June 1949 that China would "lean to one side" (i.e. align with the Soviet Union) has long been considered a benchmark in the foreign policy of the People's Republic of China (PRC). However, this statement was unexcep-

* The research assistance of Jocelyn Charles and Eileen McColgan is gratefully acknowledged.

[1] Much of the analysis that follows is drawn from my "Chinese Communist Perspectives on International Affairs, 1937–1941" (unpublished dissertation, Columbia University, 1972).

235

tional. For more than a decade the CCP had openly stated that in its anti-imperialist struggle China would be aligned with the Soviet Union. In the months preceding Mao's speech the Communist press had echoed this theme. Indeed it had been central to the CCP's world view since its founding.

More to the point is Chou En-lai's comment to General George C. Marshall during the latter's mission to China in 1946: "Of course we will lean to one side. But how far depends on you."[2] For despite its basic adherence to the lean-to-one-side principle, at certain junctures the Party had also argued for limited relations with the United States. Since the mid-1930s the central concern for the CCP had been the balance to be struck between the given of leaning to one side and the clear gains that could accrue to revolutionary China from temporary alliances with the Western imperialist states. The maintenance of this balance was the essence of the united front policy which was adopted by the Party in the mid-1930s and provided it, thereafter, with the conceptual tools for its analysis of international affairs.

The united front policy was based on the dichotomous Leninist view of the world: the forces of revolution confronted those of reaction on a global scale. The socioeconomic background of a nation determined its place in the alignment. The revolutionary camp was an entity tied together by a common outlook and a common enemy (the global capitalist system). It was a grouping of various elements—the Soviet Union, the proletariat of the world and the peoples of colonial and semicolonial countries—that was free of internal contradictions. Its members were unwavering in their commitment to mutual aid.

[2] Cited by Allen Whiting in his testimony to the House Foreign Relations Committee in "China and U.S. Foreign Policy," *Congressional Quarterly* (Washington D.C., 1973), p. 68, quoted in Donald S. Zagoria, "Mao's Role in the Sino-Soviet Conflict," *Pacific Affairs* (Summer 1974), 47(2):145. Okabe Tatsumi has also made the point about the need to understand the background to the "lean to one side" statement. See his "The Cold War and China," in Yonosuke Nagai and Akira Iriye, eds., *The Origins of the Cold War in Asia* (New York: Columbia University Press, 1977), p. 241.

The imperialist camp was quite different, according to Leninist theory as applied by the CCP. Intrabloc cohesion was a property only of the revolutionary forces. Imperialist states shared some goals but not others. The shared goals— rooted in a common desire to protect imperialist interests— provided the basis for their mutual opposition to revolution in areas open to exploitation. When the common aims of the imperialists obscured their differences, the international scene, as perceived by the Chinese Communists, most closely approached the stark Leninist picture of a world split between two irreconcilable forces. Under such conditions the CCP felt China could not find allies within the imperialist camp. It would have to rely on its own resources and on aid from the revolutionary camp.

But there were times when the differences among the imperialists were seen as overshadowing their common concerns. The colonial rivalries among the various nations of the imperialist world as well as their desire to protect their individual interests led to conflicts among them. In that event, when it was to the advantage of China, the Communists would counsel cooperation with certain imperialist powers against others.

Cooperation of this kind was, however, always regarded as temporary, based on limited mutual objectives. Certain imperialist states might join revolutionary forces in an international united front, but the intentions of the imperialists remained suspect. In the short run, it was thought, they might suddenly change their policy at China's expense. (In the 1930s, for example, the CCP feared that the United States and Great Britain might terminate their support of China and conclude an imperialist peace—a "Far Eastern Munich"—with Japan.) In the long run, it was assumed, the imperialist powers would attempt to destroy any genuine national revolutionary movement that threatened their colonial interests or the existence of a fellow imperialist state.[3]

[3] [Chang] Han-fu, "Lun tzu-li keng-sheng yü cheng-ch'ü wai-yuan" (On Self-reliance and Obtaining Foreign Aid), Ch'ün-chung (May 21, 1939), 3(1):836; and Li

These short-lived, purely expedient relations with imperialist nations were regarded, throughout the 1930s and early
1940s, as fundamentally different from the "revolutionary
comradeship" that bound China to the Soviet Union. Both
CCP leaders and rank-and-file Party members, imbued with
the Leninist interpretation of international affairs, accepted
the necessity of China's alignment with the USSR. Of course
it was recognized that global exigencies might cause the Soviets to suspend aid to the Chinese revolution or otherwise
pursue policies momentarily harmful to it.[4] But these were
seen as temporary fluctuations within a context of strong
moral unity and lasting support.

1944–1945: First Encounters

On July 22, 1944, Colonel David D. Barrett landed in Yenan
as the head of a small U.S. Army observer group, popularly
dubbed "the Dixie Mission." The mission marked an extraordinary episode in Sino-American relations. The leaders of the
CCP demonstrated the most friendly feelings toward the
United States and indicated their desire for close postwar
economic and political ties.[5] Such behavior suggested a radi-

P'ing, "Kuo-chi hsing-shih yü wo kuo k'ang-chan" (The International Situation and
Our Country's Resistance War), Chieh-fang (January 16, 1939), no. 60–61, p. 17.

[4] On the role of the Soviet Union, see Wu K'o-chien, "Su-lien ho-p'ing cheng-
ts'e ti chen i-i" (The True Significance of the Soviet Union's Peace Policy), in Shih-
yueh ko-ming ti ching-yen yü Chung-kuo k'ang-chan (The Experiences of the October Revolution and China's Resistance War) (Chungking: Hsin-Hua Jih-pao Kuan,
1939); and Hsin-Hua jih-pao (hereafter HHJP), July 29, 1940. Both Mao and Yeh
Chien-ying discussed the question of possible Soviet suspensions of aid to China's
resistance war. See Yeh Chien-ying k'ang-chan yen-lun ch'i (Collected Messages of
Yeh Chien-ying on the Resistance War) (Chungking: Hsin-Hua Jih-pao Kuan, 1938),
pp. 62–64; and Mao Tse-tung, "Lun hsin chieh-tuan" (On the New Stage), in Chung-
kuo Kung-ch'an-tang ti liu-chung ch'üan-wei wen-chien (Documents of the Sixth
Plenum of the Central Committee of the Chinese Communist Party) (Chungking:
Hsin-Hua Jih-pao Kuan, 1939), p. 51.

[5] David D. Barrett, Dixie Mission: The United States Observer Group in Yenan,
1944 (Berkeley: California Center for Chinese Studies, 1970). For other discussions
of the background and substance of the mission, see James Reardon-Anderson,
Yenan and the Great Powers: The Origins of Chinese Communist Foreign Policy,
1944–1946 (New York: Columbia University Press, 1980), ch. 3; and John Gittings,
The World and China, 1922–1972 (New York: Harper and Row, 1974), pp. 99–115.

cal change in the Party's attitude toward Sino-American relations. The important question is how sincere, basic, and du-
rable the change was.

During the late 1930s and early 1940s, consistent with
their Leninist philosophy of a world divided into two camps,
when the CCP leadership spoke of a united front against the
fascists it assumed that the alliance would be transitory. It
was anticipated that as the war progressed, allies brought
together for limited common goals would become enemies
once more because of their different social systems. More
particularly it was taken for granted that the United States
and Great Britain would again confront China and the entire
revolutionary camp.

But the CCP's world view after 1943, following the Teheran Conference held in the early winter of that year, was
very different in character. It resembled the ideas being advanced by Earl Browder, general secretary of the American
Communist Party, most fully defined in his book *Teheran
and America* published in 1944. Browder's thesis, based on
the declarations of unity made by the Soviet Union, the
United States, and Great Britain at Teheran, was that the so-
called Big Three would form a single "democratic camp"
after the war in the interests of furthering democracy and
peace.

Later, in April 1945, when the principle of solidarity had
been reaffirmed by the Big Three at the Yalta Conference,
Mao summarized the CCP's views in his report to the Party's
Seventh Congress:

> The people, and only the people, is the motivating force
> of creation. The Soviet people has created a mighty force
> which was mainly responsible for the defeat of fascism. The
> strenuous efforts of the peoples of Britain, the United States,
> China, France and other anti-fascist nations made possible the
> defeat of the fascists, after which the peoples of these nations
> will build a world peace that is durable. . . .
>
> War has educated the people. They will win the war, the
> peace and progress. This is the rule of the new situation.

This new situation is radically different from that of the first World War and the so-called era of "peace" immediately following it. *At that time there was no Soviet Union as it is today; there was no such consciousness in the peoples of Britain, the United States, China, France and other anti-fascist nations as they now possess,* and consequently there could not be the solidarity shown by the world led by the three or the five major nations. We are in a totally new situation. We now have increasingly conscious and united people all over the world, as well as their organized forces, factors determining the direction of history and the path it takes.[6] (Italics added.)

One of the themes that characterized the CCP statements from late 1943 to 1945 was, therefore, that power was coming into the hands of the people throughout the world. There would be a "new democracy" which would involve a sharing of power among many classes. As the people became an increasingly compelling force they would intensify their pressure on the Big Three to remain allies after the war and so realize the democratization of the world and the establishment of a stable world order.[7]

The CCP did not, however, hail the conferences at Teheran and Yalta only because it believed they represented an Allied commitment to postwar unity. What particularly interested the Party was the attention accorded to the issue of coalition governments and to the criteria to be used in determining which political entities would receive Allied support.

The decisions reached at the conferences suggested that support would go to those elements most effective in fighting the fascists and most committed to democracy. Although public Yalta documents did not mention Asia, the CCP in-

---

[6] Mao Tse-tung, "On Coalition Government," in Stuart Gelder, *The Chinese Communists* (London: Victor Gollancz, 1946), p. 3. This is a translation of the original speech. The version in the *Selected Works* has been extensively rewritten.

[7] For another, similar discussion of this period, see Franz Schurman, *The Logic of World Power* (New York: Pantheon Books, 1974), pp. 213–16. Chinese Communist discussions along these lines are: Teng Ch'u-min, "Jen-min ti cheng-ch'uan" (People's Political Power), *Ch'ün-chung* (March 22, 1945), 10(3–4):85–91; and Teng Ch'u-min, "Hsin min-chu chih Fa-lan-hsi hsing" (New Democratic France), *ibid.*, (April 5, 1945), no. 5–6, pp. 163–68.

sisted that these standards were applicable throughout the world. For should these criteria be applied to China, the CCP could not fail to benefit.[8] The standards were effective ammunition against the Nationalist government for, if democratization was regarded as essential, the Kuomintang was damaging the country's international prestige.[9] More importantly, the application of such standards to China might result in the provision of military aid to the Communist armies and assure the Party a prominent place in the nation's government. Once this was accomplished, the CCP would gain further sustenance through its linkage with the growing tide of international democracy. A pointed commentary on Poland in 1945 noted that the "lawful" government in exile had lost legitimation to the "democratic" provisional government because the latter was in accord with the spirit of the times.[10]

By 1944–45, the Chinese Communist leaders had also come to recognize that for the time being in many of the decisions made by the Big Three the will of the United States would be decisive. As the Soviet Union was engulfed in the war with Germany, America was inevitably the major representative of the Allies in Asia. So it was in the spirit of the Teheran Conference, later to be confirmed and amplified at Yalta, that the CCP made its extraordinary approach to the Dixie Mission. Indeed from the moment that the mission landed in Yenan the Communists, both in their discussions with the members of the mission and in the CCP press, constantly reiterated two themes—that the Communist armies were the most effective fighting force against the Japanese, and that the CCP welcomed any efforts to bring democracy to China. In the latter connection Mao said to John S. Service, then a young Foreign Service officer who had joined the Dixie

---

[8] Yü Huai, "Tsung Ko-li-mi-ya tao Chiu-chin-shan" (From Crimea to San Francisco), *ibid.*, p. 151; and HHJP in *Chinese Press Review* (U.S. Embassy, Chungking) (hereafter CPR-C) (February 15, 1945), no. 41, pp. 1–2. See also Reardon-Anderson, *Yenan and the Great Powers*, pp. 93 and 98.

[9] HHJP in CPR-C (February 15, 1945), no. 41, p. 2.

[10] *Ibid.* (February 17, 1945), no. 43, pp. 4–5.

Mission, that "Interference . . . to further the interests of the people of China is not interference."[11]

In the discussions between the CCP leaders and the members of the Dixie Mission both sides were expansive. Mao spoke warmly and positively of America's important role in the economic and political life of postwar China. But, despite his obvious awareness of the dominance of American power in Asia, his comments did not imply that the Chinese Communists wanted an exceptional or exclusive relationship with the United States. Given the Teheran—and later the Yalta—view that the Great Powers were partners working in tandem for postwar goals, the CCP leaders, according to their own statements, saw no need to choose between the United States and the Soviet Union. Indeed the dominant role of the United States in China appeared to be the result of a division of labor. As Mao suggested, the intervention of the United States in Chinese affairs in order to promote democracy might be more effective than that of the USSR given the Kuomintang's anti-Soviet feelings.[12]

The attempt of the Chinese Communist leaders at the time of the Dixie Mission to effect a rapprochement with the United States was thus neither a ploy to mislead Washington nor an unconditional request for ties with the United States government. It was sincere but very conditional. It was based on the concept of a global environment of Soviet-American cooperation in which Washington's policy was motivated by impulses other than imperialist interest. If the environment changed so would the CCP's expectations about the nature of its relations with the United States.

Would such a change occur? Despite the Party's publicly expressed confidence in the future,[13] there were always

---

[11] Joseph W. Esherick, ed., *Lost Chance in China: The World War II Dispatches of John S. Service* (New York: Random House, 1974), pp. 301–2.

[12] *Ibid.*, p. 306. Okabe makes a similar point in "The Cold War and China," p. 228.

[13] *Chieh-fang jih-pao*, July 7, 1944, and February 17, 1945; and Yü, "Tsung Ko-li-mi-ya."

strong undercurrents of doubt. Two elements of the earlier united front conceptualization persisted even after Teheran: the special place of the Soviet Union and distrust of the imperialist states. Thus in the quotation from Mao given above there is the suggestion that the very existence of the Soviet Union was an assurance of postwar peace. Other Party statements argued that because the Soviet Union was the most democratic nation and the one most committed to peace, its role would be the "greatest" or "most important" in the postwar era.[14] In the bourgeois states, it was acknowledged, enlightened elements favored continued cooperation. But popular pressure would be needed to ensure that reactionary forces did not push policy toward a restoration of the prewar system. As Mao asserted, it was "the people," with the Communists implicitly at their core, that counted.[15]

In short, although after 1943 the Party spoke of a new international system, born during the war, in which in principle all members of the democratic front were equal, it never abandoned the earlier belief that in reality gradations remained. The Party made no secret of its commitment to the Soviet Union and its concern over possible regression in Anglo-American policy.

Beginning with the close of 1944 a series of developments intensified this concern. In Europe, the conflicts over Greece and Poland indicated the persisting strength of anti-Soviet and antidemocratic forces in the United States and Great Britain and their determination to disrupt Allied unity and reverse the global democratic tide.[16] In Asia the same elements were pressing for the restoration of imperialist rule and the perpetuation of the Kuomintang dictatorship. The

[14]*Chieh-fang jih-pao*, November 7, 1944; and *HHJP* in *CPR-C* (February 10, 1945), no. 37, p. 2. For a further discussion of the special place of the Soviet Union, see Okabe, "The Cold War and China," pp. 229–30.

[15]Yü, "Tsung Ko-li-mi-ya"; and *HHJP* in *CPR-C* (February 10, 1945), no. 37, p. 7.

[16]*Chieh-fang jih-pao*, September 13, November 27, and December 21, 1944; and *HHJP* in *CPR-C* (January 8, 1945), no. 6, p. 3. See also Reardon-Anderson, *Yenan and the Great Powers*, p. 91.

pro-Kuomintang statements of Ambassador Patrick J. Hurley and America's policy of continuing aid to the Chinese Nationalists while withholding assistance from the Communists both seemed to confirm a disturbing trend. Under the circumstances, President Roosevelt's death in April 1945 must have heightened the CCP's misgivings about the future.

Mao incorporated these misgivings in his report to the Party's Seventh Congress in which he established the line for the CCP's views of the postwar world. The Yalta Conference had been warmly welcomed; the passage from Mao's report that has been quoted encapsulates his optimistic assessment. But on the pessimistic side he stated that the "disunity-advocating reactionaries" were attempting to use their "still considerable strength" to prevent the development of a progressive postwar international system. Mao suggested that certain events, if they took place, would indicate the power of the reactionaries: the negotiation of a less-than-unconditional surrender of Japan that would leave its imperial system relatively intact; the attempt, with the help of certain Chinese, to bring foreign troops to China to promote counterrevolution as in Greece; the extension of further aid to the Kuomintang; the perpetuation of colonialism; and the promotion of anti-Soviet propaganda.[17]

Should the reactionaries appear to be succeeding in their ultimate objective of moving the international world away from cooperation toward confrontation, Mao implied that the CCP would return to its pre-Teheran position of a cautious approach to the imperialists and close alignment with the Soviet Union. Mao could not have made such a suggestion publicly in April 1945 as it might have called into question the entire concept of Big Three cooperation. But in his confidential comments to the Congress, he indicated that the pre-Teheran view was never far from the surface of his thinking:

> Political reality and practice demonstrate that in the international arena the Soviet Union is our single and best friend. *All the rest are so-called Allies.*

---

[17] Mao, "On Coalition Government," *passim.*

We must resolutely stand for an alliance with England and America.

However, England has placed General Scobie in Greece for its own interests not those of the people. If they want to do this in China we will not agree. We will not permit "Scobieism."

We must be vigilant. Some foreigners support Chiang Kai-shek; they step forward as peacemakers, like some sort of gods. If we tear off their masks, then a hideous face is revealed. (Italics added. The last sentence is an obvious reference to Ambassador Hurley.) [18]

1945–1947: The Drift to Confrontation

As World War II ended, the CCP's attitude toward the international situation was thus an unstable amalgam of high expectations and profound skepticism. This attitude persisted until the late summer of 1946. Events did not seem to justify an exclusive adherence either to the Teheran faith in postwar international cooperation or the Leninist conviction that the world was divided into two basically hostile camps.

It was an unstable world during the summer of 1945. In Europe the Allies were struggling with the immense problems of the new postwar era. In Asia, where the Soviets had entered the conflict only at the last moment, the situation was still obscure. As the Great Powers jockeyed for position in both areas the Party began to express a new dichotomous world view. It spoke of "two political lines" (*liang-wu cheng-chih lu-hsien*) in international politics. The attributes of each were predictable. On the one side were those who would promote democracy, eradicate fascism, and preserve unity; on

[18] A Kuomintang source passed on to the U.S. embassy a purported CCP document that spoke of the alliance with the Western imperialists in the utilitarian manner characteristic of the united front approach. Gittings, *The World and China*, p. 108. The private comments are taken from the notes of P. P. Vladimirov, the TASS correspondent in Yenan. They are translated and reproduced in Steven I. Levine, *Mao Tse-tung's Oral Report to the Seventh Congress of the CCP: Summary Notes*, Rand Corporation Memo P6007 (Santa Monica: The Rand Corporation, 1976), p. 18.

the other were the forces opposed to those goals and dedicated to the restoration of the prewar system.[19]

The CCP consistently emphasized its strong support of the Soviet Union. Admittedly the Party must have been disappointed by the agreements Moscow concluded with the Chinese Nationalists in the summer of 1945. But it persistently defended the Soviets' actions, often at great domestic political cost, and never swerved from the line that the USSR best represented the interests of the democratic forces of the world.[20] Moreover the CCP faithfully participated in the International Communist campaigns of 1945 such as the anti-Browder movement repudiating some of Browder's earlier actions, particularly his dissolution of the Communist Party of the United States in 1944.[21]

The Chinese Communists' attitude toward the United States was far more ambivalent. They believed that Washington was under pressure from both the reactionary and democratic elements in the United States. The CCP had always expected the American reactionaries, who had opposed such developments as the conclusion of the Teheran agreements during the war, to continue their disruptive activities even after the war was over. But throughout the summer and fall of 1945, the CCP press emphasized the importance of the

---

[19] Ju Shui, "Lun Chiu-chin-shan hui-i ti-i chieh-tuan ti ch'eng-chiu" (On the Accomplishments of the First Stage of the San Francisco Meeting), Ch'ün-chung (June 1, 1945), 10(10):328 and 333, and Yü Huai, "Lun shih-chieh cheng-chü" (On the World Situation), Ibid. (June 25, 1945), 11(12):366–71, adumbrate this view.

[20] Thus, for example, in February 1946 the CCP defended the Soviets' unpopular occupation of the northeast. See English Language Supplement to News Service of Hsin Hwa Jih Pao (Hereafter Hsin Hwa Supplement), February 15 and 27, 1946; and Reardon-Anderson, "Yenan and the Great Powers," pp. 174–77. China's need to align with the Soviet Union was suggested when Ch'ün Chung published an article on Sun Yat-sen's three great policies, one of which was alliance with the Soviet Union. Tzu K'o-shih, "Sun Chung-shan hsien-sheng lun san ta cheng-ts'e" (Mr. Sun Yat-sen's Three Great Policies), Ch'ün Chung (October 25, 1945), 10(21–22):815–16. See also Okabe, "The Cold War and China," p. 230.

[21] Chieh-fang jih-pao, July 31 and August 1, 1945. In his telegram to the American Communist Party Mao did express appreciation for Browder's services to the Chinese "people's struggle." But this in no way diluted the attack on the Browder "line." Ibid., July 31, 1945.

right-wing factions in the United States to an unprecedented degree. It declared that they were urging the Truman administration to follow an antidemocratic and anti-Soviet policy worldwide.[22] It further asserted that, in regard to Asia, they were attempting to persuade Washington to settle for a less-than-unconditional surrender of Japan while promoting the conflict between the Chinese Communists and the Kuomintang, using the latter to gain control of China.[23] From this time on the CCP took the position that the civil war in China was directly attributable to the influence of reactionary circles in America.[24]

The CCP also believed however that, with the strong support of the American people and certain unnamed "government officials," the democratic forces in the United States were trying to convince Washington of the wisdom of disassociating itself from the Kuomintang and at least considering the grant of some aid to the Chinese Communists. With its staunch faith in the growing power of public opinion, the Party thought that the United States government might yet follow an enlightened course in China. It therefore adopted a flexible attitude, warning Washington and the Chinese peo-

[22] Ibid., July 13, 1945; and Yü Huai, "Tung-wen chung ti shih-chieh ta-chü" (The World Situation Is Heating Up), Ch'ün-chung (November 25, 1945), 10(21):734. The CCP went as far as to claim that some of the reactionary elements sought to take the place of Japan and that the military, in their service, was seeking to undercut a favorable policy toward China. "Mei-chün ying li-yin ting-chih tsan-chia Chung-kuo nei-chan" (The American Military Should Stop Interfering in China's Civil War), ibid., p. 774.

[23] See, for example, Yü Huai, "Lun t'o-hsieh wei-ch'i" (On the Danger of Compromise), ibid. (August 5, 1945), no. 15, pp. 507–8; Yü Huai, "Chung-yang Jih-pen yin-mou" (Alarm at Japanese Plots), ibid. (September 15, 1945), no. 17, 602–4; HHJP in CPR-C (June 3, 1945), no. 149, p. 9; HHJP in ibid. (August 21, 1945), no. 226, p. 8; and Hsin Hwa Supplement (December 8, 1945), p. A-20. Also important for CCP views during this period are Mao's articles on Hurley appearing in Chieh-fang jih-pao, July 11, 13, and 20, 1945. Only the first and third articles were later published in the Selected Works.

[24] HHJP in CPR-C (November 6, 1945), no. 300, p. 3. This bitter commentary on American policy was typical of CCP statements during the fall of 1945 as the battle for the northeast developed. The discussion that follows of American policy and Chinese views of that policy has benefited immensely from the earlier work of Gittings (The World and China, pp. 116–38) and Reardon-Anderson (Yenan and the Great Powers, ch. 6–10).

ple of the dangers inherent in America's current policy while maintaining hopes of a turn for the better.[25]

By the end of 1945 these hopes seemed justified. On November 27 Ambassador Hurley resigned, issuing a scorching attack on America's China policy. Within a few hours President Truman appointed George C. Marshall to undertake a mission to China to mediate the civil war. On December 15 the president issued a statement favoring a "strong, united and democratic China." The CCP responded to these developments by declaring that the "Hurley line" had been defeated and President Roosevelt's policy had triumphed.[26] Once again—it was to be the last time—the Party press spoke of a democratic China with American economic assistance emerging in a world of three-power cooperation.[27]

Marshall was warmly welcomed on his arrival in China. Nevertheless the CCP remained on the alert for any sign that the reactionaries might be strengthening their influence over America's foreign policy in general, and her China policy in particular.

By the summer of 1946, in the CCP's view, such signs were all too apparent. The effort to establish a genuine truce between the Chinese Communists and the Kuomintang, which had started at the beginning of the Marshall mission, broke down completely by the end of June. As a full-scale civil war developed in the north, the CCP felt that Washington was doing little to restrain the Nationalists. Worse yet, the Kuomintang armies now fighting the Communists had been transported to the areas of combat and supplied with weapons by the United States. Yet the United States continued to claim impartiality and to preach peace. To the CCP

[25] *HHJP* in *CPR-C* (November 2, 1945), no. 296, pp. 1–2. The issue of sympathetic elements in the American government is raised in *Chieh-fang jih-pao*, June 25, 1945, and July 7, 1945.

[26] *Hsin-Hwa Supplement*, December 20, 1945, p. B-41.

[27] *Ibid.*, December 8, 1945, p. A-20.

American policy seemed patently hypocritical.[28] The Party was, reportedly, convinced that the balance of power in the United States had shifted to the reactionaries who predictably were encouraging their client, the Chiang Kai-shek regime, to make war on the Chinese Communists.[29]

The sense that reactionary elements were shaping America's China policy seemed substantiated by the direction of Washington's global policy. The Chinese Communists had always believed that in order to understand the United States' actions in China it was necessary to examine its actions elsewhere. While it exonerated President Truman, the CCP saw imperialist elements behind Winston Churchill's "Iron Curtain" speech delivered at Fulton, Missouri, in March, and the growing anti-Soviet, anti-Communist mood that increasingly seemed to characterize Anglo-American policy. Indeed the Party claimed that this mood had influenced "reactionaries" in China.[30]

The slide away from cooperation and toward confrontation with the United States began in June with a strong anti-American campaign. On June 26 Mao personally denounced

[28] This point is made quite forcefully by Michael Lindsay in "Post-mortem on American Mediation in China," *International Journal* (1947), 2:207. See also Dorothy Borg, "American Loses Chinese Good Will," *Far Eastern Survey* (February 23, 1949), 18(4):38–39, for a more general discussion of Chinese public opinion. Lo Lung-chi, of the Democratic League, told Marshall that American support was the cause of CCP bitterness. See U.S., Department of State, *Foreign Relations of the United States* (hereafter FR), 1946, 9:929. Finally, Charles McLane argues that Soviet policy toward China underwent a "fundamental shift" during this period, as attacks on the Kuomintang and American policy dominated Soviet discussion. See Charles B. McLane, *Soviet Policy and the Chinese Communists, 1931–1946* (New York: Columbia University Press, 1958), pp. 249–60.

[29] Lindsay, "Post-mortem," p. 207.

[30] *Hsin-Hwa Supplement*, March 17, 1946, p. 256, and March 14, 1946, p. 242; and Reardon-Anderson, *Yenan and the Great Powers*, p. 184. For later discussions that emphasize the global context of America's retrogressive policies in China during the spring of 1946, see, for example, Ch'en Chia-kang, "Kuo-Mei ho-tso tsao-ch'eng ch'üan-mien fen-lieh" (Kuomintang-American Cooperation Is Creating Total Division), *Ch'ün-chung* (October 20, 1946), 13(1):10–11; and Ch'iao Mu, "Chieh-ch'uan Mei ti-kuo-chu-i ti ch'i-p'ien" (Exposing the Swindles of American Imperialism), *Cheng-pao* (December 30, 1946), no. 20, pp. 415–16.

a bill before the U.S. Congress designed to provide for the training and arming of Kuomintang forces.[31] The Party proclaimed that rather than condemning the Kuomintang's militaristic actions, the United States was encouraging them. The United States was no longer to be considered an honest broker. As one Party statement put it, America was pursuing two policies—one to assist Chiang Kai-shek in fighting the civil war which, it said, was "fundamental," the other to persuade Chiang to stop the civil war, which was purely "ornamental."[32]

Nevertheless there were still some limits to the June campaign. Although Marshall was not spared criticism, the Party implied at times that his mission was being undermined by other United States officials.[33] Upon occasion, it went even further and expressed the hope that Washington would return to Roosevelt's China policy.[34]

But in mid-September the Party stopped equivocating. It amplified the anti-American themes in its public statements. It ceased to draw distinctions between American policy makers and condemned the Truman administration's policy toward China as unadultered imperialism. As the Chinese Communist leaders abandoned any idea of a coalition with the Nationalists and picked up the civil war where they had left off, before the Marshall mission at the end of 1945, they told the Chinese people to "wipe out any illusions about the United States Government." The United States had "the power and means to wage the third World War and turn

[31] Mao Tse-tung chi (The Collected Works of Mao Tse-tung) (Tokyo: Kokubosha, 1973), 10:45–46. See also Gittings, China and the World, ch. 6, for a similar discussion of summer-fall 1946.

[32] Tang Tsou, America's Failure in China, 1941–1950 (Chicago: University of Chicago Press, 1963), p. 430.

[33] "Ch'i-ko yüeh tsung-chieh" (Seven-month Summary), Cheng-pao (August 21, 1946), no. 4, pp. 79–80; and "Shih-hsing Mo-szu-k'o hui-i chüeh-ting ti shih-hou tao-le" (The Time Has Come to Realize the Agreements of the Moscow Meeting), ibid., p. 81.

[34] Yü T'ung, "Shei tsai 'fan-Mei' " (Who Is "Opposing the United States?"), ibid. (July 21, 1946), no. 1, p. 8.

Japan and China into war bases." America, in short, was now enemy number one.[35]

The CCP's shift to an unconditionally hard line in mid-September was basically the culmination of the distrust that had been festering all summer. But it was triggered by two events. One was the conclusion of an agreement on August 30 by which the United States sold surplus war supplies with a procurement value of nearly $1 billion to the Chinese Nationalists at bargain rates. The other was a statement by Vice-Admiral Charles M. Cooke, Jr., commander of the Seventh Fleet, that the United States Navy would remain in China, a statement which to the Chinese Communists suggested the possibility of direct military intervention.[36]

The CCP now spoke of the Kuomintang as America's instrument, comparing it to "traitors" like the Dowager Empress and Wang Ching-wei. The Civil Air Transport Agreement and the commercial treaty (The Treaty of Friendship, Commerce and Navigation), which were negotiated between Washington and Nanking in the autumn and early winter of 1946, were condemned as the most unequal of unequal treaties. The signing of the commercial treaty became the occasion for a Communist-declared National Humiliation Day. By November the Party was claiming that Chiang had turned the economic, political, and military control of China over to the United States.[37]

The CCP's strategy for eliminating United States control was the old united front policy in both domestic and foreign affairs. At home, appealing to the broad spectrum of Chinese society that was increasingly demanding an end to American

[35] *Chieh-fang jih-pao*, in United States Information Service, Shanghai, *For Your Information*, September 14, 1946.

[36] *Ibid.; Hsin-Hwa Supplement*, August 30, September 5 and 7, 1946.

[37] Wang Tsung-i, "Kuo-min-tang tang-chü ch'u-mai Chung-kuo" (The Kuomintang Authorities Sell Out China), *Ch'ün-chung* (December 2, 1946), 13(7):10–11; "T'an Chung-Mei shang-yueh" (On the Chinese-American Trade Treaty), *ibid.* (November 11, 1946), no. 4, p. 9; *For Your Information*, December 9, 1946; and *Hsin-Hwa Supplement*, September 26, 1946, and December 2, 1946.

intervention in China,[38] the party sought to evoke the spirit that had prevailed during the halcyon days of the anti-Japanese struggle:

Yesterday we raised high the flag of the anti-Japanese national united front. Under that flag we united people of the whole country from various classes and various strata and avoided national extinction. Today we again must raise a new flag in the name of creating a national patriotic united front for independence, peace and democracy.[39]

In its foreign relations the CCP adopted a variety of measures to strengthen its connections abroad. To promote the movement in the United States for the withdrawal of the American military presence in China, an appeal was made to the United Nations and Yenan announced the inauguration of English-language broadcasts.[40]

And so, according to the CCP's perception, in little more than a year after the end of the war in the Pacific, the Teheran concept of postwar international cooperation died. The Chinese Communists never resurrected it. Instead they fell back on their old prewar Leninist assumptions about the nature of international affairs. Allies drawn together during the war by common but limited goals were now dividing on the basis of fundamental interests that conflicted. The United States was building a worldwide anti-Soviet Axis. It was following an aggressive policy in such countries as Iran and Greece as well as in China.[41] Opposing the United States and other im-

---

[38] Suzanne Pepper discusses the nature of this mood in her *Civil War in China* (Berkeley: University of California Press, 1978), pp. 52–93. See also Borg, "America Loses China's Good Will," pp. 38–40.

[39] "K'uo-ta ai-kuo t'ung-i chan-hsien" (Enlarge the Patriotic United Front), *Ch'ün-chung* (December 22, 1946), 13(10):3.

[40] *Chieh-fang jih-pao*, October 24, 1946; and *Newscast from Yenan*, October 19, 20, and 21, 1946. The latter source was found at the John K. Fairbank Center for East Asian Research, Harvard University.

[41] "Kuo-chi i-chou" (The International Week), *Ch'ün-chung* (December 16, 1946), 13(9):24; and Huang Tso-liang, "Shei shih Mei ti-kuo-chu-i k'uo-chang cheng-ts'e ti shou-hai-chih" (Who Is Hurt by the Expansionist Policies of the American Imperialists?), *ibid.*, pp. 22–23.

perialist elements were "the world democratic forces" with the Soviet Union as the "main pillar." China's place was with these forces.[42]

1947–1950: "Lean to One Side"

As indicated at the outset of this paper I do not share the widely held view that Mao's "lean-to-one-side" pronouncement, made in his speech "On the People's Democratic Dictatorship" delivered on June 30, 1949, was a benchmark in the CCP's foreign policy. Statements issued by the Party from 1946 on anticipated almost every major theme in the foreign policy section of Mao's address. Mao merely took the occasion of the Party's twenty-eighth anniversary to summarize and confirm what the CCP had been saying. As Ambassador J. Leighton Stuart reported to Washington, Mao was "simply dotting i's and crossing t's."[43]

The idea that Mao's speech was a benchmark is coupled with the assumption that until June 1949 the CCP followed an open-ended policy and could as readily have regularized relations with the United States as with the Soviet Union. But this was not the case. A pro-American policy would have required a reversal of the course the Chinese Communists had been pursuing for almost three years, the logic and momentum of which ran against any kind of accommodation with the United States. During the summer of 1949 it became clear that the CCP leadership would not, and perhaps could not, pay the political price of such a drastic reversal. With scarcely any hesitation, the Party leadership carried to its culmination the policy conceived in late 1946.

[42] Lu Ting-i, "Explanation of Several Basic Questions Concerning the Post-War International Situation," in Lyman P. Van Slyke, ed., The China White Paper (Stanford: Stanford University Press, 1967), p. 714. This memorandum was issued in January 1947. However, it clearly reflected the mood that had begun developing toward the end of 1946. See for example Ch'en Chia-kang, "K'uo-ta kuo-chi ho-p'ing t'ung-i chan-hsien" (Broaden the International Peace United Front), Ch'ün-chung (December 30, 1946), 13(11–12):26–28.

[43] FR, 1949, 8:406.

The section that follows is divided into two parts. In the first I trace the development of the lean-to-one side policy after January 1947. In the second I describe the elements that made unlikely a change in the direction of the CCP's course in 1949.

1947–1949—The United Front Against Imperialism

In January 1947, Lu Ting-yi, chief of the Chinese Communist Party's Department of Information, published a memorandum suggesting the CCP's return to the Leninist concept of a two-camp world divided between the imperialist and democratic forces.[44]

To the CCP leaders the events of the next few months only confirmed the two-camp thesis. They regarded the Truman Doctrine, proclaimed in March, as a "challenge" of war by the United States to "the people of the world." Americans were using anti-Soviet slogans to enslave all nations as the German and Japanese fascists had before them. When the Marshall Plan was announced in June, the Party leaders saw it as an attempt by the United States to rule Europe and create a West European anti-Soviet bloc with Germany at its core. They moreover believed that the United States was making a similar effort to dominate Asia and build an Asian anti-Soviet bloc with Japan at its center.[45]

The CCP leadership also became convinced that the United States government's policy toward the revolutionary movement in China was part of its policy toward revolutionary movements in general. In the Chinese Communists' view Washington was using the Truman Doctrine to smash all united front governments and to encourage reactionary

---

[44] Lu, "Explanation," pp. 710–19.

[45] Shu Yueh, "Tu-lu-men hsiang shih-chieh jen-min t'iao-chan" (Truman Challenges the People of the World to War), Ch'ün-chung (Hong Kong) (March 27, 1947), no. 9, p. 14; Newscasts from Yenan, April 25, 1947; and Shu Yueh, "Ma-hsieh-a chi-hua yü Pa-li hui-i" (The Marshall Plan and the Paris Conference), Cheng-pao (July 5, 1947), no. 45, p. 925.

factions to attack Communist parties wherever they existed. In addition, through its aid programs, the United States was attempting to compel other nations to join a global counter-revolutionary movement.[46]

In September 1947, at the meeting which marked the founding of the Cominform, Andrei Zhdanov, one of the foremost officials of the USSR, formally announced the Soviet Union's return to the two-camp view of the international order which had played such an important role in Soviet foreign policy before World War II. The CCP enthusiastically endorsed the Soviets' stand. This is not surprising given its own movement toward the two-camp doctrine since the beginning of the year.[47]

But equally importantly, the Party used Zhdanov's pronouncement to stress the impossibility of remaining neutral in a bipolar world and the necessity of choosing between one side or the other. As Ch'iao Kuan-hua, then an unofficial spokesman of the Party in Hong Kong, wrote in December 1947:

[There is] the world's great division: on the one side is the imperialist anti-democratic camp, on the other side is the democratic anti-imperialist camp headed by the Soviet Union. The struggle between the two camps has spread to all corners of the world. Any

[46] Ch'iao Mu, "Lun Tu-lu-men chu-i ti po-sheng" (The Bankruptcy of the Truman Doctrine), Ch'ün-chung (Hong Kong) (July 3, 1947), no. 23, pp. 16–20.

[47] The evolution of the bipolar view can be found in Lu, "Explanation"; Shu Yueh, "Tui Te ho-yü ti cheng-chih wen-t'i" (Questions of Disagreement in the German Peace Treaty), Cheng-pao (March 15, 1947), no. 29, p. 611; and Chang T'ieh-sheng, "Shih-chieh jen-min t'ung-i chan-hsien ti chien-yü" (The Future of the World People's United Front), ibid. (July 5, 1947), no. 45, p. 8.

Here my analysis differs slightly from that of Okabe, who, following Gittings, sees a " ' three bloc' approach to world politics" from January 1947 until the end of the year. CCP articles are quite complex in their meaning during this period because they are aimed at several different audiences including the Chinese public and, possibly, the Soviet Union. While there are some subtle differences in the foreign policy view when compared to later statements, suffice it to say that I believe the idea that there were two "lines" or "fronts" in the world and that China's place was with the democratic forces is the essence of the view even before the Zhdanov speech. The Soviet leader's speech made the two-camp idea explicit and exclusivistic. See Okabe, "The Cold War and China," pp. 230–36; and Gittings, The World and China, pp. 142–48.

person, any group, any nation must choose between these two great camps. Between these two great camps there is no independent but middle way. Even less is there a "bridge" mediating the Soviet Union and the United States.[48]

Again, after Tito's expulsion from the Cominform in the early summer of 1948, the CCP joined the anti-Tito campaign and used Yugoslavia as an example to drive home the one-side-or-the-other principle.[49] It declared that, having abandoned the Soviet Union, Yugoslavia was now being entrapped by the United States. A similar fate would befall China if it attempted to become a third force standing between the two great powers.[50]

The CCP's strong opposition to the development of a third-force foreign policy was in part due to its awareness of a growing sentiment in China in favor of neutrality between the United States and the Soviet Union. The CCP leadership felt that if such a sentiment gained ground it would detract from the Party's influence domestically since it had publicly aligned itself with the Soviet Union. But the Party was also motivated by a genuine concern that a desire for neutrality would pave the way for the restoration of American imperialist influence in China once the strong anti-American feeling, sparked by the civil war, had diminished. Support of Zhdanov's statement and the prompt denunciation of Yugo-

[48] Ch'iao Mu, "Yin shih-chieh min-chu fan-tui tou-cheng hsin chieh-tuan" (Welcome the New Stage of the World Democratic Anti-Imperialist Struggle), Ch'ün-chung (Hong Kong) (January 1, 1948), no. 49, p. 6.

[49] For the text of the Central Committee resolution on the expulsion of the Yugoslav Communist Party from the Cominform, see New China News Agency, North Shensi, July 11, 1948, p. 102.

[50] In an article written for the Cominform journal on the anniversary of the October Revolution in 1948, Mao emphasized this theme. This section was dropped from later versions of this article. Compare Mao Tse-tung chi (10 vols.; Tokyo: 1970–73, compiled by Takeuchi Minoru), 10:186, with Selected Works of Mao Tse-tung, vol. 4 (Peking: Foreign Languages Press, 1967), p. 284. The other important CCP commentary on the anti-Tito campaign of 1948 is Liu Shao-ch'i, "Lun kuo-chi chu-i yü min-tsu chu-i" (On Internationalism and Nationalism) (Hong Kong: Hsin-min Chu-i Ch'u-pan-she, 1949). See also Ch'en Yu-ju, "Kuo-chi chu-i ho Chung-kuo min-tsu chieh-fang yün-tung" (Internationalism and China's National Liberation Movement), Ch'ün-chung (Hong Kong) (August 19, 1948), no. 32, pp. 9–12.

slavia were therefore, in large measure, ways of expressing to a domestic audience the Party's disapproval of any effort to promote a neutral China.

While the CCP used the anti-Tito campaign to discredit indirectly the idea of a relationship between China and the United States, it also advanced a variety of arguments designed to undermine the American image in China more directly. The diplomatic history of the war and the postwar period was rewritten to emphasize the very conditional nature of America's adherence to the Grand Alliance and, thus, to erase the Teheran view. The United States, according to the new interpretation, had planned to pull out of the alliance from the beginning; policy was already changing in 1944 under Hurley's influence; the Marshall mission was nothing more than an attempt to fool the Chinese people; the United States had persistently adhered to one goal—the enslavement of China.[51]

Doggedly, from 1947 to 1949, the CCP criticized those who felt that American policy would change. Deals could not be made with the imperialist policy makers in Washington, whether Democratic or Republican. Contradictions between the United States and the Kuomintang could not be exploited. To suppose otherwise was simply unrealistic.[52]

---

[51] Ch'en Po-ta, *Jen-min kung-ti Chiang Chieh-shih* (Chiang Kai-shek, the People's Enemy) (Hong Kong: Cheng-pao Ch'u-pan-she, 1948), chs. 4 and 5; Chang T'ieh-sheng, "Fan fa-hsi-sze chan-cheng hou ti kuo-chi mao-tun" (International Contradictions after the Anti-Fascist War), *Cheng-pao* (March 22, 1947), no. 30, pp. 645–46; and Liu Ta-nien, *Mei ch'in Hua chien-shih* (A Short History of American Aggression against China) (Peking: Hsin Hua Shu-tien, 1950), chs. 3 and 4. The final book was a republication of a book written in 1948.

[52] Ts'ui Wei, "Ma-hsieh-a ti hsin ts'e-lueh" (Marshall's New Strategy), *Cheng-pao* (February 8, 1947), no. 24, pp. 14–15; Ch'iao Mu, "Fan-tui Mei ti chün-shih kan-she" (Oppose American Military Intervention), *Ch'ün-chung* (Hong Kong) (April 8, 1948), pp. 13–15; Ch'iao Mu, "Mei-ti ti hsin yin-mou" (New Plots of American Imperialism), *ibid.*, November 4, 1948, pp. 4–5, 24; Ch'iao Mu, *Ti Mei-kuo ti sui-ming* (Predicting America's Future) (Hong Kong: Chung-kuo Ch'u-pan-she, 1947), pp. 141–48; Ts'ui Wei, "Mei-kuo chia-shen Chung-kuo jen-min ti tsai-nan" (America Increases the Chinese People's Difficulties), *Cheng-pao* (February 28, 1947), no. 27, pp. 15–17; and Ch'iao Mu, "Fan-tui Chiang-Jih-Mei ho-liu" (Oppose the Cooperation between Chiang, Japan, and the United States), *ibid.* (August 23, 1947), no. 51, pp. 3–6.

According to the CCP's analysis, one of the key factors in the existing American policy toward China was the reconstruction of Japan. The United States was determined to control China through the use of Japanese men and materiel. It was therefore attempting to revive militarism in Japan rather than eradicate it.[53] It was also building Japan into a great industrial power while ensuring that China would remain an agricultural country. As a consequence, China was in danger of becoming the colony of a country it had supposedly defeated in a long and destructive war.[54]

In the CCP's view, the policy of the United States toward China was, moreover, only a segment of an overall plan designed to establish an anti-Communist, antirevolutionary Asia under American domination. To realize this objective, the administration in Washington was encouraging cooperation between the leaders of Nationalist China, the Philippines, and Korea; preparing to turn Taiwan into an American base; and seeking to convert South Korea into another Manchukuo.[55]

The CCP believed that the threat from the United States would increase rather than diminish as the Kuomintang

[53] "Mei-ti fu-Jih ti chen-hsiang" (The True Picture of American Imperialist Plots to Aid Japan), Ch'ün-chung (Hong Kong) (April 22, 1948), 2(15):2–4.

[54] New China News Agency, "Mei-kuo liang-nien-lai tui-Jih kuan-chih cheng-ts'e" (America's Governing Policy toward Japan over the Past Two Years), ibid., (September 11, 1947), no. 33, p. 3; "Mei-ti fu-Jih," passim; Foreign Broadcast Information Service (hereafter FBIS), August 6, 1947; Ch'iao, Ti Mei-kuo ti sui-ming, pp. 106–13; Shu Yueh, "Chiang-Jih ti kou-chieh" (Chiang and Japan in League), Ch'ün-chung (Hong Kong) (April 22, 1948), 2(15):5–6; and Ch'iao Mu, "Fan-tui hsin 'Jih-Wang hsieh-ting' " (Oppose the new "Japan-Wang Agreement"), ibid. (July 15, 1948), no. 27, pp. 7–8.

[55] Ch'iao Mu, "Fan-tui Chiang-Jih-Mei ho-liu"; New China News Agency, North Shensi, December 8, 1947, p. 1, and April 29, 1948, pp. 1–2; Shu Yu, "K'an Mei-ti ti hsin yin-mou" (Look at American Imperialism's New Plots), Cheng-pao (August 21, 1948), no. 103, pp. 4–6; Chih Chung, "Chiang-Mei tsai T'ai-wan ti yin-mou" (The Plots of the United States and Chiang in Taiwan), Ch'ün Chung (Hong Kong) (October 9, 1947), no. 37, 22; Hui Shu-yüan, "Tsung Jih-Han-Chiang t'ung-meng tao A-chou lien-meng" (From the Japan-Korea-Chiang Alliance to the Asian Alliance), ibid. (October 14, 1948), 2(40):11–12; and "Fan-tui 'Chung-Jih-Han lien-meng' " (Oppose the "China-Japan-Korea Alliance"), ibid. (August 19, 1948), no. 32, pp. 10–11.

came closer to defeat. A Nationalist collapse or near-collapse would be met by an effort on the part of the Truman administration to tighten the net it was constructing around China. In the autumn of 1948 the Communist press emphasized this theme in particular, giving broad coverage to an alleged American plan to operate out of Tokyo a counterrevolutionary spy network that would use middle-of-the-road or third-force elements to promote subversion in China and provoke splits in the revolutionary camp.[56]

By the beginning of 1949 all the pieces of the Chinese Communists' foreign policy were in place. Abroad, the CCP was adhering to the course, instituted two years earlier, of aligning itself with the Soviet Union and other anti-imperialist nations and movements against the imperialist powers.[57] Within China, the Communists were continuing their efforts to build a united front of all democratic peoples in opposition to the reactionaries abroad and at home. Here nationalism was the rallying cry. The party used it in the belief that it had an appeal not only for the Chinese people in general but also for many Chinese intellectuals who were reluctant to support the CCP partly because, on a patriotic basis, they objected to its close association with the Soviet Union.[58]

In its public pronouncements, the CCP stressed certain nationalistic themes. It persistently depicted Chiang Kai-shek as a traitor who was selling China's independence to the United States by making major concessions in return for American support. In contrast the CCP presented itself as the

[56]Lin Shih-fu, "Chung-kuo ko-ming sheng-li ho Mei-kuo tui Hua cheng-ts'e" (China's Revolutionary Victory and America's Policy toward China), *ibid.* (November 25, 1948), no. 46, pp. 4–6; *FBIS*, November 1, 1948, pp. CCC 3–7; *New China News Agency, North Shensi*, October 31, 1948, pp. 1–3.

[57]For example, *FBIS*, March 15, 1948, p. CCC-1; and Liu Ning-i, "Shih-chieh kung-lien yü Chung-kuo kung-jen" (The World Labor Union and Chinese Workers), *Ch'ün-chung* (Hong Kong) (June 26, 1947), no. 22, pp. 6–8. For a better sense of the full scope of CCP activities in these organizations, see the entries for Ts'ai Ch'ang and Liu Ning-i in Donald W. Klein and Anne B. Clark, *Biographic Dictionary of Chinese Communism, 1921–1965* (Cambridge: Harvard University Press, 1971).

[58] Suzanne Pepper discusses the problem of the Soviet connection in *Civil War in China*, pp. 215–16.

heir to the May Fourth Movement, the embodiment of
China's patriotic spirit. The Party also strongly supported the
growing popular demand for the United States to leave China
and assured the Chinese people that once the Communists
were in power they would banish all imperialist influence.[59]

Nationalism proved to be a winning issue. Admittedly
the CCP at times qualified its anti-imperialist position by
expressing a willingness to deal with any nation that would
treat China as an equal. However, other comments by the
CCP held out little likelihood of such treatment by an imperialist state. Thus, the degree of flexibility reflected in statements regarding relations with imperialism should not be
overestimated. Read in context they suggest that the Party
was attempting to allay any feeling among the Chinese people that it was being unreasonable or excessively antiforeign.
Even when the CCP said that it was willing to have relations
with the United States on a basis of equality, it did not depart
from its anti-American line. It never ceased to portray
America as seeking to perpetuate the inequality which had
always been part of China's relationship with the imperialist
powers and was now epitomized by its relations with the
United States.[60]

As the 1947–49 period came to an end the Chinese Communists' attitude toward the United States was unambiguous:
America was still China's principal enemy in a sharply bipolar world. There was no place for a demarche toward that
enemy which was surrounding and threatening China just as
Japan had done earlier. The Chinese Communists had been
nurtured on anti-Japanese nationalism in the 1930s. But 1949

[59] "Statement of the Central Committee of the Chinese Communist Party," February 1, 1947, in Van Slyke, China White Paper, pp. 719–20, and Newscast from
Yenan, January 2, 1947.

[60] For example, see "Ch'i-nien 'ch'i-ch'i' shih chou-nien tui shih-chü k'ou-hao"
(Slogans toward the Present Situation for the Tenth Anniversary of July 7), Ch'ün-
chung (Hong Kong) (July 10, 1947), no. 24, pp. 2–3; and New China News Agency,
November 21, 1948, cited in FR, 1948, 7:598. Mao Tse-tung, "Address to the Preparatory Committee of the New Political Consultative Conference," Selected Works
of Mao Tse-tung, 4:405–9; "Carry the Revolution through to the End," ibid., pp.
299–307; and "On the Outrages by British Warships," ibid., pp. 401–3.

would show that it achieved victory on a platform of anti-American nationalism.

1949–1950: Confronting the United States

The Communist armies that crossed the Yangtze in April 1949 were well disciplined, battle-hardened troops. They were euphoric as they finally entered China's great cities to garner the fruits of their victory. They were also highly politicized armies. For nearly three years the troops had been lectured on the indignities visited upon the Chinese nation by the imperialist United States. Awaiting them in the cities were workers who shared their intense anti-Americanism.

Anti-Americanism had been strong at the grass-roots level among the Chinese Communists ever since 1945–46. In August 1946, Chou En-lai candidly stated to Ambassador Stuart that resentment against the presence of American troops in China was "hotter among the lower classes than the higher classes of Communists." [61] By the beginning of 1949 hostility to the United States was rampant among the masses, especially in the major Chinese cities that contained large foreign communities. Missionaries, according to their own accounts, had to bear the brunt of much popular ill will despite the restraining efforts of Communist leaders. In Nanking members of the United States Embassy were targets of anti-American outbursts from middle- and low-ranking Communist officials. In Shanghai the pent-up animosity of the workers toward the United States erupted in spontaneous demonstrations after the Communists took over the city. Leftist tendencies pervaded the workers' movement, anxious to settle scores with foreign and domestic entrepreneurs. [62]

Prominent among the foreigners who had expected to stay in China after the Communists came to power were American businessmen in the main urban centers. Many

[61] FR, 1946, 9:1455. See also Gittings, *The World and China*, p. 122.

[62] FR, 1949, 8:1090, 1076–77, and 728. See also Pepper, *Civil War in China*, p. 362.

were eager to do business with the new China. In their own eyes, they had been compassionate observers of the Chinese scene and were now prepared to make concessions to the Chinese Communists' sensitivities. Still, like most foreign residents in China they had, consciously or unconsciously, become accustomed to occupying a highly privileged position and were unprepared to cope with the broad-based antiforeign feeling that developed in 1949 and quickly led to the elimination of their special status. By the end of the year most of the American businessmen who originally intended to remain in China had returned to the United States.[63]

Much of the anti-American and antiforeign outburst that occurred in 1949 was clearly contrary to the wishes of the CCP leadership. In the early months of 1949 the CCP had hoped to differentiate between the imperialist governments and their people. While warning the Communist troops before they entered the cities against hostile acts likely to be instigated by foreign governments they also instructed them "to protect the lives and property" of all foreign nationals in China. In the spring of 1949 Mao himself wrote: "The Chinese people wish to have friendly cooperation with the people of all countries and to resume and expand international trade in order to promote economic prosperity."[64]

The distinction between imperialist governments and

[63]FR, 1949, 8:1108–9, 1136–37, 1192–93, and 1230–31. Robert Boardman comments on antiforeign feelings among the Chinese as well as on the declining morale of the business community. See his Britain and the People's Republic of China, 1949–1974 (New York: Harper and Row, 1976), pp. 31 and 80.

[64]Mao, "Address to the Preparatory Committee," p. 408. This statement was made against a background of CCP assurances that the rights of law-abiding foreign nationals would be respected by the new government and a general mood in the foreign community that they wished to stay in China. During late 1948 and early 1949 the foreign community attempted to divine CCP intentions on this question. No clear-cut policy thrust was discerned.

On Chinese attitudes, see FR, 1947, 7:41 (statement by Chou En-lai); FR, 1949, 8:1055 (statement by Lin Piao); and Nancy Bernkopf Tucker, "An Unlikely Peace: American Missionaries and the Chinese Communists, 1948–1950," Pacific Historical Review (February 1976), 45(1):102–3. On the uncertain Western view, see FR, 1948, 7:711 and 816; ibid., 8:899–902, 907–8, and 917–18; and FR, 1949, 9:913, 916–17, 928, and 983.

their nationals proved, however, difficult to make in practice, especially in relation to the United States. Given the intensity of their feeling against the United States, the Chinese people were in no mood to draw fine lines between official and unofficial America. American nationals in China were beneficiaries of the unjust, imperialist system. If the CCP had been conciliatory toward individual American businessmen, many Chinese would have felt that the Party was violating one of its most vital tenets: the eradication of imperialism in China. To recognize or even merely to reform the old commercial system in China—a system which many Americans and other Westerners regarded as essential for the conduct of business—was patently a political impossibility.[65] As a member of the Democratic League, one of the Chinese political parties then outlawed by the Kuomintang, reported to a U.S. official:

"General intransigence of labor whether under foreign or Chinese employment is exploiting opportunity to extent which Communists disapprove but cannot afford suppress, irrespective rights and wrongs, for fear seeming to champion capitalists, imperialists, and losing urgently needed mass support."[66]

The Party leaders not only recognized the political dangers of modifying their anti-imperialist position but also realized the benefits that might be obtained from capitalizing on it. The civil war had entered a crucial phase. The Communists were now in the cities, the very places where they had the most to gain from demonstrating their loyalty to the anti-imperialist cause. Throughout the summer of 1949 the Chinese Communist press prominently published accounts of incidents in which Westerners, who had allegedly mistreated Chinese, were forced to pay compensation, indicating that the day of Western supremacy in China was over. Accounts of this nature merely intensified the public's hostility toward

[65] See, for example, the comments of the American consul in Shanghai, Walter McConaughy, *FR, 1949,* 9:1276.

[66] *Ibid.,* pp. 1193–94. For a similar assessment, see ibid., p. 379.

foreigners and thus committed the Party even more deeply to opposing the imperialists.[67]

Domestic political considerations, therefore, left the CCP little room for making any adjustments in its relations with Americans. Moreover the actions of the United States Government, as interpreted by the CCP, most certainly did not justify any moderation of its anti-American policy. America's global policy continued to be bellicose, as evinced by the founding of NATO.[68] Its China policy was seen as no different. As noted above, from the end of 1948 the Party leaders had predicted that the hostility of the United States government to the CCP would increase as the defeat of the Kuomintang drew nearer. By mid-summer of 1949 they felt their predictions had been substantiated to an alarming degree. The Truman administration was apparently acquiescing in the naval blockade imposed by the Kuomintang in June against the ports under Chinese Communist control and in August the State Department issued the famous White Paper.

From the Chinese Communists' point of view it would be difficult to imagine a more inflammatory document than the White Paper. The CCP immediately launched a massive "anti-White Paper" campaign. A large body of documentation was produced to substantiate the oft-made charge that the United States must bear a major share of the responsibility for the civil war in China.[69] The campaign was above all an attack on the hope expressed in the White Paper that "democratic individualism" would emerge in China and that the Chinese Communists would follow the road of Titoism. This American approach intensified a long-held CCP con-

[67] Ibid., p. 1166; China Press Review (U.S. Consulate General, Shanghai) (hereafter CPR-S), June 21, 1949, p. 12, June 22, 1949, p. 11, June 25–27, 1949, pp. 2 and 11, July 2–5, 1949, p. 1, and July 9–11, 1949, pp. 1–2.

[68] FBIS, March 15 and 23, 1949.

[69] Fan "pai p'i-shu" hsueh-hsi tzu-liao (Anti-"White Paper" Study Materials) (Tientsin, Chung-kung T'ien-ching Shih-wei Tsung-hsueh Wen-hui, 1949), pp. 1–51, 79–88. Included in this volume are the six New China News Agency editorials that formed the keystone of the campaign. Five were written by Mao and can be found also in the Selected Works, 4:425–59.

cern, and the Chinese Communists asserted that in attempting to foster "democratic individualism" (which they translated as "democratic individualists") the United States was trying to construct a fifth column in China.[70] They moreover took the occasion of a renewal of the anti-Tito campaign by the Soviet bloc to reemphasize their earlier position that to advocate Titoism was to be ensnared by an imperialist trick to win China over to the American side. In the international world, they were convinced, there was no middle ground between the reactionary and democratic camps. Any Chinese who favored neutrality was at best unpatriotic, at worse treasonous.[71]

As 1949 developed there seemed to be little incentive for the CCP to change its anti-American posture. Domestic restraints existed and American actions—in China and the world—conformed to the adversary relationship the CCP anticipated would develop as their victory grew nearer. China would have to confront the forces of imperialism. In August 1949 Mao wrote:

[Our course] is to expose the imperialists, irritate them, overthrow them, punish them for offences against the law and allow them only to behave themselves and not be unruly in word or deed. Only then will there be any hope for dealing with imperialist foreign countries on the basis of equality and mutual benefit. Only then will there be any hope that the landlords, bureaucratic capitalists, members of the reactionary Kuomintang clique and their accomplices, who have laid down their arms and surrendered, can be given education for transforming the bad into the good and be transformed, as far as possible, into good people.[72]

[70] Van Slyke notes this change in terminology in his introduction to *China White Paper*, n.7 (no page).

[71] For statements opposing the White Paper made by individuals or groups considered potential "third roaders," see *FBIS*, August 22, 1949, pp. BBB 1–2, and September 6, 1949, pp. BBB 6–9. Also see *Fan "pai p'i-shu,"* pp. 89–105. On the issue of the danger of being entrapped by the United States, see Mao, *Selected Works*, 4:425–31; and *Fan "pai p'i-shu,"* pp. 1–8. On the Tito question, see *CPR-S*, August 31, 1949, and September 20, 1949; and *FBIS*, September 2, 1949, p. BBB 3.

[72] Mao, *Selected Works*, 4:429. In a speech purported to have been given in March 1949, Mao spoke quite strongly of the need to do away with imperialist "eco-

Thus, only when the international and domestic sources of imperialist influence were extirpated would China again consider dealings with imperialist nations. This would take an indeterminate period of time. In the interim, the CCP saw increased international tension. At best, Sino-American relations would be characterized by mutual recriminations. At worst, the United States would continue its efforts to isolate and subvert the Chinese revolution, in the end perhaps resorting to war.

China was seen as having no choice but to turn a defiant face west. In November 1949 the Communist theoretical journal *Hsueh-hsi* implicitly established such a policy when it discussed the reasons for the downfall of the T'ai-p'ing rebellion. Readers were warned that China's most important anti-imperialist movement of the nineteenth century had failed in part because certain of its leaders entertained illusions about the imperialists. They believed they could "obtain a friendly attitude from Westerners by avoiding methods of conflict." [73]

Drawing on more recent history, a major CCP foreign affairs analyst suggested that in the perilous immediate postrevolutionary period China could benefit from the "rich educational experience" of the Soviet Union following the revolution of November 1917. Russia, he declared, had been a "semi-colony" of the Western nations which, immediately after the revolution, had subjected it to diplomatic isolation, blockades, and armed intervention because their imperialist interests had been threatened. China, in the CCP's view, was clearly in a similar position. [74]

---

nomic and cultural establishments." He did speak of a willingness to do business with foreign nationals, but this seemed a secondary matter. *Ibid.*, pp. 370–71. See also Michael Hunt's discussion of this question in this volume, pp. 198–99.

[73] Hu Sheng, "T'ai-p'ing t'ien-kuo ho tz'u-pen chu-i wai-kuo ti kuan-hsi" (The Foreign Relations of the Taiping Heavenly Kingdom and Capitalism), *Hsueh-hsi* (September 1949), 1(1):21.

[74] K'o Pai-nien, "Su-lien tsai shih-yueh ko-ming hou ch'u-ch'i tsen-yang yü ti-kuo chu-i tso tou-cheng" (How the Soviet Union Struggled with Imperialism in the Initial Period after the October Revolution), *Hsueh-hsi* (November 1949), 1(3):12–14.

Increasingly, from the summer of 1949 to the outbreak of the Korean War, the CCP elaborated upon the fears that it had adumbrated during the previous years.[75] The United States, it said, was maneuvering at China's borders and preparing to subvert the Chinese revolution through spies and fifth columnists. While supporting a resurgent Japan, Washington was building a network of bases from Korea to Taiwan to the Philippines from which to launch an invasion of the Chinese mainland. In response, the CCP developed its foreign policy for the period of imperialist threat.[76]

After its final victory and the formal establishment of the People's Republic of China in October 1949, the Chinese Communist Party moved to strengthen its ties with the Soviet Union. During the summer of 1949 the CCP had already concluded a barter agreement with the Soviet Union in northeast China demonstrating that it could rely on its friends to counteract the inimical acts of its adversaries, such as continued United States acquiescence in the Kuomintang naval blockade.[77] In October the Soviet Union quickly granted recognition to the PRC and in December Mao went to Moscow to negotiate with the Soviet leaders. By March the lean-to-one-side policy had been formalized in a Sino-Soviet mutual defense treaty and a series of economic agreements.[78] Meanwhile the CCP established closer connections with the new states of Eastern Europe that were part of the Soviet bloc.

[75] Allen Whiting notes the growing Chinese sense of being threatened in the pre-Korean War period: *China Crosses the Yalu* (Stanford: Stanford University Press, 1968), pp. 34–38.

[76] *FBIS*, September 2, 1949, pp. BBB 1–2; February 2, 1950, p. BBB 3; February 7, 1950, pp. BBB 2–3; February 28, 1950, p. BBB 1; March 22, 1950, p. BBB 1; April 26, 1950, p. BBB 1; and May 17, 1950, pp. BBB 2–3. For comprehensive discussions, see "America's New Aggressive Moves in Asia," *Shih-chieh chih-shih* in *Chinese Press Survey*, (U.S. consulate-general, Shanghai) (April 1, 1950), 9(4):102–6; and *Fan "pai p'i-shu,"* pp. 157–79.

[77] *FBIS*, August 8, 1949, p. BBB 3.

[78] For two thorough discussions of these agreements from the CCP's perspective, see Hai Fu, *Wei-shen-ma i-pien tao* (Why Lean to One Side?) (Shanghai: Shih-chieh Chih-shih She, 1951); and *Lun Chung-Su meng-yueh* (On the Sino-Soviet Treaty) (Shanghai: Hsin Hua Shu-tien, 1950).

In addition the CCP attempted to solidify its international position on a broad front. It sought admission to the United Nations and took an active part in the fight to oust the Chinese Nationalists from the Security Council. It joined the campaign against American occupation policies in Japan.[79] Peking also assumed a central role in the various international "front" organizations it had long supported, and in the growing world peace movement.[80]

As the course of Sino-British relations revealed, the People's Republic of China's attitude toward relations with imperialist states remained exceedingly cautious. During 1949 and early 1950, the CCP had stated its readiness to have diplomatic relations with any country willing to treat China on the basis of equality.[81] Throughout this period Britain had been open-minded in its dealings with China's new leaders. Ties with London seemed particularly useful given Peking's recognition that contradictions existed with the United States over Far Eastern policy.[82]

Still, as always, the CCP's statements of willingness to deal with imperialist states on the basis of equality were tempered by expressions of doubt that these states were ready to reciprocate. Specifically, it was noted that broad areas of agreement existed between London and Washington on matters of global imperialist policy and that Britain seemed slow in recognizing the changed nature of its relations with China. In addition, the CCP was concerned that official contacts with imperialism might encourage the proimperialist sen-

[79] Liang Shu-fu, Hsin Chung-kuo ti wai-chiao (New China's Foreign Policy) (Canton: Cheng-ta Shu-tien, 1950), chs. 4 and 5; Shih-chieh chih-shih in Chinese Press Survey (February 1, 1950), 8(4):97–99; and New China News Agency (London), Daily Bulletin (June 17, 1950), no. 33, pp. 3–4, and (June 18, 1950), no. 34, pp. 3–4.

[80] This was symbolized by the meetings of the World Federation of Trade Unions and Asian Women's Conference which were held in Peking.

[81] An important statement of China's attitude on this question can be found in K'o Pai-nien, "Hsin min-chu chu-i ti wai-chiao cheng-ts'e" (New Democracy's Foreign Policy), Hsueh-hsi (October 1949), 1(2):13–15.

[82] Shih-chieh chih-shih in Chinese Press Survey (January 25, 1950), 8(3):61–63.

timents assumed to be latent among the Chinese intellectuals.[83]

For all these reasons, the Chinese response to Britain's grant of de jure recognition in January 1950 was cool. Peking's statements reflected suspicion and a dogged insistence on absolutely equal treatment and renunciation of all special foreign privileges. The negotiations that followed were stormy, prolonged and, ultimately, inconclusive. The exigencies of domestic politics and the leadership's deep suspicion of imperialist motives thus severely complicated contacts with a lesser imperialist state with whom there was good reason to seek ties and whose leadership was conciliatory toward China.[84] In the case of the major imperialist enemy, the United States, the same concerns over the domestic situation and the imperialists' intent resulted in an uncompromising policy which led only to the embitterment of Sino-American relations.

As suggested above, the new Chinese leadership seemed ready for a period of tension, even conflict, with the American imperialists. The model of the October Revolution of the USSR suggested that the West would strive to destroy the new Chinese Communist regime. But it also suggested that the imperialists would eventually be forced to come to terms with it. If the history of the Soviet Union was any guide, future ties with the imperialists might be expected.[85] However, for the moment, China had to confront imperialism, solidify its relations with international friends, and get down to the business of postwar reconstruction.

[83] *FBIS*, May 24, 1950, pp. PPP 25–27; *Shih-chieh chih-shih* in *Chinese Press Survey* (February 1, 1950), 8(4):97–99, and (January 25, 1950), no. 3, p. 63; and New China News Agency (London), *Daily Bulletin*, No. 38, May 26, 1950, pp. 1–3.

[84] For a recent discussion of pre-Korean War Anglo-Chinese diplomacy, see Boardman, *Britain and the PRC*, chs. 1–3. Boardman is somewhat more optimistic regarding Sino-British ties.

[85] For suggestions of this, see Liang, *Hsin Chung-kuo ti wai-chiao*, pp. 21–22; and K'o, "Su-lien," p. 14; "Wen-t'i chieh-ta" (Answers to Questions), *Hsueh-hsi* (May 1, 1950), 2(4):18.

Although the Chinese Communists thus pursued a carefully conceived foreign policy, the outbreak of the Korean war and American intervention dictated immediate positive action. As the United Nations troops moved north, the CCP became increasingly alarmed. The fears the Party had been nurturing for years that the United States would attempt to overcome the Chinese revolution by means ranging from internal subversion to a massive invasion seemed about to be realized. Despite Washington's assurances that its intentions were not aggressive, the Chinese Communists entered the Korean War. Given their perception of the United States, there was little likelihood of their following any other course.

Lost Chance in China? An Overview
This paper has traced the policy of the CCP toward the United States from 1944 to 1950 in order to determine whether it offered any genuine possibilities for the establishment of a positive relationship between the Chinese Communists and the American government. Much of the literature on Sino-American relations during this period speaks of the "lost chance," meaning that the CCP attempted to develop friendly relations with the United States and that the Truman Administration rejected the opportunity to do so out of a blind hostility to communism.

In regard to the years before 1947, especially during the time of the Dixie Mission, many writers assert that the Chinese Communists sought to effect a rapprochement with the United States but abandoned the effort as American policy failed to meet their expectations. This, for the most part, is true. But one must go further and ask whether the CCP's expectations were realistic. For if they were not, they provided little basis for an understanding.

It is worth reiterating that the CCP's positive attitude toward the United States during the course of the Dixie Mission was inextricably tied to a very particular perception of the world held by the Party toward the end of the war. After

Teheran, the CCP tended to believe that American capitalism was becoming more enlightened and that Soviet-American cooperation during the war represented a permanent trend toward peace and democracy. While the Chinese Communist leaders were aware that there were political elements in the Western bourgeois states seeking to thwart the process of lasting accommodation, they seemed confident that more progressive forces had an equal, if not better, chance of prevailing.

This was of course an unrealistic assessment of the situation. Certainly the struggle against the fascist nations had fostered solidarity between the United States and the Soviet Union and promoted unity among the American people. However there had been no real change in the nature of the American political system. On the contrary there was ample evidence during the war that, after the defeat of Germany and Japan, the United States would remain a bourgeois nation intent on furthering its individual international interests just as the Soviet Union would remain a Marxist state determined to pursue its own ends.

Turning specifically to China, it was similarly quite unrealistic for the CCP to expect the United States to drastically alter its relationship with the Kuomintang. Indeed, men such as John Service were arguing not for disengagement but for evenhandedness in American dealings with the Nationalists and the Communists. Such a policy could not have assuaged CCP suspicions as both sides squared off for civil war. Inevitably misunderstandings regarding American relations with the Kuomintang would have arisen, especially at a time when Cold War tensions were developing in other parts of the world. An evenhanded U.S. policy might have been acceptable to the CCP if Washington's policies elsewhere in the world had seemed "progressive." But in a world rapidly moving away from the idealized goals of Teheran such a policy would have been regarded as patently deceptive.

All too often scholars have assumed that CCP-American

relations were a strictly bilateral affair, but in fact the Party leaders were convinced from the beginning that America's policy toward the Chinese Communists hinged on its attitude toward the Soviet Union. The basic assumption of the CCP was that if the United States was engaged in a Cold War with the USSR its conduct toward all Communist movements would be hostile. Consequently as the Cold War developed in Europe, the CCP's suspicions of American actions intensified.

Given the Cold War, the factor that weighed most heavily with the CCP against effecting a rapprochement with the United States was the Party's commitment to the Soviet Union. The top Party leaders, such as Mao, Chou, and Liu Shao-ch'i, were firmly convinced that China had to align itself with the USSR. The Party had certainly had its problems with Stalin and was not prepared to accept his directions uncritically. But the central fact remained that in the Communist world there was a powerful tradition of support for the Soviet Union. As the Cold War intensified the leading Chinese Communists felt instinctively that, despite all differences, China still had more in common with the Soviet Union than with any other country. I agree completely with those scholars who argue that in times of international crisis the desire to line up with the Soviet Union was as irresistible for Mao as for the Communist leaders of Eastern Europe.[86] In this respect it should be emphasized that Tito, who had maintained close relations with the British during the war and was considered the model of a "national" Communist, unwilling to subordinate his country's interests to Moscow's demands, lined up enthusiastically with the Soviet Union once the Cold War started and was even more anti-Western than Stalin. I would assert that a similar pull of Communist internationalism would have conditioned CCP policy even if the Dixie Mission had been successful. Those who compare

[86] Steven Levine, "If My Grandmother Had Wheels She'd Be a Trolley, or Reflections on a 'Lost Chance in China.'" *Contemporary China* (December 1976), 1(3):31–32; and Okabe, "The Cold War and China."

Mao with Tito ignore the Yugoslav leader's strong orientation toward the Communist world in 1945–47 and see only
his subsequent reconciliation with the West. Tito's independence from Moscow was involuntary; Stalin broke with him,
not vice versa.[87]

In connection with the post-1947 period, discussion of a
"lost chance" in China has generally centered on events in
1949, the year the CCP came to power.

The American side of the story is told elsewhere in this
volume. As the civil war developed and the Communists
gained the upper hand, the United States government was
forced to keep its distance from the CCP. While public opinion was generally permissive, the pro-KMT lobby in
Congress was strong—or at least appeared so to the poli-
cymakers in Washington. The president and the State Department were still reluctant to give a wartime ally the coup de
grâce by dealing with its enemy. In addition the administration's options were limited by foreign policy commitments
elsewhere. It was difficult to maintain simultaneously an
anti-Communist posture in Europe and an accommodating
position toward a major Communist movement in Asia.[88] In
short it was impossible, in 1949, for American policy makers
to deal with the emerging Chinese regime as it was—a pro-
Soviet, anti-imperialist movement, humiliating one of
America's wartime allies and driving uncompromisingly
against United States interests in China.

But what of the CCP? If Washington had not had these
inhibitions, would the Chinese Communists have established
friendly relations at this time? Could they have dealt with the

---

[87] See Adam Ulam's excellent discussion of this irony, in *Expansion and Coexistence: The History of Soviet Foreign Policy* (New York: Frederick A. Praeger, 1968),
pp. 469–70. Tang Tsou makes a similar point in *America's Failure in China*, p. 257.
At times, of course, Tito's instincts as a cold warrior were shunned by Stalin because
they threatened Soviet global interests or were seen as promoting Yugoslav interests.
But the fundamental point is that Tito, despite ties with the West, lined up quickly
against his former supporters.

[88] Warren I. Cohen, *America's Response to China: An Interpretive History of
Sino-American Relations* (New York: Wiley, 1972), p. 194.

United States as it was—a capitalist nation with significant economic and political stakes in China moving toward a global confrontation with the Soviet Union? I do not think so.

Unlike the pre-1947 period, in 1949 CCP statements about the United States were almost uniformly hostile. The animosity they reflected was strong and clear and any suggestions of possible ties with the United States were vague. There are, however, a few reports of Chinese Communists approaching American officials with a view to establishing friendly relations between the CCP and the Truman Administration. Of these, two have received considerable attention.

The first involves an alleged demarche by Chou En-lai through Michael Keon, an Australian journalist, in Peking in June 1949. Chou purportedly sent a "top secret" message through Keon to the American consul general in Peking for transmittal to the State Department. The message suggested inter alia that Chou was part of a "liberal" faction that was seeking ties with the United States and was eager to act as a mediating agency between America and the Soviet Union. In response the Acting Secretary of State, James E. Webb, drafted a statement of conditions for discussions with the CCP. Nothing materialized as Chou En-lai suddenly became elusive.[89]

This story has evoked much skepticism. American specialists on China, who were in Peking at the time, strongly question its validity. A few months earlier Keon had been denounced by the Chinese Communists for reportorial distortions and would therefore seem an unlikely choice to serve as messenger on a mission of this nature.[90] Moreover it is improbable that, in the period of Cominform opposition to Tito,

---

[89] For materials related to this demarche, see FR, 1949, 8:357–60, 363–64, 372–73, 384–85, 394–95, and 397–98.

[90] FBIS, February 15, 1949, pp. CCC 3–4, and February 16, 1949, p. CCC 3. For a discussion of this demarche that gives it more credibility, see Robert M. Blum, "The Peiping Cable: A Drama of 1949," New York Times Magazine, August 13, 1978, pp. 8–10, 53, 56, 57.

Chou En-lai would have maintained that China's place was between the United States and the Soviet Union.

A second account of a demarche has somewhat more substance. On June 28, 1949, Huang Hua, then director of the Communist Alien Affairs Office in Nanking, suggested that Ambassador Stuart, who had been president of Yenching University for almost three decades, might consider returning to Peking for his annual birthday visit. Huang strongly implied that, while in Peking, Stuart could hold a meeting with Mao Tse-tung and Chou En-lai. Two days later, while Huang's suggestion was under consideration in Washington, Mao delivered his "lean to one side" speech. On July 1 the proposed trip was vetoed by the State Department, to all appearances under instructions from President Truman, bringing the episode to an end.[91]

Some scholars have suggested that, if a meeting between Ambassador Stuart and the Chinese leaders had been held, it would have changed the course of history materially.[92] There is little to substantiate such a thesis. Indeed if the constant exchanges in Nanking between American and Chinese officials in the period before late June 1949 are a guide, Ambassador Stuart, Mao Tse-tung, and Chou En-lai might well have found that neither side was willing to yield on matters perceived as essential. In the Nanking meetings the responses of the Chinese officials to American initiatives were tentative and evasive. Despite the greater stature of the leaders in Peking there is no ground for supposing their reaction would have been any different. The CCP simply did not believe existing domestic or international conditions permitted the establishment of positive relations with the United States.

The domestic conditions that in the CCP's judgment

[91] This incident is discussed in *The United States and Communist China in 1949 and 1950: The Question of Rapprochement and Recognition* (Washington D.C.: U.S. Government Printing Office, 1973), pp. 7–12.

[92] Most prominently, Donald Zagoria, "Containment and China," in Charles Gati, ed., *Caging the Bear: Containment and the Cold War* (Indianapolis: Bobbs-Merrill, 1974), pp. 109–27; and Barbara Tuchman, "If Mao Had Come to Washington: An Essay in Alternatives," *Foreign Affairs* (October 1972), 51(1):44–64.

ruled out an understanding with the administration in Washington are apparent. As indicated earlier, when the Chinese Communists entered the cities and began to confront imperialism in its economic, social, and political reality, they were greatly impressed by the strength of the popular reaction to the anti-imperialist issue.[93] In the summer of 1949 the Party leaders apparently feared that to relent on the strident anti-Americanism that had characterized the CCP's foreign policy for years would incur grave political costs in the urban areas. It might also create serious organizational problems, as there was considerable hostility to the United States throughout the Party and the army. Moreover the CCP leadership was deeply concerned with the effect that any lessening of tension between the Chinese Communists and the Truman Administration might have upon the Chinese intellectuals. Although the Chinese intellectuals were firmly opposed to American imperialism, they generally still admired the United States, especially in comparison with the Soviet Union. The CCP had long feared that, under certain circumstances, many Chinese intellectuals would consciously or unconsciously promote the interests of the American imperialists. A detente between the Chinese Communists and Washington could provide just such an opportunity.

While the domestic situation, in the CCP's view, therefore suggested that there was more to lose than to gain from reaching an understanding with the United States, the international situation in 1949 seemed to point to the same conclusion. The events after 1946 had only confirmed the Party's earlier judgment that revolutionary China's struggle with imperialism was inextricably bound to the global confrontation between the forces of reaction and of progress. As the Cold War quickened, the CCP became increasingly impressed with the benefits to be derived from a policy of leaning to the side of the Soviet Union.

Admittedly there had been developments following the

[93] Pepper, *Civil War*, pp. 398–404, discusses the importance of this issue.

war—especially Stalin's advice to the CCP to negotiate with the Nationalists and the Soviets' self-serving actions in Manchuria—that might have increased the CCP's misgivings regarding the Soviet Union. Yet it would be a serious mistake to conclude that Mao's relations with Stalin in 1949 contained more areas of discord than of agreement.[94] The spirit of Communist interdependence remained strong. From 1947 to 1949, the CCP consistently supported the Soviets on matters of global policy. Such support was more than a mere gesture. The CCP adhered to its often unpopular alignment with Moscow at considerable domestic political cost. But it was obviously willing to pay the price. Whatever second thoughts the Party may have had concerning Soviet actions were more than offset by the increased American threat and the consequent importance of relying on the USSR.

It has often been stated that even if the Communists were committed to a lean-to-one-side policy they may still have been prepared to establish some limited economic or other ties with the United States. But there are a number of considerations that argue against such a thesis. In addition to the existing domestic situation and the CCP's assessment of the United States as a threat, the ideological trend within the international Communist movement in the late 1940s was against any association with the imperialist camp. The expulsion of Tito from the Cominform and the subsequent purges of other East European Communist leaders clearly conveyed the message that Stalin would not look with favor upon any dalliance with the bourgeois world. Under such circumstances the CCP was not likely to enter into any arrangements with the enemy which at best would achieve only marginal gains and might result in the alienation of the USSR, China's only real friend among the great powers.[95] While the lean-to-

[94] See, for example, Zagoria, "Mao's Role," p. 140.

[95] For a summary of Chinese statements regarding Stalin's suspicions of their "Titoist" sentiments, see Okabe, "The Cold War and China," p. 243. Obviously my argument above, that Sino-American policy must be considered in a global context, has much in common with and complements Okabe's argument in this fine article. See especially pp. 245–46.

one-side policy need not have precluded ties with the West, the CCP had long recognized that under certain circumstances it might do so. Such was the case in 1949–50.

It is common to view the crisis-ridden beginnings of Sino-American relations as the result of a "failure" of American diplomacy. While some impugn the motives of the Truman administration, more sympathetic proponents of this view depict the administration as severely constrained by political considerations of a domestic and international nature. Discussions of the Chinese side rarely mention comparable constraints. Mao and the CCP leadership often seem to be making policy in splendid isolation from such factors.

This paper asserts, to the contrary, that an appreciation of similar constraints on the CCP leaders is indispensable to an understanding of United States-China relations in the years from 1944 to 1950. Peking, too, was constrained in what it could do by the weight of past policies and perceptions and, more immediately, the pressures of domestic public opinion and international commitments. There was no "lost chance" for the simple reason that neither side was in a position to take a chance.

PART IV
Broader Perspectives

American China Policy and the Cold War in Asia: A New Look

Waldo Heinrichs

A brief explanation of the form and intent of the following paper is in order. My assignment was to summarize the papers and discussions at the end of the conference. Rather than to recapitulate the proceedings, I thought it would be more valuable to draw the papers and discussions together into one picture that might give us some early sense of what the conference as a whole was contributing. The limitations of such instant history are obvious, but it has the virtue of immediacy: it does at least reflect what seemed most important to one person in a setting full of intense intellectual interaction and fresh thinking. Therefore, I have decided to adhere as far as possible to the substance of those original remarks.

Since the Chinese side has been enlarged for publication, and since my remarks were in any case largely addressed to the American papers, I have confined this version to the American side. In addition, my original comments have been considerably revised and amplified for the sake of clarity and in response to criticisms raised in the ensuing discussion.

THIS CONFERENCE and book provide the first opportunity to take advantage of newly available documents to reexamine Sino-American relations in the context of the rising Cold War in Asia and the transition from Nationalist to Communist rule in China. In doing so, we have been asking the following interrelated questions. How did the Cold War come to East Asia? To what extent did exogenous Cold War concepts, assumptions, methods, balances, and swings spill over into East Asia from the areas of their inception—Europe and the Middle East—and with what effect on Sino-American relations? Alternatively, to what extent did events and circumstances within the region, especially in China, precipitate the extension of the Cold War into East Asia? How do we account for the American shift from relative apathy and passivity on China questions to confrontation with the People's Republic of China? Why was the path of accommodation not taken? How promising was it? Had the shift toward confrontation reached an acute stage before the Korean War? Or was the Korean War the decisive factor that not only ruled out any possibility of accommodation but established China as a major focal point (perhaps at times the major focal point) in the Cold War throughout the next decades.

A convenient point of departure is early 1948, on the eve of the great battles that brought the downfall of Nationalist rule in mainland China. What was the American outlook at this time of relative quiescence in East Asia? What conditions and assumptions affected the American view of China?

The United States was intensely preoccupied with Europe, to the point where East Asian problems must have seemed an unwelcome distraction. Containment in Europe, along established, finite boundaries on familiar ground of the highest strategic importance, presented powerful, clear-cut demands. With aid to Greece under way, setting up of the Marshall Plan, and movement toward an independent West Germany and NATO, the European policy of the United States was proving imaginative and increasingly rewarding, but each evolving stage required deeper American commitment. June 1948 brought the long, harrowing crisis of the Berlin blockade. Compared to this vivid drama, East Asian developments seemed remote and nebulous.

In 1948 the government of the United States was not inclined to undertake risks or costly involvements in East

Asia. Military resources were scarce, defense dollars getting scarcer. Atomic advantage over the Soviet Union still provided a sense of security, but the United States possessed surprisingly few of these weapons. The American policy leadership was cautious and conservative. With respect to Asia it had some grounds for confidence. Revolutionary nationalism threatened the old empires, but so far the transition from colonial rule to independence had been relatively successful. Witness India, Indonesia, and the suppression of the Hukbalahaps in the Philippines. One could identify with the new nationalism and still contain it. Time seemed on the side of the United States.

The principal feature of American foreign policy at this time was the doctrine of containment, the determination to resist the expansion of Soviet influence. Taken as rhetoric, containment was worldwide in scope and assumed that communism anywhere was an instrument of Soviet expansion. Practically speaking, there were qualifications and limitations. Containment emerged in a European-Middle Eastern context at a time when, I am persuaded—though others disagree—the Yalta assumption of accommodation with the Soviet Union still prevailed for East Asia. The Marshall mission goal of a reformed Nationalist China still lay within the Yalta framework, based on the premise of Soviet acceptance of the existing regime in return for imperial concessions in Manchuria and Inner Asia. Containment, furthermore, did not dictate resistance beyond the resources of the United States or reasonable prospects of success. The assumption after the Marshall mission was that no strategic purpose would justify use of American combat forces in China and that no other form of assistance was likely to sustain the Nationalists. Containment reflected a mindset that tended to spur confrontation, to be sure, but it was nonspecific as to means, allowing widely different tactics and considerable policy flexibility. As of 1948 American policy makers were still free to take a fresh look at their options in China.

During the following year the Nationalist regime in

China steadily disintegrated, and it became more and more likely that the United States would face a communist China. The question was what to do about it.

The starting point was the defensive perimeter concept. This was not a containment line, not a means of obstructing Soviet advance or communism. Rather, it represented the irreducible minimum the United States would fight to defend under any circumstances against any foe. It had a retrospective quality, recalling similar island perimeters much farther eastward in the Pacific which described the limit of American capability and critical interest before Pearl Harbor. The new perimeter was not a likely battleline. What naval, air, or amphibious force existed opposite to challenge American positions? It was simply a line that could be held with existing small sea-air capability. Southeast Asia, I would suggest, was not immediately relevant to the perimeter. It was still perceived as a colonial region, by way of Europe. Only the rise of Communist China fused East and Southeast Asia in the American strategic conception.

Using the defensive perimeter as a base point, two streams of policy emerged that did address Asian mainland questions. They had common features but were nevertheless distinct. The first of these may be described as the Peking policy, and it was closely identified with Secretary of State Dean Acheson.

The Department of State and Acheson in particular were totally convinced of the ineptness of the Chiang Kai-shek regime. Nancy Tucker has described the confusion and cross-purposes characterizing the propaganda activities of the Kuomintang in the United States and how these reflected the precarious internal balances of the regime itself. This disjointed effort reinforced existing convictions inherited from Secretary Marshall and China hands in the department that Chiang and his various cliques were totally incompetent. Reports from the field that Chiang was intervening in battles with disastrous consequences did nothing to improve the image. The overwhelming feeling was one of distaste and desire for disentanglement. Livingston Merchant captured this attitude when he wrote in February 1950 of "regaining our complete freedom of maneuver and disassociation in the Chinese mind with the Kuomintang as rapidly as events at home and abroad permit."

Dean Acheson, tall, bristling, lucid, imperturbable, did not don or doff decisions lightly. China, he concluded, was relatively unimportant to the United States, so survival of the Nationalist government was not critical. Its collapse and the fall of Taiwan seemed inevitable, and eventually the United States would have to recognize and deal with Communist China. He would encourage whatever divergences existed or might arise between Peking and Moscow and above all keep hands off Taiwan. Identification with the Nationalists on the island would create an irredentist issue barring the road to Peking. Warren Cohen has clearly established the saliency, strength, and consistency of this Acheson position, which I identify as the Peking policy.

On the face of it this Peking policy seems more imaginative and resilient than Acheson's hard-line Cold War policies elsewhere. But on closer examination the differences seem not so great. Acheson's China policy was no less a containment policy, only the line of containment would run not along the rim but across the inner frontiers of Asia. He and his Foreign Service advisers, George Kennan, John Davies, Walton Butterworth, and Merchant, were operating in a realpolitik framework, seeking balance of power at the Soviet border by way of a nationalist, although communist, China. The function of containment for that sector of the Soviet periphery would be filled by China. However sophisticated, this approach did not address Communist China on its own terms, in the light of its own experiences and sensibilities. The Peking policy was urgent on disassociation from Chiang, theoretical about association with Peking. It was stronger in abhorrence of Chiang and his followers than on understanding Mao and his.

Acheson was determined to fight as hard as possible to

keep open the possibility of recognition, but when that would occur remained unclear. It would be an evolutionary process. As the People's Republic of China recognized its obligations and permitted the United States a graceful transfer of recognition from the Nationalists to Peking, normalization would proceed. The pace would depend on Chinese behavior; the burden of proof was on them. The Peking consular compound issue of January 1950 is illustrative. The Peking authorities requisitioned an American embassy building on the grounds that it was a barrack for stationing troops under the abominated unequal treaties. The United States, after giving due warning and pointing out that the building in question had been converted to a consular office, protested violation of treaty rights and withdrew all remaining officials from mainland China. Acheson would undoubtedly have been prepared to renegotiate the treaties ultimately, but the Chinese Communists would have to accept them as a starting point. To him full equality lay at the end of the normalization process; to Peking it was the indispensable beginning. Meanwhile, restrictions on American officials in Communist China became so frustrating and insulting that even their continuing presence was a liability to improvement of relations, and they were withdrawn.

Acheson's policy had a patronizing tone typical of him and Westerners dealing with China. Discussion of the Chinese Communists at the State Department, Cohen notes, was like a seminar in adolescent psychology. This attitude is captured in the concern of American officials that the Chinese Communists should be made aware of their economic dependence on the United States. Contrast this view with Mao's statement that China hoped for foreign aid but could not allow itself to become dependent on it. On an analytical level Acheson could envision the same result as Mao: equality and reciprocity. On the perceptual level, however, they were worlds apart.

Paradoxically, Acheson depended on a sovereign display of force by the People's Republic even to begin normalization. He could do nothing until Communist conquest of Taiwan eliminated the Nationalist regime from Chinese territory and thereby, he hoped, from American politics as well. He must have awaited the invasion anxiously. It was a tenous policy Acheson pursued so doggedly, potentially constructive but burdened by contingencies and liabilities of the past.

The second policy stream, emerging in 1949–50, aimed at the containment of communism along the periphery of East and Southeast Asia. It might be called Asian rim containment. Not a national decision or choice, lacking comprehensive and coherent formulation, it was rather a syndrome of discrete decisions linked by a new disposition. Like the Peking policy it presumed a worldwide, Soviet-inspired communist challenge, but it did not play for a Sino-Soviet split. Instead it assumed Communist China to be a satellite of the Soviet Union and a springboard for Soviet expansion. It was anchored in the defensive perimeter but converted it: where the perimeter had previously served to guarantee control of the Pacific basin, now it would provide bases for controlling approaches to the Asian mainland. Whereas the defensive perimeter had been an offshore position reflecting a hands-off attitude toward mainland affairs, rim containment encouraged involvement in Asia; it was partly an onshore line. It did not contemplate use of American combat forces in mainland Asia, but it did involve use of such typical containment methods as military and economic assistance. Above all it reflected the belief that a firm American posture at selected points would have broad psychological benefits for the American standing and position in Asia and the rest of the world.

The disposition to contain Sino-Soviet communism along the periphery of Asia originated in diverse sources and spread through the American government in 1949–50. It was notable among the military with their faith in firmness and their habit of drawing sharp lines between friend and foe. Asia was a minor theater, it is true, not the place to fight a war. By 1950 the navy may have been thinking of the budgetary rewards that would flow from larger East Asian responsibilities, but generally the institutional interests of the services lay elsewhere. On the other hand, rim containment seemed neither risky nor costly. Military advising and training and provision of arms was turning the tide in Greece. Repertoires established for that intervention could easily be applied to improving the defense capabilities of small Asian states bordering China. Thus one finds the Joint Chiefs of Staff taking a greater interest in this type of containment and upgrading the strategic value of the region.

Such thinking was by no means restricted to the military. It was percolating upward through the Department of State too. Edmund Gullion, the chargé at Saigon, for example, warned that twilight zones where the United States had established no firm commitment tempted Communist aggression. Dean Rusk called for drawing the line against communism in Asia. NSC 68 reflected an official mind seized with worldwide confrontation of Soviet menace.

President Truman remained tethered to Acheson's policy of keeping the road to Peking open but seemed to strain against it. His tendency to take an undifferentiated view of communism and his "penchant for clarity and confrontation" noted by Martin Sherwin made him receptive to the new containment thinking. In 1949 he intervened on several occasions with decisions that hobbled the Peking policy. He refused permission for Ambassador John Leighton Stuart to journey to Peking for talks with Chou En-lai and refused to challenge the disguised Nationalist blockade of central and south China ports. Above all he was sensitive to the mood of the country and Congress. He was undoubtedly paying close attention, for example, to committee chairmen in Congress who stood for a display of firmness towards all communist regimes and at the same time controlled the flow of domestic legislation.

Dramatic events of 1949–50 intensified public pressures for a more militant foreign policy. The weathering of the Berlin crisis demonstrated to policy makers that firmness in an outpost paid off. The August 1949 Soviet explosion of an atomic device appeared to alter the strategic picture profoundly: the United States faced a long-term, desperately serious struggle for existence. Staying ahead required all the resources, will, and friends the nation could muster. Time pressed; worst-case assumptions prevailed. Prestige became critical: the balance of power must be perceived as evolving in America's favor, or at least not to American disadvantage. Small events gained significance as measures of the state of that balance. In October 1949 another catalytic event occurred: the establishment of the People's Republic of China. Policy makers were determined to allow no more lost Chinas; the line must be drawn. Finally, the Sino-Soviet alliance of February 1950 reinforced the monolithic view of communism and sharpened and extended the cleavage set forth in the Truman Doctrine between the free and totalitarian worlds. At this time the Klaus Fuchs spy trial in Britain revealed Communist acquisition of thermonuclear secrets and Senator McCarthy began his crusade against traitors in the State Department. Public officials, especially the president, sensed a rising public demand for firmness against communism everywhere.

Early in 1950 China policy, especially Taiwan, became an issue of particular public interest. The major policy statements of Truman and Acheson on January 5 and 12, 1950, implying abandonment of Taiwan, brought the pot to a boil. Previously the China lobby had been somewhat successful, but the Democratic leadership in Congress had dominated the debate. Now Chiang resumed formal leadership of the government on Taiwan, thereby providing his supporters in the United States with a familiar and highly visible symbol of the continuity of the Nationalist regime. However inept Chiang's agents in the United States appeared to State Department officials, their free-wheeling propaganda apparatus attracted widening attention.

The confrontationist thinking that arose from these sources, events, and attitudes led to a number of policy results. Of course the United States was determined to maintain its positions on the off-shore chain. It expected to hold Korea as well, but reinforcement of its position there did not seem warranted. The Syngman Rhee government could with existing forces and assistance programs take care of internal subversion. An external threat would arise only in the context of general war, it was assumed, and then an American troop commitment to Korea would be a liability.

Policy for Japan shifted into a containment format. The United States, determined that the defeated enemy should never again present a threat to its security, insisted on a dominant role in Japan's reform and reintegration into the world community. By 1948 completion of the reform phase, the financial burden of occupation, the increasing restiveness of the Japanese people, and the weakness of their economy compelled American officials to consider afresh the means of accomplishing their fundamental aim. By reduction of the American presence, relaxation of controls, and encouragement of Japanese initiative and autonomy, they hoped to make Japan into a self-sustaining, stable nation with a stake in its own future and in a close, equal relationship with the United States.

The rise of Communist China gave added incentive to this fresh approach, at least within the State Department. Ensuring against a resurrection of Japanese militarism became less central than protecting Japan from Soviet attack or subversion. By 1949 officials at State would hasten a peace treaty to achieve Japanese-American partnership.

For the military the reverse was true. The Joint Chiefs of Staff dug in their heels against a peace treaty. More than ever they perceived the crucial importance of Japan's position astride the Asian littoral and interlocked with the offshore chain of islands. The navy, dissatisfied with Okinawa as a forward base, looked to Yokosuka, while the air force sought bases in Japan for atomic offensive against the Soviet Union in the event of general war. In this light, the military preferred retention of broad existing occupation rights rather than a more dubious future within an independent Japan.

This issue between State and Defense was not resolved before the Korean War, but consensus was building. The original concept of a demilitarized, neutralized Japan was dismissed. General agreement existed on ensuring American bases by way of any peace treaty. In this regard, the United States was entirely prepared to override Sino-Soviet objections. What remained to be settled within the American government was the extent of retained military privilege and the manner of achieving a treaty.

China now loomed over Southeast Asia. Peking's assistance to Ho Chi Minh across their common border, added to Soviet assistance, posed a new threat. In January 1950 came a quick drawing of lines: Sino-Soviet recognition of Ho, matched by American recognition of Bao Dai. In April and May 1950 the United States established a military advisory group in Vietnam. It undertook to provide military and economic assistance there and elsewhere in Southeast Asia.

Steadily, from January to June 1950, an arc of containment formed. On January 10, 1950, before the Senate Foreign Relations Committee, Acheson pointed out on a map a semicircle or "crescent" of countries bordering China, starting in Japan and ending in India. Here, he said, "the real center of our interest in Asia must lie." Others would end the line in Southeast Asia. Offshore it was a military line, onshore more political and psychological. This was containment at the Asian rim.

Pressure to include Taiwan rose, and it was here that the Peking policy and rim containment clashed. Taiwan seemed far more important in the new context. Enemy air forces located there could intercept American planes flying from the Philippines to Okinawa. Even so, a glance at the map would suggest that the island was not substantially more threatening in hostile hands than the whole of the China coast behind it. Now, however, every piece of territory counted. In March 1949 the Joint Chiefs' planners advised holding Taiwan in case of war with the Soviet Union, and in December the Joint Chiefs adopted that position. Through the latter part of 1949 and into 1950 State and Defense waged bureaucratic warfare over the issue, Acheson making concessions under intensifying pressures but holding the inner redoubt of his Peking policy, namely that the United States must not create an insuperable obstacle to recognition of Peking by intervening in this last stage of the Chinese civil war. He looked to the possibility of Taiwanese autonomy, a UN trusteeship, a liberal-democratic substitute for Chiang, even a coup to rescue him from his dilemma. As these alternatives failed, he held stubbornly to his course, demanding of the military whether they were prepared to invest American forces in the defense of Taiwan against China; the military responding no, at last, no. Containment would not go that far yet.

With the North Korean attack June 25, 1950, pressure to defend Taiwan became irresistible. Acheson may have satisfied himself that naval intervention would be temporary, tied to the Korean emergency. The military may have seen it as implementation of the war plan denying Taiwan to the Russians in a situation of impending general war. But the order to the fleet was also a result of powerful pressures generated in 1949–50 by the rise of Communist China in the context of a perceived shift in the Cold War balance. These pressures led to Asian rim containment. Taiwan fitted neatly into that arc of containment.

The Korean intervention had many roots. It sprang directly from global Cold War concerns and from the belief that the lessons of the past—of Manchuria and Munich—taught that aggression must be met condignly at the outset. It also emerged from regional policy development. Most especially, the Korean War created its own dynamic, with profound regional consequences. It reinforced containment at the rim of Asia and destroyed what was left of the Peking policy, with consequences that were to last for over two decades with shattering results.

As stated in the prefatory remarks to Steven Levine's introduction which appears earlier in this volume, Steven Goldstein's paper was written following the conference at Mount Kisco and so could not be discussed during the course of the meetings. It is therefore impossible to write a summary of the discussion of the Chinese papers comparable to Waldo Heinrich's preceding commentary on the American papers. In lieu of such a summary Steven Levine undertook to write the following essay which, in effect, is an addition to the Hunt and Goldstein papers in that it focuses on certain aspects of the Soviet factor in the Chinese-American relationship which Hunt and Goldstein deal with only in passing.

NOTES ON SOVIET POLICY IN CHINA AND CHINESE COMMUNIST PERCEPTIONS, 1945–1950

Steven I. Levine

THE CHAPTERS by Michael Hunt and Steven Goldstein represent different approaches to the study of Chinese Communist foreign policy in the late 1940s. As noted above, Hunt's situational approach suggests that Mao Tse-tung was seeking to avoid an exclusive dependency upon the Soviet Union. Mao's prior experience, his knowledge of China's economic weakness, and his basic political instincts were reflected in his preference for an autonomous foreign policy that would allow China to benefit from relations with all countries while being beholden to none. Goldstein's approach, by way of contrast, stresses the importance of the CCP's Marxist-

293

Leninist ideology in defining the Party's foreign policy. The emerging Cold War helped to eradicate the CCP's hope that the Kuomintang-Communist conflict might be settled short of civil war, and that the United States might play a key role in promoting democratization in China. The CCP's ideological legacy inclined it to accept the sharply defined Leninist duality of the Cold War world. Alliance with Russia and enmity with the United States followed naturally.

In reflecting on these contrasting versions of Chinese Communist foreign policy, it may be appropriate to raise several interrelated questions. These concern the nature of Soviet policy in China, the implications of that policy for the CCP, and how the CCP probably appraised its alliance with the USSR at the time it signed the Treaty of Friendship and Alliance in 1950.

As Goldstein shows, until mid-1946 the CCP wavered between an optimistic "Teheran view" of the United States as a potential partner for building democracy in postwar China, and a classical Leninist view of America as an imperialist power certain to revert to a counterrevolutionary stance once the slapdash unity of the anti-Hitler coalition was superseded by victory. The Teheran view, as Goldstein notes in passing, was expressed most distinctly in early 1944 by Earl Browder, head of the American Communist Party.[1] Browder, whose misfortune it was to mistake a transient ripple for the coming wave of history, interpreted the Big Three's rhetoric of unity at Teheran as presaging the postwar continuation of the Grand Alliance since "capitalism and socialism have begun to find the way to peaceful coexistence and collaboration in the same world." The political formula that Browder commended (specifically for Europe, but by extension elsewhere too) was a "broad, all-inclusive anti-fascist democratic camp . . . in each country within which all relations are determined and problems settled by free discussion, free political association and universal suffrage. Such a democratic camp

[1] Earl Browder, *Teheran and America*, (New York: Workers Library, 1944).

of necessity must include the Communists. . . ."[2] Finally, while diminishing not a bit his admiration for and loyalty to the Soviet Union, Browder hailed the dissolution of the Comintern as signifying the maturation of communist parties to the point where they could begin to act independently without prompting from Moscow.[3]

Browder's views are worth pondering because what he voiced then was in fact Stalin's own view of the future of the Grand Alliance as well as the widespread conviction within the communist movement that participation in the antifascist struggles represented a turning point in the legitimization of communist parties throughout the world. Mao and the CCP certainly shared both of these views toward the end of the war.

As William McCaggs demonstrates in his provocative reinterpretation of Stalin's foreign policy in the 1940s, Stalin's notion that the Soviet Union should make preservation of the Grand Alliance in the postwar world the foundation of its foreign policy represented a major although implicit departure from Leninist orthodoxy.[4] Lenin, of course, had counseled his followers to take advantage of inevitable splits among the imperialist powers to forge *temporary* alliances in order to oppose the primary enemy of the moment. Leninist united front strategy (which Mao later termed one of the "three magic weapons of the revolution") was premised on a transient commonality of interest vis-à-vis a specific enemy. The Stalin-Browder view of the Grand Alliance, however, was something very different. It presaged long-term political

---

[2] *Ibid.*, pp. 14–15.

[3] *Ibid.*, pp. 43–45. Of course, the Comintern still continued to function after a fashion despite its formal dissolution, and Moscow continued to provide cues to the other members of the international communist movement.

[4] The following analysis is very much beholden to McCaggs' insights into this period. See William O. McCaggs, *Stalin Embattled, 1943–1948* (Detroit: Wayne State University Press, 1978). McCaggs sees Soviet foreign policy in this period as primarily a function of the various domestic political battles Stalin fought against powerful Soviet interest groups and leaders and equally powerful pressures within the international communist movement.

and economic cooperation between the first socialist state and the two major imperialist powers in the absence of a clearly defined enemy. This orientation reflected Stalin's statist preferences as well as his fear of exposing the war-devastated Soviet Union to the hazards of war with the much stronger Western powers.[5] Moreover, Stalin believed that by remaining within the Grand Alliance he could play on the mounting friction between the declining imperialist superpower (Great Britain) and the rising imperialist superpower (the United States) to advance the Communist goal of seizing power without the need to resort to an insurrectionary strategy. It was in this context that Stalin in 1944–45 signaled foreign communist parties to eschew direct revolutionary tactics and to support broad popular coalitions so as not to jeopardize the Grand Alliance.[6] Communist parties in Western and even in Eastern Europe fell into line for the most part, but not without considerable misgivings and internal opposition.

The source of discontent with Stalin's conciliatory tactics was both doctrinal and visceral. Classical Leninism viewed the disorganization, uncertainty, crisis of legitimacy, and general chaos characteristic of postwar periods (especially in nations directly scarred by the war) as an unsurpassed opportunity for revolutionary initiatives. To this were added the natural feelings of many Communists that the appropriate reward for their struggle and sacrifices in the resistance movements was not a reconstitution of the prewar bourgeois social and political order but rather an advance toward socialism, the ultimate object of their efforts.[7]

Such a mood, of course, was particularly acute in the Chinese Communist Party given the peculiar conditions of political struggle in China. An analysis of the concept of co-

---

[5] McCaggs, *Stalin Embattled*, p. 14.

[6] Gabriel Kolko, *The Politics of War* (New York: Random House, 1968), pp. 36–37; McCaggs, *Stalin Embattled*, pp. 35ff.

[7] McCaggs, *Stalin Embattled*, p. 45.

alition government, which both Stalin and Mao subscribed to in this period, may best reveal the divergence in the Soviet and Chinese Communist perspective.

For the Soviet leader, the concept of coalition government, which was pressed upon European communists in 1944–46, was a means of consolidating Communist Party strength (which in many cases had grown dramatically during the war), involving communists in government as a step along the road to ultimate power and, above all, avoiding inciting the suspicions of the Western allies about Soviet motives and objectives. By working responsibly with bourgeois parties within parliamentary systems, communist parties could broaden their appeal internally while simultaneously serving the Soviet state.

Although such a strategy held little appeal for the more impetuous left Communists, it made sense in a European context. In Central and Eastern Europe the presence of the Soviet Red Army ensured that if parliamentarism faltered, local communist parties could still take power almost at will. In Western Europe democratic political systems were the best guarantors against repression by hostile internal forces of communist parties like those of Italy and France that surrendered their arms at the end of the war.

In China, of course, where politics had long since become militarized, no such assurances were available. CCP leaders realized only too well that to surrender their armies in the name of national unity would be political suicide. At the Seventh CCP Congress in April-June 1945, Mao subscribed to the concept of coalition government that his communist brethren in Europe were also endorsing, but with a difference. For Mao the primary question was certainly not the preservation of the Grand Alliance, but how to take power in China. Coalition government (which the Soviets commended to the CCP in 1945) might serve Mao's purpose if Chiang Kai-shek could be pressured into transforming the Kuomintang one-party rule into some semblance of a federal democratic system. Then the CCP could continue to exercise power in its "liberated" base areas, share power at the center, and use its legalized position to build additional power bases in the cities. The key questions for Mao as always were those of hegemony, autonomy, and security in the united front type of coalition. What seemed like a reasonable tradeoff to many CCP leaders in 1945 was to concede temporary hegemony to Chiang and the Nationalists in return for the continued de facto autonomy of the areas the CCP already controlled and the security afforded by the Communist armies.

As Goldstein indicates, the United States in its democratic "Teheran" guise could be a positive force in pressuring Chiang Kai-shek into compliance, and therefore it was worth the candle to cultivate the American connection. This was done in part by emphasizing Communist desires for American trade, technical assistance, and so forth, as Michael Hunt observes. (It may be noted, incidentally, that most Communists anticipated a depression of crisis proportions in the United States once the war boom was over unless burgeoning overseas trade could fill the gap. Thus the Chinese Communist and simultaneous Soviet interest in American trade was as much an offer to help the capitalists as it was a plea for assistance.) Acceptance of the coalition government objective also satisfied Moscow's concerns, as we have noted.

The CCP's power drive, however, was not premised solely on the success of a coalition government strategy. In fact, from the very outset there may well have been some skeptics in Yenan's camp who doubted the prospects for an approach that may have seemed both too passive and too novel for what had long since become a highly militarized movement. However, Goldstein suggests, as long as international events and the main thrust of American policy sustained the "Teheran view," the Party leadership pursued a coalition strategy. But at the same time, in North China, Manchuria, and wherever circumstances allowed, Communist armies moved at the war's end to seize new territories and extend their control over more people. In Manchuria, in particular, this created a very delicate situation for the Soviets who were bound by treaty to support the Chinese National Government. Moscow's response was complex, but the upshot was to assist the CCP in its struggle for Manchuria.[8]

During the civil war years, although the Soviet Union generally maintained diplomatically correct relations with Chiang's Nationalists and counseled caution on the CCP, Moscow funneled small but crucial amounts of industrial and technical aid to the Communists in Manchuria.[9] It is there that the military momentum for nationwide victory was accumulated and the first great victories were won. Thus, notwithstanding the initial divergence between Soviet and Chinese Communist perspectives in 1945, it is misleading to argue that Stalin and the Soviet leadership were indifferent or hostile to Mao and the CCP.[10] The latter may well have understood the Soviet Union's prudence in seeking to avoid unnecessary provocation of the United States. In any case, open support of the Chinese Communists who were winning handily on their own was hardly necessary. Evidence of active Soviet support of the CCP during the civil war years was the one thing that might have triggered as escalated American intervention in China and delayed the Communist march to power.

Those who argue that the U.S. lost a chance to establish good relations with the Chinese Communists in the 1940s make the assumption that alliance with the Soviet Union was a last-chance option for the CCP. Yet it seems questionable whether Stalin's embrace was so uncongenial that only a political movement in a desperate and utterly isolated position would have gladly accepted alliance with the USSR. The experience of the 1940s suggests that many Communist leaders as well as millions of rank-and-file members in many coun-

[8] See my "Soviet-American Rivalry in Manchuria and the Cold War," in Hsüeh Chün-tu, ed., *Dimensions of China's Foreign Relations* (New York: Praeger, 1977), pp. 10–43.

[9] O. B. Borisov, *The Soviet Union and the Manchurian Revolutionary Base*, (Moscow: Progress, 1978).

[10] See McCaggs, *Stalin Embattled*, p. 299, for a contrary evaluation.

tries saw a close association with the Soviet Union as highly desirable. For such people internationalism (defined as support of the Soviet Union) supplanted the narrow "bourgeois" concept of patriotism. (Recall in this context the famous statement by French Communist leader Maurice Thorez that his followers would fight against their own country if the Soviet Red Army entered France in an anti-imperialist war.)[11] Of course, Mao was no Comintern apparatchik, and the history of Soviet-CCP relations was scarred with frequent discord, but one should not read the Sino-Soviet enmity of the late 1950s and after back into this earlier period.

It seems doubtful, therefore, that in the context of 1949–50 Mao would have seen an alliance with the Soviet Union as a form of dependency that ran against the grain of his self-reliance policies. The dependency which Mao rejected as intolerable was the type of exploitative relationships that had hitherto characterized relations between China and the imperialist powers. Despite the history of disagreements between the CCP and the Soviets, it is difficult to believe that the Chinese Communist leadership anticipated a repetition of such an exploitative relationship between the new China and the socialist Soviet Union. In fact, it was not until some years later that Mao and his associates not only began to question the Soviet developmental model, but also to express dissatisfaction with the quantity and quality of Soviet economic assistance. Mao's latter-day comments on the difficulty of extracting aid from Stalin are rather poor evidence for his contemporary views since by the time he issued them he was having to justify his own prior faith in the Soviet big brother.

Actually, even leaving aside the crucial security aspect of the 1950 Sino-Soviet alliance, the economic assistance that the Soviets extended the new Chinese regime was not nearly so niggardly as it is sometimes depicted. The $300-million-

---

[11] Witold S. Sworakowski, ed., *World Communism: A Handbook, 1918–1956* (Stanford: Stanford University Press, 1973), p. 142.

dollar five-year credit was, to be sure, a drop in the bucket of Chinese need, but it should be recalled that in 1950 the Soviet economy itself was still recovering from the devastation of war and was short of capital, technology, and trained manpower. If one compares the simultaneous Soviet exploitation of the East European communist states, one can see how generous Stalin was towards Mao, in his own terms to be sure. Although Stalin may have seen in Mao a potential Chinese Tito—prone to disloyalty and insubordination—he was realistic enough not to treat China as an overgrown Balkan state. And though he may have used Manchurian regional boss Kao Kang as a conduit for inside information on Politburo politics in China, Stalin knew he lacked and probably could not hope to develop the kinds of control mechanisms over China that he possessed in Eastern Europe.[12]

It is true that even after Mao's lean-to-one-side speech, he and Chou En-lai undertook diplomatic initiatives aimed at undermining the American policy of diplomatic isolation of China and broadening diplomatic ties beyond the USSR. This seems only reasonable. No state wants to limit its diplomatic relations to a single partner. There is no reason to suppose that the USSR would have wanted to prevent China from developing formally correct relations with other countries. Once the basic political and security relationship between China and the USSR was established, foreign trade between the PRC and the West would not have posed a threat to Moscow. One may even suppose that if the West had been willing to help resuscitate the economy of an avowedly communist China allied to the USSR this could only have redounded to Moscow's benefit by reducing the burden on the Soviet economy and strengthening the Soviet Union's major ally.

In hindsight Dean Acheson's prediction of an eventful

[12]Nikita Khrushchev, *Khrushchev Remembers: The Last Testament*, translated and edited by Strobe Talbott (Boston: Little, Brown, 1974) pp. 243–44; and Zbigniew Brzezinski, *The Soviet Bloc: Unity and Conflict* (Cambridge, Mass.: Harvard University Press, 1967), pp. 105–38.

split between Moscow and Peking looks remarkably pres-
cient, but in contemporary policy terms the idea that some
American officials entertained of luring Mao away from Moscow in 1948–1950 seems more than a little farfetched. Stalin
may not have tried to keep Mao on as short a leash as he did
the East Europeans, but the Soviet dictator would certainly
have reacted swiftly to any indications that the Chinese Communists were playing Acheson's game. More important, Mao
and his associates would certainly have perceived American
attempts to split them off from the Soviet Union as imperialist tricks and maneuvers to which their ideology had forewarned them. CCP reaction to Tito's expulsion from the Cominform is instructive in this regard. In the early postwar
period (1945–46), Stalin commended the relative autonomy
of Communist parties, separate roads to socialism, and a
loosely structured international Communist movement. But
by 1948–49 in the wake of the Tito episode, a process of Soviet enforced unification within the Communist movement
occurred. This was symbolized by the ideological redefini-
tion of people's democracy (previously termed a new type of
government) as simply another form of the proletarian dictatorship.[13] Challenged from within by Tito and facing a hostile Western coalition outside, in effect Stalin was closing the
doors of the fort, and the Chinese Communists had no difficulty in choosing whether to come inside. Of course China
would stand with the Soviet Union.

Did the anti-imperialist ideology that informed Mao's
and the CCP's world view seriously impair their ability to
conduct foreign policy? Deducing his view of the United
States from his ideology, Mao apparently felt no need to seek
the truth from facts. Therefore, his understanding of the
United States was superficial and seriously distorted. Burdened by such blinders, the argument goes, Mao was unable
to achieve the flexibility necessary for China to avoid depen-

---

[13] McCaggs, *Stalin Embattled*, pp. 57–62, 276–77; and Benjamin I. Schwartz,
Communism and China: Ideology in Flux (New York: Atheneum, 1970), pp. 47–65.

dency upon the USSR and a hostile confrontation with the United States. Thus Mao's pro-Soviet and anti-imperialist revolutionary line was irrational and counterproductive.

One cannot quarrel with the assertion that in 1945–50 Mao's knowledge of the United States (and of the Soviet Union one might add) was superficial and deduced from his ideology. Mao's perception that the United States was fundamentally hostile to his revolution and stood as the major status quo power in a rapidly changing world was basically accurate. Here, if anything, Mao's ideology sharpened his perception and facilitated his decision to align with the Soviet bloc. This choice was not without its costs as well as its benefits, but it hardly seems irrational in the context of 1948–50. Although Mao had already adumbrated the notion of a Third World by talking of the intermediate zone separating the imperialist United States from the socialist Soviet Union, conditions were not yet ripe either in China or in the Asian-African world to act upon such a notion. And so Mao and the CCP reached for the Soviet alliance, which seemed their only safe harbor as they commenced the monumental task of transforming China into a modern state. At the same time, relations with the United States remained solidly fixed within the Marxist-Leninist scheme of world politics.

Chronology of Events, 1947–1950

Compiled by Michael L. Baron

(Events occurring in Asia or Asia-related are starred)

1947

January

3   80th Congress convened, first Republican majority in both houses in 14 years.

*7   Gen. George C. Marshall issues statement upon his return from China reporting on the mediation mission.

21   Marshall sworn in as secretary of state replacing James F. Byrnes.

*29   U.S. announces formal termination of its mediation efforts in China.

February

21, 24   British notes to U.S. government indicate inability of British government to provide additional aid to Greece and Turkey.

*28   Rebellion of native Taiwanese suppressed by mainland Nationalist troops.

March

*2   Chinese Communist delegation leaves Nanking for Yenan, ending face-to-face Nationalist-Communist negotiations.

4   Senate cuts Truman's proposed FY 1948 budget by $4.5 billion following a $6 billion cut by the House.

10	Truman and advisers meet with Congressional leaders to outline proposed aid plans to Greece and Turkey. Moscow Conference of foreign ministers opened.
12	Truman Doctrine presented to Congress.
*19	Yenan occupied by Nationalist troops after its abandonment by Communists.
21	Truman establishes Federal Employee Loyalty Board, Executive Order 9835.
31	Wartime draft ended.

April

| *2 | U.S. granted UN trusteeship over former Japanese mandates in western Pacific. |
| 24 | Moscow Conference ends. |

May

*3	Japanese constitution put into effect. It includes clauses by which Japan renounces war and which prohibit maintenance of military forces by Japan.
8	Undersecretary of State Dean Acheson makes speech in Cleveland on need for European aid program.
22	Truman signs Greek-Turkish aid bill providing $300 million in economic and military aid for Greece and $100 million in military aid for Turkey.
29	Marshall instructs Gen. Lucius D. Clay, in charge of the occupation administration in Germany, to strengthen bizonal organization with the British government and expedite expansion of the German economy.
30	Premier Ferenc Nagy resigns in Hungary as Communist party leaders assume power.

June

5	Marshall proposes European aid plan in commencement address delivered at Harvard.
19	Truman vetoes Taft-Hartley labor act.
30	Robert A. Lovett assumes position of undersecretary of state following Acheson's resignation.

July

| | George F. Kennan's "Mr. X" article appears in *Foreign Affairs*. |

2   Soviet Foreign Minister Molotov walks out of Paris Conference in process of formulating response to Marshall's suggestions of June 5.

*4   Chinese Nationalist government orders total mobilization for war against Communists.

10–26 Russia concludes trade agreements with Eastern European states.

12   Eastern Europe boycotts initial session of Committee for European Economic Cooperation, convened to draw up detailed plans for American economic aid.

26   Truman signs Armed Forces Unification Act setting up new national security apparatus and creating office of secretary of defense. James V. Forrestal named as first secretary of defense.

August
*15   British imperial control of India ended. India partitioned, Pakistan established.

*   Wedemeyer mission to China begins.

September
2   Inter-American Treaty of Reciprocal Assistance (Rio Pact) signed.

*19   Wedemeyer's final report submitted but not released due to Marshall's objections.

22   European nations request more than $22 billion in U.S. economic aid for European reconstruction.

October
5   Soviet-directed COMINFORM created.

23   Truman calls Congress into emergency session to deal with inflation in U.S. and crisis in Western Europe.

30   General Agreement on Tariffs and Trade (GATT) signed.

November
17   Congress convened in emergency session. Truman requests $570 million for third interim aid bill.

29   UN General Assembly adopts partition plan for Palestine. Arab League begins hostilities.

December

19   Truman presents $17 billion European aid program, $6.8 billion in first 18 months.

*   Congress approves $540 million interim aid for Italy, Austria, and China, of which China is to receive $18 million.

*25   Mao Tse-tung makes speech on CCP tactics in Civil War, claims "turning point" has been reached.

29   Henry A. Wallace announces third party candidacy for presidency.

1948

January

1   Finletter Commission issues report calling for creation of credible American counterforce air capabilities to meet challenge of Soviet possession of nuclear weapons expected by 1953.

12   Truman submits FY 1949 budget to Congress, the second largest peacetime budget in American history ($39.7 billion).

February

*18   Truman presents China Aid program to Congress, proposing $570 million economic aid and reconstruction plan over 15 months.

25   Czech coup. President Eduard Beneš yields to ultimatum of Premier Klement Gottwald.

29   Britain, France, Belgium, Luxembourg, and the Netherlands agree to form Western European Union.

March

5   Gen. Clay cables from Germany that war with Soviet Union might come with "dramatic suddenness."

10   Czech Foreign Minister Jan Masaryk falls to his death from office window.

14   Economic Cooperation Administration (ECA) passed by Senate, 65–7.

*15   Communist military forces recapture Yenan.

17   Brussels Pact, 50-year defense treaty, signed by Britain, France, and Benelux countries.

*22   Undersecretary of the Army William Draper arrives in Tokyo to study plans for revision of occupation policies.

31   ECA passed by House.
Soviet troops begin obstructing military traffic into West Berlin.

April
*3   ECA and China Aid Act signed. ECA calls for $5.3 billion during first year (cut by the Congressional appropriations committees to $4 billion); China Aid bill provides $338 million in economic aid (cut to $275 million) and $125 million in unrestricted grants intended for use as military aid.

6   Paul Hoffman appointed ECA administrator.
Finland and Soviet Union announce 10-year military alliance.

*19   Chiang Kai-shek elected president of China by National Assembly, Li Tsung-jen elected vice president (April 29) despite Chiang's opposition.
Christian Democratic Party led by Alcide de Gasperi wins Italian elections.

May
2   OAS (Organization of American States) charter signed.

14   Israel proclaims its independence and within minutes is recognized by Truman.

17   Truman asks Congress to enact universal military training and reinstitute draft.

*20   Truman allocates $100 million in budget for rehabilitation of Japan's economy.

*31   Syngman Rhee elected leader of Korean assembly following UN-supervised election held only in South Korea (May 10).

June
7   London Agreement, planning rehabilitation of German economy and creation of federal state.

11   Vandenberg Resolution passed by Senate supporting establishment of regional and collective self-defense arrangements.

18   Western powers announce impending currency reform in West Germany to include Western sectors of Berlin.

24   Soviet Union cuts off all land access to Berlin. Blockade begins. Republican Party nominates Thomas E. Dewey for president, Earl Warren for vice-president.

28   Stalin-Tito break becomes public knowledge as Cominform denounces Tito.

July

15   Truman receives Democratic Party presidential nomination; Senate Majority Leader Alben W. Barkley nominated as vice-presidential candidate.

30   (through August) House Un-American Activities Committee hears former Communists name alleged Communists holding high-level positions in Washington.

August

*15   U.S. occupation of South Korea ended. Republic of Korea formed, with Syngman Rhee as its first president.

September

*9   Establishment of Democratic People's Republic of Korea formally announced in North Korea with Kim Il Sung as prime minister.

17   Zionist terrorists in Jerusalem assassinate UN mediator Count Folke Bernadotte. He is succeeded by Ralph Bunche.

*24   Ch'angch'un, key Manchurian city, falls to Communists with heavy Nationalist losses.

November

*1   Communists take Mukden, signaling loss of Manchuria.

2   Truman reelected. Democratic Party regains control of Congress.

*12   Seven Japanese war criminals convicted, later executed.

December
* *1   Mme. Chiang Kai-shek visits U.S. to try to secure more aid.
* 9   Truman characterizes House Un-American Activities Committee hearings as "red herring."
* *12 UN General Assembly passes resolution naming Rhee government as the only lawful regime in Korea.
* 15   Alger Hiss indicted for perjury.
* *31 Soviet troops withdrawn from North Korea.

1949

January
* 3   81st Congress convened with Democratic Party in control of both houses.
* 7   Marshall resigns as secretary of state, Dean Acheson named his successor.
* 20   Truman in his inaugural address introduces Point Four Program of technical assistance to less developed countries.
* *21 Chiang retires from presidency of China in favor of Li Tsung-jen.
* *22 Communists gain Peking without a fight.

February
* *7   51 Republican House members send letter on China to Truman indicating concern over potential defeat of Nationalist forces.
* *25 Senator Patrick A. McCarran introduces bill calling for $1.5 billion loan to Nationalist China.

March
* 4   Vyshinsky succeeds Molotov as Soviet foreign minister.
* *10 50 senators sign letter supporting Chinese Nationalists.
* 28   Louis A Johnson replaces Forrestal as secretary of defense.

April
* 4   North Atlantic pact signed.
* 8   Western allies merge occupation zones in West Germany, plan to set up unified government.

*14   Congress authorizes extension of China portion of ECA, permitting president to spend remaining $56 million through February 1950.

*20   Chinese Communists cross Yangtze River in force.

*23   Nationalists abandon Nanking and move capital to Canton.

Secretary of Defense Johnson orders work on supercarrier halted, Navy Secretary John L. Sullivan resigns in protest.

*24   Nanking occupied by Communist forces.

May

12   Berlin blockade ended.

23   (through June 20) Council of Foreign Ministers meets as concession to Soviet Union in return for lifting blockade.

*25   Communists capture Shanghai.

June

*24   Statement issued by 21 senators opposing American recognition of any Communist regime in China.

*29   American troops withdraw from Korean peninsula.

*30   Mao issues speech "On the People's Democratic Dictatorship."

July

*16   Chiang organizes Supreme Policy Council, which begins to remove forces to Taiwan.

*20   Chiang flies to Philippines to confer with President Elpidio Quirino on possible anti-Communist pact.

23   Truman submits to Congress military assistance program providing for $1.5 billion to support European defense efforts.

August

*2   Ambassador John Leighton Stuart leaves China.

*5   China White Paper released by State Department.

*8   Chiang visits South Korea to promote anti-Communist alliance.

10   Truman approves amendments to National Security Act

of 1947, creating a stronger secretary of defense, a Department of Defense, and a reorganized National Security Council.

September

Government of German Federal Republic formed early in month.

8　　Export-Import Bank approves $20 million loan to Yugoslavia.

23　　Truman makes public U.S. government knowledge of Soviet atomic bomb.

*27　　W. Walton Butterworth confirmed as assistant secretary of state for Far Eastern affairs after Senate repeatedly passes over his nomination.

28　　Soviet Union denounces 1945 treaty of friendship and mutual assistance with Yugoslavia.

October

*1　　People's Republic of China formally proclaimed.

5　　Admiral Arthur W. Radford leads "revolt of admirals." Navy officers condemn U.S. reliance on air power, Congress is implored to increase share given to navy in military budget then under consideration.

*6　　Truman signs Mutual Defense Assistance Act providing for $1.3 billion, including $75 million for use in general area of China.

7　　German Democratic Republic established in Soviet zone.

*12　　Acheson lists three conditions for recognition of new Chinese government: 1) effective control of territory; 2) acceptance of international obligations; and 3) consent of the population.

*24　　Communist authorities arrest U.S. Consul-General at Mukden Angus Ward, held under house arrest since November 1948, for directing espionage ring. Ward is deported in December.

December

*7　　Chinese Nationalist government evacuated to Taiwan.

*16　　Mao arrives in Moscow to negotiate for Soviet aid.

*23   State Department sends secret circular to diplomats abroad warning of impending fall of Taiwan.

*27   United States of Indonesia becomes a sovereign state.

1950

January

*3   Contents of Taiwan circular leaked from MacArthur's headquarters in Tokyo, followed by repercussions in Congress.

*5   Former President Herbert Hoover demands American naval protection of Taiwan.

*6   British government recognizes PRC and breaks off relations with Nationalist government.

Truman delivers speech asserting that no military aid or advice will be given to Taiwan.

*10   Jacob Malik walks out of UN Security Council protesting continued presence of Nationalist Chinese delegation.

*12   Acheson delivers National Press Club speech on defensive perimeter in Asia.

*14   U.S., French, and Netherlands compounds in Peking seized on grounds that they contain military barracks. U.S. recalls all official personnel.

*18   Ho Chi Minh's Democratic Republic of Vietnam recognized by PRC; Soviet recognition extended January 30.

25   Alger Hiss convicted of perjury.

*29   France recognizes Bao Dai regime in Vietnam.

31   Truman instructs Atomic Energy Commission to proceed with development of hydrogen bomb.

February

*6   U.S. recognizes Bao Dai government.

9   Senator Joseph R. McCarthy attacks alleged Communists in State Department in speech at Wheeling, W. Va.

*15   Sino-Soviet communiqué announces conclusion of new agreements in Moscow, including 30-year defensive alliance against Japan and its allies, an agreement concerning Soviet rights in the Chinese Ch'angch'ün railway, Port Arthur, and Dairen, and provisions for a Soviet $300 million, five-year credit to China.

March

1   Klaus Fuchs convicted of espionage in Britain.

7   Judith Coplon and Valentin Gubitchev convicted of espionage in U.S.

8   Senate Tydings committee begins hearings on McCarthy's charges.

19   Soviet-sponsored World Peace Conference adopts Stockholm Appeal calling for abolition of nuclear weapons.

*27   Sino-Soviet agreements concluded providing for joint stock companies to exploit resources of oil and nonferrous metals in Sinkiang and for a joint civil aviation company to operate routes between China and USSR.

April

17   Truman provisionally approves NSC-68 subject to submission of cost estimates.

*23   PRC captures Hainan island.

May

9   French Foreign Minister Robert Schuman announces plans for European Coal and Steel Community.

June

5   Point Four Program passed in scaled-down version.

*25   North Korea launches large-scale attack against South Korea.

*27   UN Security Council condemns North Korean attack and demands immediate withdrawal. U.S. air and sea units sent to aid South Korean defense efforts and U.S. Seventh Fleet interposed in Taiwan Straits to prevent Nationalist-Communist clashes.

*30   UN calls on all members to repel armed attack in Korea. U.S. sends ground troops from Japan.

July
20   Tydings committee report castigates McCarthy.
*30   Chiang Kai-shek and MacArthur meet on Taiwan.

August
1   Malik returns to UN to assume presidency of Security Council.
*10   Karl Rankin dispatched to Taiwan as U.S. chargé d'affaires.

September
9   Truman announces increase in American troop strength in Europe.
12   Louis Johnson resigns as secretary of defense and is replaced by Gen. Marshall.
*15   MacArthur launches successful landing at Inchon.
23   Congress passes over Truman's veto Internal Security Act mandating registration of Communist Party members.
*26   Joint Chiefs of Staff call for destruction of North Korean armies; MacArthur prepares to cross 38th parallel; Seoul retaken.
27   Congress appropriates $26.9 million for Point Four Program.

October
*1   MacArthur issues unapproved ultimatum to North Korea demanding unconditional surrender.
South Korean forces under MacArthur's command cross 38th parallel.
Chou En-lai warned through Indian Ambassador K. M. Panikkar against crossing the parallel; warning repeated October 10.
*7   UN-approved movement of UN forces north of 38th parellel.
*15   Truman and MacArthur meet on Wake island. MacArthur reassures Truman that Chinese will not intervene in Korean fighting.
*24   MacArthur informs Joint Chiefs of Staff of final push to unify Korea.

25   Pleven Plan introduced to speed integration of German troops into unified European force.

*26   First Chinese prisoners captured in Korea.

November

*3   Because of deadlock in Security Council, U.S. promotes "Uniting for Peace" resolution allowing General Assembly to decide on matters of security upon which only Security Council had previously acted.

*6   Joint Chiefs of Staff give MacArthur permission to bomb Yalu River bridges.

7   Republicans record gains in elections but Democrats retain control of Congress.

*20   Parts of U.S. 7th Division reach Manchurian border.

*26   Chinese massively intervene in Korea, forcing retreat of American forces.

*28   MacArthur heralds start of "an entirely new war."

Participants

Conference participants, their affiliations, and some of their major publications (1978).

MICHAEL L. BARON. Doctoral candidate, Department of Political Science, Columbia University (dissertation, "Sino-American Relations and the Policy Process, 1946–49").

ROBERT M. BLUM. Doctoral candidate, Department of History, University of Texas, Austin (dissertation, "Containment in the General Area of China: The Impact of Section 303 of the Mutual Defense Assistance Act on U.S. Far Eastern Policy"). *The United States and Communist China in 1949 and 1950: The Question of Rapprochement and Recognition* (1973) and *The United States and Vietnam: 1944–1947* (1972), Staff Studies for the Committee on Foreign Relations, U.S. Senate.

DOROTHY BORG. Senior research associate, East Asian Institute, Columbia University. *Pearl Harbor as History: Japanese-American Relations, 1931–1941*, co-editor (1973); *The United States and the Far Eastern Crisis of 1933–1938* (1964).

WARREN I. COHEN. Professor of history, Michigan State University. *The Chinese Connection: Roger S. Greene, Thomas W. Lamont, George E. Sokolsky and American-East Asian Relations* (1978); *America's Response to China* (1971); *Dean Rusk*, volume in series "American Secretaries of State and Their Diplomacy," edited by Robert H. Ferrell (forthcoming).

BRUCE CUMINGS. Assistant professor, School of International Studies, University of Washington. *The Origins of the Korean War* (forthcoming).

ROGER DINGMAN. Associate professor of history, University of

Southern California. *Power in the Pacific: The Origins of Naval Arms Limitation, 1914–1922* (1976); "The Origins of the U.S.-Japan Security Treaty of 1951" (in preparation).

ROBERT J. DONOVAN. Fellow, Woodrow Wilson International Center for Scholars, Washington D.C. Two-volume study, *Conflict and Crisis: The Presidency of Harry S. Truman, 1945–1948* (1977) and *The Devastating Years, 1949–1953* (in preparation); *Eisenhower: The Inside Story* (1956).

JAMES FETZER. Assistant professor of history, Maritime College, State University of New York. "Congress and China, 1941–1950" (dissertation).

JOHN LEWIS GADDIS. Professor of history, Ohio University. *Russia, the Soviet Union, and the United States: An Interpretive History* (1978); *The United States and the Origins of the Cold War, 1941–1947* (1972); *Strategies of Containment: From Kennan to Kissinger* and *The United States and the Escalation of the Cold War, 1947–1953* (both volumes forthcoming).

STEVEN M. GOLDSTEIN. Associate professor of government, Smith College. "Chinese Communist Perceptions of International Affairs, 1937–1941" (in preparation).

WALDO HEINRICHS. Professor of history, Temple University. *American Ambassador: Joseph C. Grew and the Development of the U.S. Diplomatic Tradition* (1966).

MICHAEL H. HUNT. Associate professor of history, Colgate University. *Frontier Defense and the Open Door: Manchuria in Chinese-American Relations, 1895–1911* (1973); "The Making of a Special Relationship: The United States and China, 1784–1914" and "The United States and Communist China at the Crossroads, 1948–1950" (both volumes in preparation).

AKIRA IRIYE. Professor of American diplomatic history, University of Chicago. *The Origins of the Cold War in Asia*, co-editor (1977); *Mutual Images: Studies in American-Japanese Relations*, editor (1975); *The Cold War in Asia: A Historical Introduction* (1974); *Pacific Estrangement: Japanese and American Expansion, 1897–1911* (1972); *Across the Pacific: An Inner History of American-East Asian Relations* (1967); *The Chinese and the Japanese: Their Political and Cultural Interaction*, editor (forthcoming).

DONALD W. KLEIN. Associate professor of political science, Tufts University. *Rebels and Bureaucrats: China's December 9ers*, co-author (1976); *Biographic Dictionary of Chinese Communism, 1921–1965* (2 vols.), co-author (1971).

WALTER LaFEBER. Professor of history, Cornell University. *America, Russia, and the Cold War* (4th ed., 1980); *New Empire: An Interpretation of American Expansion, 1860–1868* (1963).

STEVEN I. LEVINE. Research associate, East Asian Institute, Columbia University. "World Politics and Revolutionary Power in Manchuria, 1945–1949" (in preparation).

ERNEST R. MAY. Professor of history, Harvard University. *American-East Asian Relations: A Survey*, co-editor (1972); *"Lessons" of the Past: The Use and Misuse of History in American Foreign Policy* (1973); *American Imperialism: A Speculative Essay* (1968); *Imperial Democracy: The Emergence of America as a Great Power* (1961); *The World War and American Isolation, 1914–1917* (1959).

ROBERT L. MESSER. Assistant professor of history, University of Illinois at Chicago Circle. "James F. Byrnes and the Origins of the Cold War" (in preparation).

JAMES WILLIAM MORLEY. Professor of government, Columbia University. Editor of multivolume series "The Origins of the Pacific War," of which *Deterrent Diplomacy: Japan, Germany, and the USSR, 1935–1940* is published (1976) and *Fateful Choice* is forthcoming; *The Japanese Thrust into Siberia, 1918* (1957).

THOMAS G. PATERSON. Professor of history, University of Connecticut. *On Every Front: The Making of the Cold War* (1979); *American Foreign Policy: A History*, co-author (1977); *Soviet-American Confrontation* (1973).

STEPHEN E. PELZ. Associate professor, University of Massachusetts, Amherst. *Race to Pearl Harbor: The Failure of the Second London Naval Conference and the Onset of World War II* (1974); "America Goes to War: The Politics and Process of Decision, 1914–1941" and a second volume dealing with the years 1945–65 (both volumes in preparation).

JAMES REARDON-ANDERSON. Associate professor, School of Advanced International Studies, Johns Hopkins University. *Yenan and the Great Powers* (forthcoming).

DAVID ALAN ROSENBERG. Consultant to the Naval Research Advisory Committee Task Force on Historical Perspectives of Long Range Planning in the Navy, Office of the Secretary of the Navy; doctoral candidate, University of Chicago. "Long Range Planning in the Navy, an Overview," Appendix to *The Maritime Balance Study: A Strategic Planning Experiment in the Maritime Balance Area* (1979); *History of the Strategic Arms Competition, 1945–1972*.

322   **PARTICIPANTS**

Supporting Study: U.S. Aircraft Carriers in the Strategic Role: Naval Strategy in a Period of Change, 1945–1951, co-author (1975).

WARNER R. SCHILLING. James T. Shotwell professor of international relations, Columbia University. *American Arms and a Changing Europe: Dilemmas of Deterrence and Disarmament*, co-author (1973); *European Security and the Atlantic System*, co-editor (1973); *Strategy, Politics and Defense Budgets*, co-author (1962).

MARTIN J. SHERWIN. Lecturer in history, Princeton University. *A World Destroyed: The Atomic Bomb and the Grand Alliance* (1975).

RONALD STEEL. Visiting lecturer in government, University of Texas, Austin. *Imperialists and Other Heroes* (1971); *Pax Americana* (1967); *The End of Alliance* (1964); *Walter Lippmann* (forthcoming).

NANCY BERNKOPF TUCKER. Adjunct assistant professor of Asian history, New York University; doctoral candidate, Department of History, Columbia University (dissertation, "Patterns in the Dust: Why the United States Did Not Recognize the People's Republic of China in 1949 or 1950").

LARRY WEISS. Instructor, Brooklyn Friends School; doctoral candidate, Department of Political Science, Columbia University (dissertation, "Storm Around the Cradle: The Korean War and the Consolidation of the People's Republic of China, 1949–1952").

SAMUEL F. WELLS, JR. Secretary, International Security Studies Program, Woodrow Wilson International Center for Scholars, Washington D.C. *The Ordeal of World Power: American Diplomacy since 1900*, co-author (1975); *Escalation of the Cold War: The Impact of Korea, 1950–1954* (forthcoming).

ALLEN S. WHITING. Professor of political science, University of Michigan. *China's Future: Foreign Policy and Economic Development in the Post-Mao Era*, co-author (1977); *The Chinese Calculus of Deterrence: India and Indo-China* (1975); *China Crosses the Yalu: The Decision to Enter the Korean War* (1960 and 1968); *Soviet Policies in China, 1917–1924* (1968); *Siberian Development and East Asia* (forthcoming).

Index

Acheson, Dean: on aid to Kuomintang, 21-24; attitude toward China, 286; on Bao Dai, 100n.112; basis for China policy decisions, 48-49; and Chiang Kaishek, 43, 49, 54, 67, 173, 284; and China White Paper, 24-25; and Chinese Communists, 16, 23, 32, 34-35, 54-55; and containment, 5, 16-17, 285; and Davies, 16; and defensive perimeter concept, 106-7; and Dulles, 16; effect of Korean War on policy making, 42-48; on French in Indochina, 94-95; on Ho Chi Minh, 96; on importance of Asia, 50; on importance of China, 16, 53-54; on importance of Europe, 68; and Kennan, 16, 19-20; and Korean War, 51-52, 57-58, 113; on lean-to-one side policy, 37; on Mao-Stalin meetings, 41-42; meeting with Lie, 41; and Mutual Defense Assistance Act, 29; National Press Club speech (January 12, 1950), 61-62, 65-66, 67; on Nationalist air raids, 30; on Nationalist blockade, 205; on Pacific security pact, 159; *Present at the Creation*, 13; and public opinion, 40, 50, 56; and recognition of PRC, 32, 34-35, 37-39, 42, 46, 285-86, 292; roles of, 55-56; and Seventh Fleet decision, 90; on Sino-Soviet relations, 26, 32, 37, 49-50, 56, 69-70, 301-2; on Southeast Asia, 94n.92; staff of, as secretary of state, 16-21; on Stuart meeting with Communists, 36; on support of Nationalists, 13, 24, 47; on Taiwan and U.S., 85; on Taiwan autonomy, 79-81; and Taiwan defense, 80-81; on Taiwan question, 25-26, 28-29, 30-31, 32, 46, 48, 50, 89-90, 92, 125, 286-87, 289, 292; and third road, 219; on 38th parallel decision, 46, 57-58, 112n.146; on Truman, 16, 21-22, 39-40; on UN forces in Taiwan, 91; on U.S. consular property, 40-41; viability of policy, 57; on Ward case, 40; *see also* State, U.S. Department of

Allison, John M., 110-11
American China Policy Association, 165
Attlee, Clement, 92

Badger, Oscar C., 71, 167
Bank of China, 146-47
Bao Dai, 95, 100n.112, 291
Baron, Michael L.: discussant, on U.S. China policy, 11, 178-79
Barr, David, 144n.25
Barrett, David D., 238
Blum, Robert M.: discussant, on Acheson, 56; on U.S. China policy, 174; on U.S. strategic planning, 122
Bohlen, Charles E., 108, 110
Bradley, Omar N., 85, 89, 89n.79, 124
Browder, Earl, 239, 246, 246n.21, 294-96
Butterworth, W. Walton, 16, 81, 164n.78; and aid to Kuomintang, 13-14; attitude toward China, 18-19; and China lobby, 19; and Chinese Communists, 19; and containment, 285; Koo view of, 21; on recognition of PRC, 33, 38; replaced by Rusk, 31; on Stuart meeting with Communists, 36; on Taiwan question, 25-26, 27, 28; on U.S. China policy, 49

Cabot, John M., 34, 162n.71
Cairo Declaration, 92

323